Robert Timsol

An Alien from the Commonwealth

The Romance of an Old Young Man

Robert Timsol

An Alien from the Commonwealth
The Romance of an Old Young Man

ISBN/EAN: 9783744679442

Printed in Europe, USA, Canada, Australia, Japan

Cover: Foto ©Thomas Meinert / pixelio.de

More available books at **www.hansebooks.com**

AN ALIEN

FROM

THE COMMONWEALTH

The Romance of an Odd Young Man

BY

Robert Timsol

AUTHOR OF "A PESSIMIST"

BOSTON
CUPPLES AND HURD, PUBLISHERS
The Algonquin Press
1889

To C. S.

CONTENTS.

BOOK THIRD.

THE OAKLANDS EPISODE.

BOOK FOURTH.

IN HARNESS.

AN ALIEN
FROM THE COMMONWEALTH.

CHAPTER I.

PROLOGUE.

"THE trouble with you, Dick, is that you don't go at things in the right way."

"No doubt of it, Bob. But that is a very general statement."

"Oh, I can make it more definite, if you wish. Mostly you don't go after things at all, but wait for them to come to you, which it is not their nature to do."

"So it seems. I wouldn't care whether they came or not, if I could do as well without them."

"Precisely; but you can't. In this world, men are largely dependent on things."

"That's what I object to, Bob. It's humiliating

and absurd. I can't believe we were made to expend our whole energies on beggarly carnalities, — money-getting and the like. Men are greater than things, and ought not to be enslaved to them."

"But they are — or principally by lack of the things. Present arrangements have no respect for our abstract dignity, my boy. What you are is judged by what you do, and what you can do depends largely on what you have got. Moreover, what you have got is supposed by many — in fact, by nearly everybody — to be the proof, and test, and measure, of what you can do, and so of what you are."

"That is low materialism. I despise these mere external valuations. A man ought to be appraised for what he is, not for the clothes he wears or the house he lives in."

"Very likely, Dick ; but what ought to be is one thing, and what is, another. You live in a world of your own, and pay too little attention to received opinions."

"But the opinions are wrong, and ought to be changed."

"Set to work to change them, then ; you'll have your hands full for life."

"I would, if I thought there was any use of trying, and saw my way to keep above ground and out of debt while I was at it. But the difficulty would be to get an audience — unless I paid them to come. They certainly wouldn't pay me for attacking their traditional position."

"They might, if you were more of a fanatic : a reformer has to be that, you know. But you are only a critic. I don't say you lack the courage of your convictions, but you have no evangelistic zeal. You are not yearning to convert others; you care only to coddle your doxies, and go your own way."

"Well, it does seem to me that every tub ought to stand on its own bottom. I am willing to let my neighbors alone, if they will return the compliment."

"Oh, they will; have no fear about that. But will that suit your book ? It seems to me you can't afford to be let alone. You see, so independent a mind needs an independent fortune. As you are situated, you have to keep on terms with the world."

"I want no favors; only a chance to exercise such talents as Heaven has given me. I propose to fill any post I may occupy, and give an honest dollar's worth for every dollar I take."

"Undoubtedly. But whoever pays you a dollar, or gives you a chance to earn it, does you a favor, until you get your name well up and your services in demand. That's the way they look at it, and you can't change the fact. The competition is great; and he who wants work must put his soul into the search for it, as well as into the doing of it after he finds it. And that is what you won't do ; you might the last possibly, but not the other, which is the more important of the two. You're too proud and too wilful."

"Very few pursuits seem worth investing one's whole soul in, Bob ; a fair measure of brain and conscience ought to be enough for them. One should keep most of his force in reserve for higher occasions, and use some of it to find out what is worth doing."

"All that is for your private satisfaction, and practically useful only as a means toward doing something that will tell. The world cares nothing about your observations and your reserve forces ; it asks only, 'What has he put into the common fund ? What has he to show ? What is he doing that contributes to his own and the general interest ?' You see, it must tell somehow."

"Always this everlasting doing, Bob ! They make such a fuss about it, and it amounts to so little. I don't like the world and its ways ; I can't take its point of view."

"If you announce that, you will have a bad time in it, Dick. Since you are compelled to live in it, and not in some distant planet constructed according to your own ideas, you had better conform to its customs and requirements."

"I am willing to do my part, since, as you say, I have to make my own way and get my own

living. I wish I hadn't ; the whole thing is a bore.
I'll work if they will let me ; but I can't get up
any great enthusiasm about it, or pretend that
dross is gold."

BOOK FIRST.

EARLY DAYS.

CHAPTER II.

It might be inferred from the above conversation that my poor friend was younger than his actual age, or else a cowardly imbecile, which was far from true. He was at this time about twenty-six, and a person of very fair parts and excellent principles, or what would have appeared such had he been in harmony with his environment. But it was largely a case of heredity, and I had better begin the tale pretty far back.

The Graftons used to be people of consequence, with large estates bordering on the Chesapeake. One of them sat for a while in Congress, which was perhaps no discredit in those days ; his father had rendered service in the Revolution. Long before that, as long after, they were local magnates, keeping open house, and living easily on slave labor. This sort of thing does not last forever, and the race was slow to learn modern manners. On the eastern shore, it was said, the lower orders continued to hurrah for George Third at the beginning of the century, and to vote for Jackson long after he was under ground. In the Grafton neighborhood, within the memory of men yet living, were two ancient spinsters of illustrious name, who could not read — let us hope they had once learned but forgotten — and maintained themselves in squalor by hiring out a pair of negroes, the meagre remnant of their personal property. Dick's family kept up their traditions somewhat better; the men were sent to college, and came home to ride, shoot, fish, and occupy themselves with dying out. What vitality was in the blood generally passed to the eldest son; his brother (there were seldom more than the two) neither founded a new house nor long encumbered the old one. It was a startling novelty when the last of these cadets, after some unusual escapades, disappeared during the infancy of our unheroic hero, and was believed to have gone West.

Of Dick's grandfather an edifying incident was remembered. The heir of a Philadelphia merchant-prince, travelling in that benighted region, called at the manor-house to present a letter of introduction. The old gentleman glanced it over, recognized the signature, and was heard to mutter, "Damned tape-seller!" before rising to discharge the duties of lavish hospitality. His son was of gentler and less bigoted strain, but ill-fitted to increase any of his belongings except the library. There he mostly passed his time, a reader and theorizer, meditating plans that came to nothing, while servants idled and overseers gathered acres and bank accounts.

The boy, an only child this time, grew up at will, wandering over woods and streams, but his tastes were quiet and bookish ; unguided, he learned as much as he might have gained in school. The war passed by them little heeded : they were not politicians, and newspapers were infrequent visitors at the remote plantation. The father died when Richard was twelve ; the mother, placid and colorless, responded mildly to his mild affection, and exerted little influence upon him. Thus outward life made no strong impression ; its activities never came within his ken. He read of cities and foreign lands with no eager curiosity to see them ; the march of history, the strife of nations and of trade, the adventures of love and war, of travel and of business, seemed to him but a curious panorama, a puppet-show better to look at than take part in. He had few comrades of his own or any age, nor did he pine for them ; to sit on the veranda with a book, to paddle lazily on the creeks and inlets, was occupation enough. His mind was never idle, but it had little hold on externals ; it was his kingdom, and he wanted no other. He took matters " by and large ; " he early learned to generalize, and became impatient of details. Man to him was more than men ; he was at home in abstractions, puzzled and wearied before the concrete. As he grew older he mused much upon the fallen fortunes of his line, but no thought of restoring them occurred to him as a definite possibility ; he was the last, and the tale of what had gone before seemed to impose a law on him. These things went as they were ordered, and how could he resist the ordering, or succeed where his fathers had failed ? The ends that men were said to value so highly might be well enough if one had them and could take them quietly ; but surely they were not worth setting one's heart on and struggling for so furiously. To be useful, — that might be good if one knew how and had a· gift that way ; but taken selfishly, wealth, honors, power, were nothing except for their effect upon the mind ; and if the mind did not care for them, why then as well be without them. No ; exemption from the strife, to be away from the madding crowd, was best. A decent competence, shelter from the storm, peace and leisure and liberty, were all one need desire ; and if he could not have these, he would at least compromise, and take life on a small scale.

> "Sound sleep by night; study and ease
> Together mixt; sweet recreation;
> And innocence, which most does please
> With meditation."

Many a youth of introspective cast has thus mused in salad days of greenness, and changed the opinion when he was older ; but with poor Richard

the choice was sincere and wise. Had he been
differently trained from infancy — had some firm
hand persistently drawn him out of himself, and
fitted him against his will for the battle of life, he
might perchance have been able to win and hold
his own, or even to make his mark; for he lacked
not power of brain and will, but only direction of
these; a direction he never received till given
by hard necessity, and accepted under protest.
There may be many who fall under the burden
and heat of the day, unlamented, and scorned as
imbeciles, who might have deserved honors and a
better fate, — idealists like Sidney Lanier, lacking
his high resolve to do and die ; souls manly and
capable as Bayard Taylor's, could they have believed with him that it is possible ·to serve both
God and Mammon, and that the prize is worth the
race. The world has no respect and little pity for
them, for they do not follow its paths ; but I suppose the saying that heaven is for such as have
failed on earth applies to these whose failure
came by no inherent vice or weakness, but from
lack of harmony with their surroundings, from inability to worship the gods the popular Nebuchad-
nezzar has set up. If we take them into the
account at all, it certainly needs the prospect of
another world, managed on broader principles than
this, to save one's faith in the general ordering.
If success be the only test of merit, it is not easy
to see that we have advanced much beyond the

feudal notion disclaimed by Rumbold under the
gallows, that some are brought into the world
booted and spurred to ride, and others saddled and
bridled to be ridden.

Dick Grafton, if you took him intrinsically, had
as much force of character as anybody I ever
knew ; but it was his curse that his character
expressed itself negatively. No one could over-
rule him, or lead him where he did not choose to
go ; no force of circumstances could make him do
what he thought wrong ; but — looked at from outside — he had not the same will-power for doing as
for refusing. He was not stubborn in a vulgar
way, like so many stupid folks who call their obstinacy firmness, and are proud of it ; he was not
actively or consciously wilful, though I often called
him so. He was always willing to hear both sides,
to discuss a matter to its roots ; but he seemed to
be governed by an inward law that made it impossible for him to take the popular and conquering
course. The genesis of this intractability should
appear from what has been told of his childhood.
He never was under tutors and governors when
he ought to have been ; left thus alone, his nature
turned in upon itself, and stiffened and hardened
at the core, when outwardly it was soft and pli-
able.

I believe there are more people than we usually
think who hide this dogged immovableness under
a mild exterior, and without the least hypocrisy

or affectation. When they can take care of themselves, it is all well enough ; but when they cannot, it is very difficult to help them.

CHAPTER III.

A HAZING PARTY.

THE pressure of visible need might have awakened Dick from his dreams, but no such pressure was felt while, his mother lived, for she kept the place together somehow, and they never went away from home. Emancipation had destroyed the last vestige of their wealth, for the land was worn out and heavily mortgaged ; but the barnyard and the creeks supplied abundant food, and thus far there was no lack of clothing. Thus matters went on in a slovenly, careless fashion till Mrs. Grafton died, when Dick was just seventeen. He mourned her sincerely, but not violently ; whatever passions might exist within him had not yet been called forth. After the funeral his guardian, a distant relative, came to the front.

"Young man," said he, "you will never make a farmer, but I hear you are good at your books. The house is going to pieces; to repair it and make the fields productive would more than exhaust your capital. Education will be a more

profitable investment for you. There is nothing
to keep you here, and you ought to see the outside
world. I think we had better let the place go;
it will yield enough, with economy, to carry you
through college, and give you a start in life."

This sounded wise, and Richard had nothing
to say against it: as to where he should go and
what he should do he was quite willing to be
guided, if any one would take the trouble to guide
him. So he said farewell to the familiar water-
ways, shed a few private tears over the old dog
that had been his comrade almost since he could
remember, and started for a cooler and more
energetic clime. Yale was among the family traditions; a few months of preparation qualified him
for entrance, and there I first met him in the fall.

A little contact with his kind had taught him
much; he was not afflicted with hobbledehoy
shyness, and no one suspected how hermit-like
his life had been. I was a sophomore then, and
the custom of hazing had not been abandoned.
Dick had few acquaintances; but his room-mate,
a little fellow blest with a brother among the
juniors, was posted, and had given him the necessary points. So, when a party of us called on
them one evening, we were politely but warily
received. They set up the beer; our leader,
noted as a "bad man" and freshman-hater, poured
into Dick's portion, unseen as he thought, an
infusion of something stronger. Presently Dick,

with more success in escaping notice, exchanged
glasses : one or two of us, who detected the ma-
nœuvre, found no opportunity to warn Jones before
he swallowed the compound. Soon our hosts were
invited to contribute vocal music to the amenities
of the occasion. "Unfortunately, I don't sing,"
said Dick; "but Mr. Jones here is good at it, I
am told." Jones, who was by this time in a state
of maudlin amiability and ready to fraternize with
his worst foe, promptly complied, and made a
sufficient exhibition of himself. So heterodox a
turning of the tables deeply disgusted us, for when
had a sophomore ever made mirth for freshmen?
The Marylander was asked, with some urgency,
to display his powers in other directions ; but all
these suggestions he coolly declined.

The hazing fervor at that time had received
some discouragement from tales, probably apocry-
phal, of a wild Arkansan who, being beset in his
room at Ann Arbor, had turned off the gas, picked
up a heavy chair, and "gone for" the crowd in
the dark with good will and too marked results,
and of a Carolinian who had knifed his assailants
nearer home. Much respect was felt for Southern prowess, and it was agreed that students from
Spanish-American lands should be exempt from
domiciliary visits. At a council held on the first
night of term, the truculent Jones himself remarked, "Understand, boys, these foreign ducks
are to be let alone. They're not up to our customs,

and it's not fair or hospitable to bother them; I
don't go into any arsenal. And I say, fellers, let's
look out for these coons from the cotton states, and
inquire whether a man carries a bowie before we
drop in on him. We want to do it gentlemanly,
and not get into rows with any dashed duellist."

The committee of investigation had satisfied
themselves that Grafton was harmless, and so
instructed the squad which took his case in hand;
but when the critical moment arrived, our *a priori*
doubts returned. He was from the wrong side
of the line after all, and he had a Southern look.
He was well grown and muscular for his age,
with very dark hair, a firm chin, and an eye that
looked as if it could flash. His easy manners
showed good blood, and hinted at dignity in
reserve, if there should be any call for it; his
tranquil presence of mind was more than we had
expected. Veal is better adapted to the hazing
process than precocious beef; so after looking
at each other awhile, and answering his civil
questions rather tamely, we rose to go, on the
best terms with our entertainers, and feeling
that we had furnished too much of the entertainment ourselves. Our ex-hero Jones was in no
condition to rise; as we lifted him, Grafton observed, in a tone of dispassionate criticism, "His
head must be weak. I'm not much used to beer
myself, but I can't imagine its affecting me like
that."

Having thus begun his college course with *éclat* my friend (as he soon became) continued it with decent credit, but without fulfilling the expectations to which his first exploit had given rise. Several fraternities sounded him, but he said he had not much cash to spare for luxuries, and did not care to branch out just then. His classmates, at first disposed to rally round him, soon found that he was a peaceable youth with no pretensions to leadership. He went into athletics enough to meet their demands, and into junketings sufficiently to avoid being thought mean or unsocial, but he was not bigoted to such. "I don't know how to take Grafton," the great Van Snoozer was heard to state. Van Snoozer was an F. F. and plutocrat in one, handsome, envied, and courted, who held his head high, and had a right to. "He's friendly enough when you drop in on him, and always has time to hear what you've got to say. He'll go out with you when you ask him — sometimes. He's not a mere grind, nor the least of a cad in any way, and you can't say he's offish. But he doesn't seem to appreciate your attentions, nor to value his opportunities." At this point Tufts, who stood listening reverently on the outskirts, sighed at the thought of such a waste, and groaned and frowned over the sacrilege of it. "O, yes, I know he'll stand by a friend; but how much does he care for his friends, or for anything, as far as you can see? If this

were England now, and he a duke's son, with
rent-roll and the rest to match, it might do; but
as it is, I'm blanked if I can understand his
being so dashed indifferent."

This was delivered with some feeling. It *was*
difficult to patronize Grafton ; and Van, whom he
had pulled and pushed through a tough examination,
and whose usage it was to pay for such
services in suppers, introductions, and the like,
was naturally puzzled, as were some others. But
Dick fell into no snares and made no enemies.
The only sins you could lay at his door were
negative. He was not this, that, or the other,
one or sundry of which a youth generally is and is
expected to be ; not gluttonous nor a wine-bibber,
nor a friend of jockeys and actresses ; no toady to
wealth or station or office ; no devotee to football
or waltzing, nor yet even to chemistry and calculus;
neither pietist, bookworm, nor worldling of
any ascertained and labelled type, but just a quiet
fellow who did his daily tasks and somewhat
more, asked no favors, and liked to look about
him and see how men disported themselves and
how things were done. Now observation of character
and manners is not a recognized profession,
nor is it easy to see how one may make a living
by it. If you have a definite aim indeed,— if
you mean to be a politician, and secure people's
votes ; or a blackmailer, and realize on their
secrets ; or a novelist, and expound their weak-

nesses,—there may be profit in this calm study
of your kind. But none of these was likely to
be Grafton's "lay:" the trouble about him was
that he seemed to have no "lay"—no serious
purpose in life, such as the rest of us pursue.
Even his observations sometimes bored him, because no mastering sympathy entered into them.
A man must take his line, and follow it as if it
were liable to lead to something, or what would
the world come to? Little Tufts, perhaps the
only man in college who actively disliked Dick,
used to say, "The feller's a fool, don't yer see?
Why, he's poor, he is, and yet he never borrows,
though Van Snoozer would lend him fifty any
day. Don't even return half Van's visits;
dash such an ass, I say. Plays a good hand at
whist and billiards, and never makes any money
by it—won't gamble, he says! I wish to Jove
I had the chances he throws away. Would you
believe it, at the last hop old Billion's daughter
took a shine to him,—the old lady too, and
invited him to their swell place by the Park; and
the blanked idiot's never been !! I wish to Zeus
she'd take a shine to me. Don't even go to
Prex's, or to the profs', though a dozen of 'em
have asked him; hasn't sense enough to see that
somethin' can be made out of the Faculty. What
the demon does he mean by such conduct? Just
grubs and looks at Life, he says. What the
hades is the use of lookin' at Life, unless you're

on spec, goin' to make a pot out of it, eh? No make in him at all; he'll never do any good in this world. Dod gast such a gosh blasted loafer, anyway."

CHAPTER IV.

ECHOES OF ALMA MATER.

THESE comminations, and such occasion for them as their object may have furnished, were of later date. I do not propose to afflict the reader with a detailed narrative of Dick's four years in academic halls. They constituted the happiest portion of his life — at least that is the received and canonical opinion as to all of us. And yet, however important and blissful that early and formative era, there is seldom much to say about it afterwards. How flat and stale the recollection of experiences once full of zest, — the surreptitious joys of evenings in oyster-cellars ; the well-planned assault on freshman windows ; the breathless retreat, hotly pursued by minions of the law ; the ecstasy of painting Professor Z.'s horse blue, and painfully leading him up the stairs ; the delirious rapture of skulking through snow half the night, picking a few locks, and bearing away in trembling triumph the clapper of the big bell ! Why is it that when graybeards

meet to exchange reminiscences of lang syne,
their sedate tongues babble of grovelling class-
room imbecilities? — How, during the brief career
of Jugs and Grogson, they would enter with
unsteady step, lean heavily on the back of a
friendly bench, fix on the blackboard a glassy
stare, thickly answer in the very words of the
book, and fall wofully at the first departure from
that sacrosanct order, or question of how and why.
How Shirk used to pin his faith to Diddle, and
drink in wisdom from his monitory lips, and from
them alone ; how in history, gently wooed to name
some of these Elizabethan free lances of the sea,
— " Now, Mr. Shirk, who was Raleigh's half-
brother? I am sure you know. Sir Hum-
phrey — ? " He bent toward his chosen guide,
caught two magic syllables, and cheerfully responded, "O, yes, sir, of course! Sir Humphry Davy."
How in chemistry, required to state the properties
of gold, he turned to the same unfailing source
of light, and rejoiced professor and class with
the priceless information that " All is not gold
that glitters." But in the Latin room no such
vicarious wisdom was accepted, for Syntax knew
boys; no getting around him. You remember
Dummy's handling of the intricate passage that
began, *Et insignum* — ? By rule he was allowed
five minutes. For two of them he stood with the
book close to his nose, then looked up and ventured with dubious inquiry, " *Et* — and ? " This

being admitted, three minutes more passed in solemn silence; then, with more confidence, "*Insignum* — the ensign?"

Grafton's enjoyment of such feats was less vociferous than that of the rest. Not that he and I were ever in the same class : I would not have you suppose that I was dropped a year. But he surveyed most phenomena with placid tolerance, feeling nowise responsible for idle dullards like Shirk and Dummy; as for Grogson and Jugs, — why, if men chose to mistake themselves for lower animals, that was their affair. Obviously, Dick would make but a fourth-class missionary. But it was not safe to practise gross meanness or injustice when he was by. He never fought, but he had a way of drawing himself up and staring at you from under lowered brows that was unpleasantly suggestive. Once there was a contest between Truman and Caddy for a prize, and we all knew who deserved it. While others were talking about what ought to be done if it should fall to Caddy, Grafton went to him and said, " If you like to cheat through an examination and avoid a flunk, I have nothing to say ; but you ought to know that honors and scholarships are not to be got that way. If you get this one, I will tell the authorities how you did it."

"You will? Play informer, eh?"

"Just so; and you can't say you had no warning."

There was no more trouble about that. He was a generous fellow too. He rather laughed at philanthropy, but he used to do more good turns than most of us. I stopped one night to take him to a show; a very decent show it was, of the mildly improving kind. I thought he had been working too hard, and needed relaxation.

" I can't go, Bob; too busy, you see."

"What's all that exercise? It's never yours."

"No," he said reluctantly, "it's Featherton's. He had an engagement to-night, and I promised to do it for him."

"How's this? Helping the camel to go through the needle's eye? I thought you were down on cheating."

" Yes; but he's in a hole rather, and can't get out by himself. It can't hurt anybody, and I don't want to see him dropped."

"I say, what does he pay you for this?"

He flushed. "Pay? What do you take me for? You'd do it, or anybody."

Now, "anybody" would not, as far as my experience goes ; but that was Dick all over. He would let himself be imposed on by a careless ne'er-do-well, who would forget the service to-morrow ; he would waste an evening to do another's work in misplaced good nature, and anxiously avoid getting any credit or profit from it, then or ever after,

CHAPTER V.

INFANTILE CONFERENCES.

STUDENT customs have — or had in my time — a rigidity which the outside world cannot comprehend, and which even to an alumnus of a dozen years seems somewhat mediæval. However badly a junior might want a light for his cigarette, an unwritten but Median law forbade him to accept it — on the campus — from a lower classman. But this rule was relaxed indoors and as graduation approached, and during my last year Dick and I came to be as intimate as he ever was with any one. .

"Grafton," I asked him one night, "what are you going to do when you get through here?"

"I am not sure. There's over a year yet. Take to the law, I suppose."

"What for? You don't care for law, do you?"

"Not especially. How many fellows have any marked taste or talent for anything in particular — I don't mean in the way of beer, tobacco, dinners, dances, and the theatre, but occupation, line of

life? Not one in twenty. How do we know what
we are best fitted for? Aptitudes are seldom
developed at our time of life. I rather envy those
who escape the bother of choosing, and have a
way marked out plain before them, like you. I
might go into business in that way, — if I had it
all fixed, and paternal prestige, and skilled clerks
to conduct it for me. Otherwise, I have no turn
for it."

This he said not the least enviously, but simply,
as one who states a case. He was frank enough,
and ready to discuss any subject, but in a general,
impersonal way. When he brought himself in —
which he was as ready to do as others — it was as
illustrating the principle or case in hand; not as if
his fortunes, or any external fact or set of facts,
could be a prime consideration. He seemed to
have no secrets, no ambitions, no prejudices, no
passions worth mentioning, and scarcely any
interests.

" By the way, what has become of your farm in
Maryland?"

" My guardian took that. It was encumbered,
you know."

" Makes a good thing of it, does he?"

" Better than I should. I wouldn't mind living
there as my fathers did, if it were still mine. But
I know nothing about land and crops, and that.
Oh, it will come right somehow."

" You have no relations?"

"None of any account. The guardian never cared for me, nor I for him. There was a brother of my father's who went off ages ago and died, we supposed ; he was never heard of again. No, I'm all alone ; have to stand on my own pins, or tumble."

"Would you mind telling me how you're set up, Dick ? "

"Not the least, if I knew ; but I've not en-quired into details. Time for that when I come of age. I believe there's enough to keep me a while yet, and then I must get up and go to work. So I thought of law. They say it leads everywhere."

" I doubt if it leads where you want to go ; politics are not in your way, surely. To do any good at law you've got to persuade yourself that you believe in it — or pretend to, anyway. Remember Dummy, when he was plucked, and Smith asked him what he would do next : 'I shall read law; the study of the law is the most gentlemanly excuse for doing nothing.' That might do for him, but not for you."

" I'm not conscious of any wild longing to do anything in particular, Bob ; and I presume I could do one thing about as well as another. No tormenting desire to show the world how to keep house disturbs my sleep o' nights. I could be content to sit still and see how folks do it of their own motion."

"So most of us feel; we'd like to take it easy and let others do the work. But that's not exactly your style either."

"What I object to is the practical part — the competition and the scrambling. I can do my own work if it's cut out for me, but I don't want to push myself, and stand in some other fellow's light. I suppose one can learn to do it, though, when he has to."

"Why not try teaching? You're an intellectual chap — you like books and ideas, and all that."

"District school, and board around, as Hobbs did last summer? Thanks; such ambition as I have flies a little higher than that."

"Well, journalism, then; that might get you on the literary line."

"You have to begin with reporting. I haven't the cheek to ring people's door-bells and ask 'em about their daughters' elopements. Do you believe I could be an author, Bob, — write big books, and be one of the few immortal names?"

"You ask me too much, Dick: time alone can tell. But you might be a writer. You generally get ten on essays, don't you?"

"Who'd want to print our essays? They're mere 'prentice work. O, yes! with practice I might do conundrums for the story papers, and see my initials in the poet's corner. That might suit Bardie here, but I don't seem to care about it."

At this point his chum, who had just come in,
took a hand. He was a wiry, nervous little boy,
with curly hair, blue eyes, and ideas far above his
stature; said to be addicted to verse of his own
construction, but free from other vices. The roy-
sterers of their class called him and Dick the pair
of doves.

"You never do seem to care about anything;
that's what's the matter with you. I wish you'd
take him out and shake him, Tim."

If any of my class had been present, I might
have felt obliged to resent a junior's making thus
free with my name. They all did it themselves,
but this was too unconventional. But, alas! I was
never, like General Banks at New Orleans, great
on dignity; and Bardie meant no harm. So I let
him go on.

"It's too bad! Here are a dozen great careers
waiting for a chap that's got a head on him, and
a soul inside him; and —"

"Which of 'em do you mean to follow, Bardie?"

"I? Oh! we're not talking about me; Dick's
the theme just now. I don't mind you, Tim. You
waste your time dreadfully, and keep some pretty
rough company; but you're not half as bad a lot
as you'd like people to think, and I for one believe
you've got a heart. Keep still now, and let me
go on. — Why, he might be a statesman, and make
his voice heard in the council-halls of his state, or
even of the nation; there's need enough of reform

in Baltimore, close to where he came from. Or he
might be a doctor, and carry the balm of healing
to suffering thousands — hough I don't think so
much of that, for the body isn't the man. Or he
might make a big fortune — wait, now, and hear
me out; not that that's of any account in itself, of
course, only think what good he might do with it!
There's a lack of large-minded and public-spirited
millionnaires, as we all know. Or he might be a
great scholar, and shed abroad the light of science,
and perhaps get to be president of this concern in
time; even here some improvements might be
made. He's got capacity, if he had any ambition.
Or —"

"Or he might be a thumping preacher, only he
never could compete with you," Dick interrupted,
reaching for the tobacco jar.

"Or he might be a poet, and write beautiful
songs to bring tears to every female eye," said another; "but he doesn't seem to care for it, because
there you'd be ahead of him again."

"Well," said Bardie, flushing a little, "anyway
you both know he ought to be stirred up, and have
a noble aim, and go in for something great and
useful."

CHAPTER VI.

CUI BONO?

BUT enough — perhaps too much — of this innocent childish talk.   Alas poor infants, who think
the world is all before them where to choose, and
they can do pretty much anything if only they
make up their minds to this or that !   We smile
at the raw conceit, forgetting the sadness of the
spectacle in the light of what lies ahead.   What
more pathetic than to hear green youth exclaim,
"I will be a statesman — or a famous artist — or
a great author !" or what not ?   Dear child, what
does the world care for you and your roseate
schemes ?— How do you know it has any room for
you at all ?   You may be thankful by and by if
through any sort of tolerably honest drudgery you
can pay the rent in an obscure back street, and the
butcher's and grocer's bills as they fall due.   Bardie is now a meek little minister in a New Hampshire village, raising a fine family on seven hundred
dollars a year.   The light has gone out of his eye,
and he has forgotten more poetry, written or un-

written, than I ever knew ; but his sentences are
still neatly turned, and the old ladies of his flock
say he reads Dr. Watts's hymns beautifully. And
Dick — poor Dick, dear Dick, who had more in
him than any of us, if only he could have brought
it to bear — ah well, let us not look ahead so
eagerly, or so disconsolately. The evil day will
come soon enough ; there is abundant time to tell
of his struggle with environment. Let him repose
in the arms of Alma Mater while he may. His
tasks there are congenial and definite ; as yet
no vague responsibility for managing events and
shaping life perplexes his brain and dulls his
spirit ; the day has not arrived for half-envious
wonderment at those who, with far less mental
range and furnishing, solve easily the baser problems that were not included in his curriculum.

For such as Dick, and for multitudes little like
him, grave doubts may be raised as to the value of
a college course which prepares for and leads to
nothing. In a semi-feudal society, where a gentleman has his ancestral acres to retire to and perhaps parliament to enter, he wants the traditional
accomplishments of his order ; to keep on terms
with his Homer and Lucretius may be amusing
and appropriate. But that is another case than
ours. Of what use are Greek roots and metaphysics to those who have to fight for a foothold,
and for every inch of advance ? They give tone
to the mind, perhaps, but not the tone that is

wanted for real life. A university atmosphere is
not that of the outside world : it may be purer
and finer, but when one descends from scholastic
heights into the marketplace, his lungs are poorly
fitted for the transition. Contact with books and
abstract ideas has given his brain a stamp which
does not recommend the goods, and turned it into
other roads than that of commerce. Not only is
the graduate distrusted in newspaper offices and
counting-rooms, but he feels himself too good for
the work that is open to him. It is coarse, and
he is fine, if not superfine : what a waste of his
acquirements, — to hide them behind a desk or
counter ! His nature has been subdued to what
it worked in, and now it must soak in another
vat and take a different dye. The aristocrat of
thought is but a poor plebeian before the aristocracy of shares, and his careful speculations vain,
since they look to no returns of cash. Laboriously he must unlearn what he has been learning,
and begin with another alphabet — a Volapük of
trade, in which men compute and calculate to out-
wit each other.

I buy my cigars of Schnabeling, whose shop is
under the Hungarian theatre ; a fluent and travelled exile, whose conversation is improving. "O,
yes," he informs me, "dis is better dan de oder.
Ven I teach Greek and Latin, my vife haf to do
de vashing ; now she vear silk and go to de play.
Tobacco pay vell, yes ; but classic — ach !" He

has introduced me to Professor Von Bamberg, who holds several titles and a creditable post in one of our erudite institutions. " I am too oldt to schange," he says, " but our friendt here vas vise. For vhat I spendt so many years at Heidelberg and Berlin? I am ghentleman, yes ; but vhat of dhat? I am an employé. My neighbor de plumber, he employs oders, and earn ten dollar vhile I earn von. He enjhoy life; he feel no deficiency; he leave his schildren providedt for. I live on a higher plane, you say, I haf mental resources? Ach, but dhat is not practical, not American. It is de *gelt, pecunia, l'argent!* "

If my boys had their way to make, I should aim to begin their training for it at the earliest possible moment. You send a youth to West Point or Annapolis : only get him in, and he is all right if he can stand the pace, and if the navy is not cut down again. He goes forth with a profession, such as it is, a position, a salary. They give him some nominal work to do, whatever it may amount to, and keep him at it ; at least he is not left out in the cold, he does not have to think what he can turn to next. That is one use of government ; and that is the main argument for socialism, — the difficulty of finding and keeping a footing in the crowd, the incompetence of many to do it. Why should not education recognize the facts of modern life, and, instead of merely enlarging the circle of one's wants, teach him how to supply them?

From time immemorial we have had schools of
law, physic, and divinity, and more recently of
engineering, agriculture, and finance ; yet about
even these hangs a suspicion of the visionary and
unsubstantial.   Is theory naturally hostile to practice, and learning at variance with doing?   I
have heard ministers say that all their theology
that was worth insuring was gained after leaving
the seminary, and engineers, that their diploma
signified no more than a plan after which their
house of professional knowledge was to be built.
As the country becomes more crowded and the
struggle for existence fiercer, our schemes of
study will have to be modified more and more,
until the college offers an avenue leading to, and
not away from, the paths of after-life.   General
culture, "the humanities," a wider range of mental
vision and sympathy, are very fine things ; but
work in the world is for the most part neither
humane nor liberal, nor in any wise refined or
rarefied, but narrow and rough and hard.   Our
time-honored plans of instruction appear to assume
that anybody can make a living, or a fortune if he
should need or care for it, much as Dogberry held
that reading and writing come by nature ; and one
position is about as well justified as the other.

You say I am preaching base materialism.   Am
I responsible for the present state of things, for
Life as it is, and its hard laws?   It seems time
we began to face the facts and try to mend them,

by sending forth our rising generation — our *élite* and elect youth, if you like — fitted as well as may be to claim and keep their own. Nobody else is likely to look after them if they cannot do it for themselves; and it is a pity to see so many learned titles strewn about the country, battered and rusty because the owners have not wherewith to keep them in repair.

CHAPTER VII.

THE SOCRATIC IDEA.

My family being in business, and not ashamed of it, I had more inkling of these facts, or principles — call them which you prefer; we will not quarrel about a term — than Grafton could be expected to possess; though the bulk of such usable wisdom as either of us ever acquired (or any other fellow, for that matter) was laid in by slow degrees long after taking our B.A. During his junior year my friend, more through his own reading than from class-room requirements, became inthralled by the ancient philosophy, or what he supposed to be its leading ideas. Not being a German or a Scotchman, he had no very pronounced taste for pure metaphysics; but the moral and rudimentary part of those notions, as outlined in the fourth century and expounded by sympathetic Occidentals, gripped him hard. I never believed that the old masters themselves, with some few exceptions, cared half as much for this doxy as did their belated disciple; for the Greek mind, while vastly delighted with dialectical puzzles, had no bigoted attachment to questions of faith and conscience. But poor Dick thought he had found a rule for the conduct of life. He said all the antique schools branched from the trunk of Socrates, laying stress on whatever part of his teaching they happened to like best, as all the Christian sects did from Jesus. This, I suppose, may have been so; but it was not the main point. He fell in love with the Socratic idea that the end of man was to recognize Truth and be in harmony with it; to look things in the face, and call them by their right names; to respect facts, and order his life according to them. When he burst upon us with this discovery — for, incredible as it may appear, these pale abstractions had more charm for him than a boat-race or a ball, and waked him to new life — we told him that was all simple and obvious, and nothing to make a fuss about.

"But how many remember it, or live by it?" he cried. "To cast aside prejudice and passion and self-interest, to look steadily at and care simply for the Truth — here's a chart to steer by! Original and absolute truth voiced and shadowed forth in existing facts, in the phenomena of life; why, that makes heaven accessible, and gives us a noble law at once for thought and action."

"See here, Dick," said I; "according to this, whatever is is right. You'll not find it so — not by a jugfull. I know better."

"You mustn't take it so narrowly," said he. "It doesn't mean that your cutting so many classes is right, or staying out so late nights; but the general concourse of events, the harmonies of cause and effect, the ordinances of nature. Rightly understood, these are a law to our minds, a law of magnanimity and veracity and wisdom. All events, characters, and thoughts are parts of the whole, and we may learn from any source."

"That sounds transcendental," I said, "and I don't believe it. Have you been to Concord lately? Dick, if you go on like this, you'll get to be a mere muddle-headed theorist."

"He's right, of course," Bardie shouted joyously. "He wanted just this to rouse him. You shut up, Tim."

"There's no harm in being a theorist so long as you're not a dogmatist," said Dick. "Why, man, how can you live without theories?"

"You certainly can't live *on* 'em," I replied. "That's the point; you make a note of it." But he would not heed; with all his talk about being open to truth, he would take it only in such shapes as suited him. Ah, what green goslings we were in those days, with our Ideals and Phenomena and such! Yet even I, though I was but a year or two older, and the President (who was prejudiced against me) might not think me the best guide for my juniors, could have taught Dick a thing or two, had he listened. At that time, alas! he had no ears for any instructor less venerable than Socrates and F. D. Maurice. The sins of the fathers are visited upon the children, and the self-indulgences of youth return to plague us in maturity. That was a wise man who said that of all his sins those of omission weighed heaviest on his accusing conscience — though I think he had committed arson and several burglaries. If Grafton had done no worse than amuse himself like the rest of us with a moderate amount of drinking and gambling, he might not have been so heavily punished afterwards; but when a fellow goes off mooning with toploftical theories, and turns a deaf ear to prudent counsels, what can he expect or what can his friends expect for him?

CHAPTER VIII.

MRS. MAGELLAN'S.

AFTER graduating, I was supposed to be closely occupied learning the business in New York; but I went to New Haven now and then, and persuaded Grafton to come to me at Christmas. Here I strove to induct him into metropolitan society and its canons.

"You go out too little, old man. It's not what a man knows, so much as *whom* he knows, that tells. You ought to be making acquaintances that may be useful to you."

"I can't take that view, Bob. A man must depend on his own exertions."

"Yes, but his own exertions may need backers. If you make the right impression on the right people, they can put things in your way, and open various channels to your beneficent activity. See?".

"No, I don't. There's time enough for all that yet. I've got my studies to attend to. And then I know a lot of fellows."

"Much trouble you ever took to know them, staying in your room and grubbing at your old pagans. We live in the nineteenth century A.D., man, not in the fourth B.C. Did you ever make an effort to cultivate anybody that was worth knowing, now?"

"Why no, not especially. My friends usually come to me. Affinity and taste regulate these matters."

"You can't live on your tastes. There's Van Snoozer, for instance. He feels grateful to you, and would like to show it. He's not a bad fellow, and with his wealth and influence—"

"What do I want of his wealth and influence? He's not my sort; he's too rich. You don't suppose I would make a trade of friendship? That will do for Tufts."

"Do you remember what Tufts said about you once? Well, there was truth in it, though he put it coarsely. You're far from a loafer, and you're not a fool in the broad sense, but if you go on in this way, people will think you are. You neglect your opportunities, and you won't think of your interests. I tell you, these things go for more than scholarship and abstract ability and character. People don't care for the abstract: it's the concrete that wins."

He looked disgusted. "Do you want me to be a male Becky Sharp? I should be ashamed to look people in the face if I were thinking of what

I could make by them. Relations must be free and natural and spontaneous, or I don't want them."

"What do you suppose people go into society for, dear child?"

"A few to study character and manners, or brush up their wits by contact, and most to meet their friends and enjoy themselves, I presume. That's all right, though I don't care for it."

"They are like Mary's little lamb, eh? Love of their kind and pure affectionateness — was that your idea? They go to secure or improve their positions; position is everything in this world, and it involves relations with a lot of people. There may be exceptions, but as a rule we're all on the make, in one way or another."

"I don't like to hear you talk like this, Bob. It seems to take all heart and soul out of life. You are not so mercenary as you pretend, or you wouldn't care to have me about; there is nothing to be made out of me. I had better get back to college."

"Not yet for a few days, sweet youth. You've got to take in at least one crusher, and see the world that lieth in wickedness."

The next night I took him to Mrs. Magellan's. He was not altogether a hermit, but accustomed to do his duty as a classman, some small part of which was social. Thus he had several times been obliged to entertain ladies at the hops, a task requiring no vast intellectual outlay. If he possessed but a moderate fund of small talk, he could at least smile politely and look like a gentleman in his decent though not oppressively new dress coat, which dated from early in his sophomore year; and I did not fear his appearing awed by so much splendor, or talking Greek philosophy unawares. He had already met several persons, and I introduced him to others who would know how to handle him and not mind the trouble too much; besides, there was my sister to look after him at need. He could dance in a way, and a good-looking youth who has that merit can get on well enough, as he seemed to do. On the way home I asked him,

"Well, what do you think of it?"

He answered in his usual placid and summarizing way, "It was all right. Very well done, no doubt; very nice for those who like that kind of thing."

"Several pegs above what we had at New Haven, eh? Yet you don't seem impressed by it."

"Impressed? No; why should I be? It was simply one of the phenomena, and not so much in my line as some others."

"O, hang up your phenomena. Weren't you struck by any of the girls?"

"They didn't carry clubs, that I saw. What would I be struck for?"

"Well, fellows sometimes are. How is it that you don't care for female loveliness?"

"How is it that I don't care for race-horses, or editions *de luxe*, or fancy farming, or the stock market? They are not in my line. It's just as well that I have no expensive tastes, isn't it?"

We had dropped into Delmonico's, and were consuming some light refreshment. As my guest, I wished him to see things that were beyond his usual range; but it is sometimes hard to know what to say to such a fellow.

"Bob," he went on, "I had better get out of this. You're very kind, but I don't care to play the country mouse sponging on his city cousin when he can't respond in kind. You see, it's all so different; I can't set up the champagne, nor entertain you and others as you do me."

"Who expects it of you? Are you putting down in your mental accounts, 'To R. T., *Dr.*, one pint Mumm and one shrimp salad'? We don't do things that way, my dear boy. Have you been oppressed by our haughty state at the house? I thought we were rather unpretentious and homelike."

He blushed. "No; you're all right. But it isn't even; it isn't fair. I felt as if I had no business at Mrs. M.'s to-night."

"Because you're not triple-plated? Did you think you owed her a return blow-out? The gilding on some of those swells is pretty thin.

You noticed Dacres and De Shyster? They sleep in little hall bedrooms on the fifth floor, dine at cheap places on Sixth Avenue, and save their pennies to come out strong on these occasions."

" I can put my pennies to a better use, preferring as I do a simpler life. There was that dinner Van Snoozer gave us ; I tried to get out of it, you know, but couldn't. He means well, but these things leave me with an unpleasant sense of obligation."

" That's all nonsense, I tell you. Your pride will be the ruin of you ; put it in your pocket, and take things as they come."

" I prefer to pay my own way, and live within my income. However narrow that may be, a man can at least preserve his self-respect. To do that, he had better not mix too much with those who are differently situated ; the fitness of things forbids it."

To this notion he stuck as Quixote to Rosinante, nor could my arguments budge him from his high horse.

CHAPTER IX.

THE DE GROUTS.

OF course I attended the next commencement, where Grafton had the valedictory and went off in a blaze of glory. He was a fair speaker, and one of the best writers in his class; not that what they write there bears any relation to what is wanted outside — as he had the sense to know, and had once acknowledged. His effort dealt with the Relations of Thought to Life, and was hugely applauded. Its ideas, as you might expect, were wholly abstract, unfounded, and misleading, but an audience will put up with any amount of philosophical foolishness at such times. Tufts had withdrawn long before (in fact, he had worked his principles for more than they were worth, and been caught cheating at cards, as well as at the blackboard), so Dick had not an enemy in the place. Now was his chance, if it had been anybody else, to come into something good; but his high-toned obstinacy stood in the way, of course. Van Snoozer, whose younger brother was wild, wanted Grafton to take the boy to Europe and act as bear-leader for a while; but Dick, suspecting patronage in it, declined an offer which you or I, in his circumstances, would have jumped at. Harker, who had no more cash and less qualities than our misguided friend, secured the berth, and to that auspicious start in life owed his subsequent fortunes: diligently cultivating the connection, he married judiciously on the outer edge of the charmed circle, set up as a stockbroker, got points from Van's uncle, the railroad magnate, and was rich before he was thirty. Dick never could have done all that, I own; and he had made up his misjudging mind to try the law. One or two of the professors advised him to take pupils, and sent him a few, for he was too proud to seek them. This occupied his vacation, and his leisure through part of the fall.

In the winter I induced him, much against his will, to make me another visit. He was warmly received by my people, and by others of the Yale set, who knew of his high standing and blameless record: solid old-fashioned men, who liked to see the virtues of their youth repeated; matrons who admired pink cheeks, pure brows, and guileless frankness in a boy, and were not apt to find them in their own sons; some young girls even, who saw the halo of commencement yet about his head. We dined with the De Grouts, who still display the plate of their Huguenot ancestor, and some mahogany nearly as old; but perhaps you will kindly excuse me from describing the furniture. As we sat solemnly over some extra regalias, the head of the house thus accosted his principal guest, who was not myself.

"My dear sir, it is not my custom to use many words; but I have not forgotten what you did for my unhappy boy. If ever I can—"

Here, with what seemed to me a gross breach of his usual good manners, Dick hastened to interrupt. "O, thank you; but it was nothing—nothing at all." I kicked him under the table; why will he flout the goddess Fortune whenever she tries to smile on him?

"My son thinks differently; but it is a pleasure to meet, in this degenerate day, a young man who is unwilling to discuss his own good deeds. You will at least permit me to say that I appreciate your influence on Clinton. That of our friend Robert here might not have been equally beneficial." And he looked at me rather grimly.

I knew I was asked there only on Dick's account; but I answered loyally, "Well, sir, you can't expect us all to be such paragons as Grafton. He's a sort of *lusus naturæ*, he is. He can row a fair oar, and catch a tolerable ball; and yet he was always well up near the head. He was class treasurer once, and I believe his accounts came out straight, or very near it. He never got into any scrapes or rows at all, which is unusual, sir, I assure you. Quite popular with the boys, he was; and yet the faculty thought a heap of him."

"So I have heard," said the old gentleman, smiling gravely, while Dick fidgeted on his chair, and scowled at me. "By the way, Mr. Grafton, your great-grandfather married into a branch of my family then resident in Virginia, now, unhappily, extinct. Yes, your great-grandmother was a second cousin once removed of my grandfather's half-brother Hugh, who was killed at Eutaw, as you may remember; there hangs his sword. She was a reigning beauty in her day. We are among the few New Yorkers, my dear sir, who are not indifferent to the past." And they went off into the depths of a genealogical discussion, while I escaped to the parlor. Madame and her handsome daughter received me civilly, but looked as if they would rather see the beneficent and irreproachable Dick.

"Well," I asked later that night, "did you pass examination on the battle of Eutaw? At least you remember your great-grandmother's beauty?"

He did not seem to see the joke. "My ancestors may not have left me much, but I keep their pedigree if not their acres. I enjoyed Mr. De Grout's conversation."

"A good thing you did; I don't grudge it to you. What was that about the son? You never told me of that."

"It wouldn't interest you, as you knew the boy

but slightly.   He was a soph then, and inclined to
be fast.   He got into a scrape, and I happened to
be near by; I had coached him once or twice.
The particulars are of no account."

" No, I suppose not.   And after that you played
Rhadamanthus and Boanerges, made him see the
error of his ways, and snatched him as a brand from
the burning.   Yes, you could do that better than
I, as the old gentleman said."

" He was behind with his work — had to stay
half the summer, and I was asked to coach him
again, as a matter of business this time.   They
paid for the lessons; I didn't like it altogether.
It seemed as if I ought not to be dining there to-
day, having been in their employ."

" Bright idea that, Richard.   When we go to
Washington, and call on the President, no doubt
he'll be ashamed to shake hands with us, being in
our pay."

" Well, you can exaggerate, and you can laugh,
Bob; but I feel as if I had derogated from my
dignity, and lost caste."

" You'll have to go on derogating and losing —
unless you marry an heiress soon.   Are you a
feudal baron, or an American democrat?   There
was a doctor once who felt as you do, and never
could bring himself to take a fee.   The people
were so grateful that they elected him to a public
maintenance in the prytaneum — which was in his
case the poorhouse."

"I dare say it's absurd, Bob, and of course I have to support myself; but I would rather do it among strangers. The De Grouts paid me near fifty dollars last summer; it was almost the first money I ever earned."

"Well, you did earn it, I judge, and they can afford it."

"Yes; but this mixing business with social relations doesn't seem right. When they received me almost as a friend, I felt that I was in a false position."

"Babe of the woods, your position in that house — or what you could make it in a week, if you chose — would be envied by half the men about town. I wouldn't mind taking it myself, if it were transferable. You've struck oil, my son, and struck it rich."

He stared at me. "I don't understand. What do you mean?"

"The father, for all his quaint ways, is one of our leading men. The mother can do what she pleases socially. In a quiet way they are cream of the cream; didn't you know that? I tell you, that invitation was an honor, and I was in it only perforce and on sufferance; they are particular to the last degree. Not only do they feel indebted to you, but they approve of you, and like you; tastes vary. The boy is evidently attached to you — I suppose he has reason; and the others are inclined to follow suit; their domestic feelings are strong.

There are but the two children, Clint and Miss Edith. She is just out, and said to be a very superior young person. By the way, what do you think of her looks ? "

"I scarcely noticed — or not especially."

"You didn't? Where were your eyes, man? Hers are better; she noticed you, I am able to inform you. Didn't you meet her last commencement ? "

"Yes, and danced with her, I believe. O yes, her brother introduced me; but there were so many others. All that is a matter of form."

"It is, eh? Your fine mind was on Plato and Confucius, probably. If I had been your father and had you in hand early enough, I would have interviewed you in the woodshed about twice a day till you learned to keep your eyes open."

"I *am* unobservant at times, perhaps. But what are you so excited about?"

"About your innate depravity. Why, Bartimæus, that girl is counted the fairest of this season's buds. She has been beautifully brought up, and is said to be at once amiable and spirited. She'll come into about two millions, D. V., and meantime she has a hundred and fifty thousand of her own from an aunt who died four years ago."

He looked rather bored. "Well, what of it ? "

"What of it ? Excuse me; profanity is against my principles, and ordinary language fails to meet an occasion like this. Ought you not to take a primary course in social economy? They have them now, and I presume you can get one at Yale."

"I'm not sure I understand you, Bob; I hope I don't. If you mean that it is considered the correct thing in your circle to make up to a lady in cold blood because she has money, I must beg to remain outside it." He spoke with dignity, but with an undertone of feeling; he actually looked shocked, as if I had said something immodest.

I hastened to pacify him. "Don't mistake me, Dick. I quite agree with you. I am the last man to defend, not to say recommend, mercenary unions; couldn't do such a thing myself if my salvation depended on it. But there is some sense in the old Quaker's advice, 'My son, don't thee marry for money, but go where money is.' Why should you object to people because they happen to be well off, if they are otherwise unobjectionable? I've already tried to show you the importance of associating with the right sort. We've got nothing better than the De Grouts, and you have lots of things in common with them, — blue blood, and high notions, and cultivation, and all that. A studious chap like you needs feminine society: any of the moralists will tell you so. Miss Edith likes you, and so does her mother; and they don't take to everybody — far from it. And now you're prejudiced against the poor girl because her aunt died and left her a trifle. I ask you, is that fair? is it manly? is it generous?"

"I'm prejudiced against fortune-hunting, and the odious motives you seemed to suggest. That apart, we went over this ground last year. No doubt your friends are very worthy people, but—"

"They're not *my* friends; they're yours, or they wish to be. Why not let them? Meet them half way; give them a trial."

"I can't meet them on equal terms. Best leave me to my own, Bob."

"Perhaps I will, if you'll tell me what your own may be. Not relations, for you have none. Not your old classmates, for they are scattered. Hardly even your den at New Haven, for you must soon leave it to go out into the cold world. I wanted you to start fair, under decent auspices; and here you are taken into the arms of an excellent man who admired your great-grandmother. There's a providence in it. Have you no filial feeling?"

But all he would do was to make a single call at De Grout's, where a cordial reception had little visible effect on his stoicism.

BOOK SECOND.

TACKVILLE AND MILETUS.

CHAPTER X.

HAD Dick played his cards properly, he might have secured in time a tutorship at Alma Mater. That is no towering height of greatness, but it would have kept him in the scholastic seclusion which seemed his native air; so placed, he could have gone on spinning his beloved theories, and shunned the loathsome contact of practicality. Or, had he been less unlike others, he might have found some sort of position in the metropolis, with a few influential friends to stand by him, protect him from bunco-steerers and confidence sharps, and see to his advancement as soon as he had learned the A B C of useful accomplishments and business life. Van Snoozer, though justly incensed at his refusal to take the dancing-bear contract a year before, still felt that something ought to be done for him, and would have recommended him as private secretary to the golden uncle; but then, as Van remarked, Grafton was so blanked unmanageable, he might not understand

the exigencies of such a post, and the implicit
deference due to a somewhat imperious twenty-
millionnaire. Mr. De Grout, I always believed,
would have treated Dick like a son, and found an
innings for him somewhere in the circle of his
extended operations, had he been given the
opportunity.

But the object of all this unavailing good-will
adhered to his wild idea of beginning the battle at
a distance, that those who had known him while
spending his modest inheritance like a gentleman
might not witness the degradation of efforts to
earn his bread and cheese, nor his pride be hurt by
taking a dollar, for whatever service, from a familiar hand. The dwindling of his resources was
like the dying out of his race; by rights, he should
have changed his name, as well as his habitat,
when he began to work for pay. Commonly the
frankest of men, on this topic his lips were sealed;
he would tell no friend his situation, lest he should
be affronted with the offer of a loan. His wilful
thoughts turned westward, echoing the dubious
advice of Mr. Greeley; there men were fewer to
the square rod, and there another year might fin-
ish his legal course. This saving of time was
important, for his finances with straitest economy
would hardly last beyond a twelvemonth more.
So he turned his face to the Mississippi, with little
more thought of the future or sense of adult responsibility than when he had abandoned his child-

hood's home five years before. No eager hope
lured him on, no heavy fear deterred him; to borrow trouble, or anticipate Eldorados, was not his
way. A change had to be made, and this seemed
to him the correct way to make it. It might be—
as it proved—the great mistake of a life made up
of blunders; but his uncalculating mind, as yet
unawakened to the value of tangible questions
and impotent to deal with them, saw no other
road open, and committed his fortunes to the elements with careless trust. Had it been an affair
of verities, of that metaphysic gardening which
cares not for raising fruit, he would have given his
best powers to its consideration; but so long as it
concerned merely such trivial carnalities as where
he should go and what he should do, what mat-
tered it, so long as he went out of reach of patronage and help?

The remote law school offered little that was
more memorable than his trip thither. By one so
introspectively absorbed the break from old associations was not greatly felt, nor any longing for
new ties. His diligent application soon bridged
whatever gap there might be between the point
at which his studies had arrived and that the
graduating class were supposed to have reached.
Without active effort in that direction, he won the
favor of professors and measurably of his compan-
ions. A winter course of lectures admitted him
to the bar, and then his shingle was put up in a

town to which casual advice and acquaintanceship
directed his listless steps.

For a time his letters were tolerably cheerful;
but they dwelt rather on the inexpensiveness of
living than on any rapid professional advancement.
He seemed to be taking notes after his manner.
The people were unpretentious, their manners
democratic, he said; he rather liked that, it was
so American.   Nobody was rich, judged by Eastern standards ; all had begun humbly like himself,
and the few who had risen highest retained the
simple habits of their earlier days.   Every one
worked, and there need be no embarrassment
about his pocketing any fees that might come ; it
was no unusual thing for the daughters even of
the comparatively wealthy to accept a position
behind the counter or at the telegraph wires.
Thus the Dignity of Labor was appreciated, and a
little money would go a long way where all were
economists, and no allowance made for fashion
and nabob pride.   Nor was the spirit of the place
wholly materialistic; societies flourished for the
promotion of literature and art, or of the interest
of the members therein.   "Not that they know
much about these," he admitted, "but they evince
a creditable desire to learn."   The country was
sufficiently settled, and had been more or less so
for some decades; not only buffaloes but prairie
chickens were things of the past, and emigrants
were moving to "the West."   Society had out-

grown border rudeness ; the condition depicted in
certain works (some of them more recent than
this period, but I may draw on subsequent literature to eke out the impressions received from
my friend's epistles) of Messrs. Twain, Eggleston,
and Howe belogned to a region further south, or
to a time long past.   It was said to be a fine farming country, but this was not in his line, and I
would be more interested to know that the fishing
was of a superior character.

As months rolled by, these communications
became more vague and, as I thought, less en-
couraging in tone.   When he had been "in practice" about a year and a half — it was not easy to
connect the idea of practice with poor old Dick —
business took me to Chicago and St. Louis, and I
went out of my way to see for myself how he was
progressing, or to spy out the nakedness of the
land.

I would willingly describe the approaches to
Tackville, but there can be little to tell where
there is nothing to see.   A painter would have to
go far for subjects, for the only variation was from
flat to "rolling" prairie, and the roll in the latter
case was very mild.   Never a rock, and rarely a
tree except upon the streams and in the villages,
which are usually called cities.   One does not get
from car windows a favorable view of these busy
haunts, and a single sample, I thought, would
probably be enough.   The dreariness of the iso-

lated farmhouses oppressed me; rude, meagre, and generally unpainted, like the shanties of Paddies and Kanucks near our northern boundary, but with all picturesque surroundings eliminated — what must it be to live in them! At a certain junction I had to wait two mortal hours, for trains run long distances, are often behind time, and usually fail to connect. There were few passengers, and my reading matter had given out. I paced the platform and inspected the settlement: — three habitations, the inevitable grocery and blacksmith shop, and a wretched saloon, ambitiously but uncertainly labelled "St. Nichols Hotel." I turned to the prairie, — ten miles of bleak unbroken flatness under a sombre sky; no tints, no foliage, hardly a sign of life.

"Pretty dashed poor country," said a drummer at my elbow; "too poor to support a decent road."

"It must be exceptional just here," I ventured. "The state is prosperous and growing, isn't it?"

"O yes; this is rather worse than usual. Raises a lot of corn and wheat, and shows civilization in the river towns. The inland places are mostly mere centres of a little country trade, and pretty blanked mean to stop in over night, some of 'em. Why, sir, I've struck cities around here that might be in Vermont — reached their high-water mark, and going down hill; less of 'em now than there was five years ago. What line did you say you were in?"

The rest of the journey was not so bad; but where was that mellow richness one sees anywhere in the East — that air of being not only inhabited, but lived in? There, men have made homes in country as well as town — and better, some think; here, nature has supplied only fields, and human nature seems to have done nothing but work them. But tastes differ; we cannot all live in New York or Boston, and for those who like this region, I suppose, as Artemus says, it is a kind of region they will like.

CHAPTER XI.

LAW AT TACKVILLE.

Dick was waiting at the station; but for the smile of welcome in his eyes I should not have known him at first, for he had grown a beard. I told him I preferred to walk and see the town; he said it was not much to see, but we could take it in before supper, and send my bag by the 'bus. So he marshalled me through the principal streets, and pointed out the abodes of such wealth, fashion, beauty, and learning as the place contained. It might not be much, but it was a vast improvement on the country; the saying about the respective makers of these two does not always apply. It was a relief to see trees, and decent houses, some of them standing back from the street, and two or three with an attempt at lawns and shrubbery.

"This is our West End," he said. "The business portion is not so remarkable; hardly equal to Broadway, in fact."

" Is it true," I asked, "that the percentage of insanity is unusually high in this state ? "

" Yes. The farmers came here young, with no money or but a few hundreds each. They had to borrow to get stock and implements. Then a bad season, or a plague of grasshoppers, would ruin them ; they couldn't pay their interest, and the mortgages would be foreclosed. The fear of this, and the anxious effort to avoid it, sent them to the asylums in shoals."

" Their game wasn't worth the candle, I should say."

" They thought it might be ; hope springs eternal, you know. They took their chances like the rest of us. But that's not all. You've been over a good deal of ground to-day ; you noticed the aspect of things? Well, the farmer's wife sits all day in one of those attractive homelike edifices, while her husband is out in the fields ; nothing to look at, nobody to talk to, for neighbors are few and far between. The lonesome life, and her share of the anxiety, send her too to the asylum. The state is well provided in that way."

" A cheerful prospect ; but you're better off here in town, surely ? "

" O yes. We live off the farmers ; sell them tools and sugar and calico, and then foreclose their mortgages and send them to the asylum."

" This is unpatriotic, Dick. But at least you individually are growing practical ; taking an interest in the humble pursuits and fortunes of your neighbors."

"O yes: you have to, out here. But this is the tavern, and supper will be ready."

When that not too elaborate repast was ended, I inspected my companion more closely. "Old man," I said, "you're changed. You look older."

"Naturally; it's over two years since we last met. Then the transition from boy to man goes for something, and from the Atlantic coast to the prairies. I've missed the refining influences, you see; you may expect to find me deteriorated."

"If you mean you've grown less visionary, I'm glad to hear it. How is Lady Law?"

"Only so-so to middling. Law out here, Bob, is merely business. Nobody cares for the science of it, and it is not so much a profession as a trade, whereby to command a little cash, as one might at carpentry or hardware. You saw those men at the next table; where would you place them?"

"Freight conductors, I should say, or bar-keepers. No? Possibly tinsmiths?"

"Three of them are my learned colleagues; getting on, too. One of them is aiming at the legislature. That's the way of it; education is not required. They take a great deal of pains with the public schools, and the state proudly cherishes thirteen alleged universities; but attendance at any of these is optional. A boy may pass from the plough's tail to the village store, and

thence, if he is sharp, to the law school, where
about ten months, or two winter courses, qualify
him to shine at the bar. Nobody thinks the worse
of him for not having been to college; to go or
not to go is a question for inclination or circumstances to decide, and discrimination would be undemocratic. Nor does it make so much difference,
as far as manners and appearance go. A necktie
is not *de rigcur* in classroom, and pantaloons may
be worn inside the boots, though that is not so
customary. Some of the professors you might
take for machinists, but they all are posted in
their departments. I saw something of the college while I was finishing my law at Hector; it
stands as well as most state concerns, after
Michigan of course. The brighter fellows aim at
teaching or politics; the course is regarded as an
instrument, a means to an end, not as an intellectual necessity. That's all right, I presume, or
you ought to think it so. You see, in a new and
mainly poor community things are necessarily
different from what you've been used to; and
it's to their credit to think as much of education
as they do."

"No doubt. But you were telling me about the
lawyers."

"Strange that I could digress from so inspiring
a theme. Well, there are gentlemen among them
—in the effete eastern sense of the word; we're
all gentlemen here, so long as we keep out of jail

—and a few scholars, in the larger towns. And two of those you saw are good fellows in their way. But some of the older men are mere pettifoggers of a low type. Oh, I know you have such in New York, but scarcely at the head of the local bar. You should hear them abuse each other in court by the hour, as if their clients and their cases were nothing beside their personalities. In pure impudence they could give a lesson to your shysters at home. To see them with their judicial air on, their huge assumption of wisdom and power and importance, their lofty contempt for whoever is on the other side, is a study. I often wonder whether all this conceit is genuine, or merely put on for effect. Probably the latter; if they were idiots enough to take themselves at their own pretended valuation, they could hardly impose on anybody else. As it is, one or two of them make as much as twelve hundred a year by their humbug. I'm speaking of a certain class, mind; not of all."

"Not of yourself, certainly, for you're one of them. I fear you've been disappointed in the results of this move, Dick."

"Not greatly; blessed is he that expecteth nothing. I've learned to heed some of your advice, and take things as they come."

"Does it pay you? Financially, I mean."

"My office-rent, and mostly my board. No, I don't want any money, thank you; the rest I eke out by copying papers. If I can't live by law, I can try something else. But there's time for all this yet."

He looked at his watch. "It might be pleasanter to stay here and talk, but I promised to take you to a party at Mrs. Claybank's. We're very hospitable here; I tried to get off on the plea that you were coming, but she would not forgive me if you were not there too, and so on. Distinguished strangers don't arrive every day. Prepare for a flutter in sundry female breasts."

"Glad you've got to be a society man, Richard. Who's Mrs. Claybank?"

"The leading lady of our small local drama. Lives in the biggest of those houses you saw; husband one of our foremost merchants. She is a very active person, socially, ecclesiastically, philanthropically, every way; president of this and secretary of that; gets up most of the circles and art clubs, and to some extent runs the town. Very good woman in her way."

"I can't do it, Dick. Sorry, but haven't a dress-coat along."

"That garment is allowed in Hector and the larger towns, but is *taboo* here. I wore mine once, but found it attracted too much attention, and caused me to be regarded as a haughty and obtrusive worldling, which is not my character, as you are aware. The ladies dress, but not the men; that is, clean collars are expected, and cuffs dis-

played by those who are particular. We can go
as we are, or, if you want to be stylish, in dark
frocks."

"Any dancing? What sort of girls?"

"An estimable sort, versed in the useful and
the ornamental both; see and judge for yourself.
Square dances, and figures called at every change.
No round; it's a religious house, though liberal, as
you will hear."

"I'm in your hands; but hadn't you better give
me some more pointers?"

"That's unnecessary; only don't talk too much,
and bewilder our damsels with too many scintilla-
tions of New York wit, or expect them to understand the latest gags. This is a simple and somewhat Puritan community. Let Mrs. Claybank talk
to you; she'll save my explaining sundry matters.
You're on a tour of observation; you'll find her
instructive."

CHAPTER XII.

MRS. CLAYBANK.

OUR hostess, a lady of commanding presence and alert air, a trifle floridly attired, received us warmly. "So pleased to meet any friend of Mr. Grafton's, and especially a gentleman fresh from the gilded saloons of the metropolis."

Somewhat alarmed, I hastened to assure her that I knew of the gilding in those resorts only by hearsay; had Grafton been misrepresenting my habits?

"O no; you mistake my meaning. But we hear so much of the gorgeous East, which showers pearls and gold on its inhabitants, as the poet says; and yet I see you wear very little jewelry. Not that I am unfamiliar with the East myself; I have relatives in Indiana, and have visited in Cincinnati. But we too have our own local pride. We may be recent, but the future belongs to us, — the vast prairies, the well-nigh illimitable expanse, the boundless agricultural resources! Really, you Easterners are to be pitied, hemmed up in a nar-

row space, with your stony fields, your barren
mountains, and your narrow and tyrannous restric-
tions. Society is very stiff with you, is it not — all
etiquette and conventionality? Now, don't imagine for one moment that I would reflect on your
own manners, which are excellent, I am sure ; one
might think you had been brought up among us.
But I am told that in your parts objections are
made to a lady's earning her own living, and that
people are actually ashamed of .the shop by which
they rose. With us, Thought is free, unfettered as
the eagle's flight ; though we are all orthodox, —
oh yes. There is indeed a struggling Universalist
society on River Street, but they can't support a
minister — a poor affair. O no, we do not look
down on them ; they too are human, as Stuart
Mill says. But we are mostly Congregationalists,
Methodists, or Baptists. We live in perfect harmony; all religions are welcome here, — even Jews
and Catholics, though we see little of *them.* The
Presbyterians are so bigoted, and the Lutherans
— ah, well, so Teutonic, and one may say un-
refined. Yes, there are a few Episcopalians ; very
worthy persons, but too liturgical, not to say papist-
ical ; and, only think of it, their minister doesn't
exchange with ours : so narrow ! Your own views,
Mr. Tinsel ? Tolerant, liberal ? Ah yes. I am
so glad, in one coming from the East. We are all
liberal here ; at least we ought to be, with our
advantages, and that is the prevalent opinion.

Your first visit? It will not be your last, I predict. You have so much to see, to learn. If you
stay here a month or two, Mr. Timmens, you will
never be willing to return to the East — not to
reside there. You will become so attached to
our ways; rooted to the soil, I may say. It is
the universal experience. Those who have once
breathed our free and bracing air, and been accli-
mated, so to speak, can no longer endure the
crowded existence, the belittling routine, the effete
traditions, of the older States."

The lady's eyes were flashing with what Mr.
Gilbert calls superior gleam, when her disclosures
were strangely interrupted. An elderly being of
unadorned appearance, with a rough gray coat, a
sprawling collar, and a blue and pink tie, had been
hovering near. A rustic grin now overspread his
countenance; he thrust forth a huge and horny
paw, and poked my entertainer violently in the
ribs — or thus I would express it had the victim
been a man; as it was, let us say he indented her
corsage. "Don't ye run the young feller too hard,
Melindy; let him down easy, now." Then to me,
benevolently, "Ye mustn't mind her; it's only a
way she has. She don't mean no harm."

I had been meditating the propriety of defence
and rescue; but my hostess smiled tolerantly,
introduced the assailant as her uncle Jacob, and
sent him off to talk to a female of lonesome, not
to say grewsome, appearance, stranded in a corner.

Then she took my arm, smoothed her rumpled plumage with the left hand, and marched me in another direction.

"A most excellent man, Mr. Tims, and highly respected. Plain and unassuming ; but we are all plain people here. Not ashamed of our origin — as why should we be? An honest man and a free self-respecting American is the noblest work of God. We have no kings and dukes here, thank Heaven ; and so we make no idle pretensions to be what we are not. You easterners are not always very good Americans : you should come to us to learn to prize your birthright. I must present you to some of our belles ; but first I want to talk to you about Mr. Grafton. There is a touch-me-not air about him, as if he had been a prince of the blood and cradled in luxury. Were his family anything very great ? "

"They are dead now," I replied ; "peace to their ashes. They lived on the eastern shore of Maryland from time immemorial, you know, but the war and what not reduced them, I suppose ; so he had to make a new start. But he's a fine fellow, true as steel and good as gold."

"O, I see ; worn-out southern aristocracy. But that ought not to be counted against him, poor man. What is birth ? I was born in a dugout and raised in a one-roomed log cabin. My father carted his corn — when he had any — with a mule and a cow, and I was proud to go along

with a basket of eggs. I went barefooted till I
was fifteen ; and yet my husband praises my
complexion. That is Americanism, Mr. Timlow.
But we must not despise those who have been
differently raised. No one can say that I have
not always appreciated Mr. Grafton's qualities;
that pure classic brow, that winning manner. But
do you think he is very practical ? "

"Possibly not ; but I hope your free and bracing air, and the example of your noble and vigorous democracy, may make him so. He needs
stimulating influences."

The lady stiffened visibly. "Don't let Mr.
Claybank hear you say that ; he abhors alcohol
in every form. Your friend will get neither stim-
ulants nor political sympathy here, with my consent. Democrats indeed ! Why, we are all
Republicans, of course. I am not prejudiced, not
the least ; but what is there on the other side but
Irishmen, rumsellers, and rebels ? You said you
were liberal, Mr. Tipton ; and I always thought
Mr. Grafton's habits were correct."

Her tones were full of reproach, indignation,
and disappointment. I hastened to explain ; a
task of some difficulty, but at length happily accomplished.

"O well, as you assure me that he is not a
rebel, he was wise to come here, of course. But
I sometimes think he lacks animation, energy,
ambition — decision of character, almost."

"Not that, my dear madam ; only direction."

"He's not easily directed either. He wouldn't teach in Sabbath-school when I asked him ; and he appears indifferent to our young ladies. One might almost fancy he held himself above us — though that is hardly possible."

"Certainly not: he has too much sense, and is not what some would call 'stuck up' at all. You see, I've known him from a boy. His pride is of the sensitive kind, harmless unless to its owner. He never cared for girls ; that is a grave fault, I own. But he looks up to you."

"No doubt. I have tried to be a mother to him ; I will continue to try. Poor Mr. Grafton, he needs it, as you say. His own mother must have been a shiftless, incompetent person : those southern women generally are. And he never had a sister. Well, Mr. Timothy, *you* are not indifferent to young ladies, I trust? We have some lovely ones : in fact, they are all lovely. You must come to our sociable and our prayer-meeting — the Congregational, of course. And wouldn't you like to lecture before the art club? No? Well then, the literary circle. It is almost wholly composed of ladies ; the gentlemen are too busy to attend. We have gone over nearly all the poets ; Milton is the next subject. But we would be charmed to hear you on any topic. No formality, you know."

Presently Dick came up with a Major Way.

"This is our great fisherman, Bob. He'll take us up stream to-morrow, if you say so, and show you more bass than you ever saw." We had barely made an appointment, when Mrs. Claybank carried me off to her bevy of attendant maidens, whose varying charms I need not inventory here.

CHAPTER XIII.

NATURE AND HUMAN NATURE.

It was hardly past midnight when we reached Dick's office, an upstairs room in a corner building. "You see our humble efforts at festivity are small and early," said he. "Do you want to sit up and talk, or are you tired? Not from the dissipation, but your journey."

"O no! There's not so much to see that I need be fatigued by it. Your scenery is not what you can call overpowering."

"That's our weak point. In the East you can fall back on Nature when you are tired of men, and she has something to say to you. Here we have nothing except the river: I prize that as a relief. It's not merely the water, but the land keeps such beauty as she has for the banks. We'll take the day to it, if you like. Will a cold lunch content you?"

"Surely, if there's any sport. But can you spare the whole day?"

"O, business is not so pressing; I often do it.

Then Way is worth knowing; more companionable than most. He fought through the war, and came out of it with broken health; has his pension, some property, and a nominal business, but really represents the leisure class, which is rare in these parts. He goes off in winter, and when here spends most of his time on the river. It's a wise choice, for the river is the best thing about here. Fishing is his passion, and we get the benefit of his skill and tackle."

"Good. But we were to discuss your social phenomena. Who's that Miss Edwards?"

"I thought you'd notice her. She's a Yankee, one of the numerous descendants of Jonathan; teaches in the schools, and helps support a widowed mother; would rather do it at home if she could, I fancy. O, there are a few eastern people here; but most of them are to the manner born, or come from not far across the Mississippi. They think this section is the world's garden and granary and treasure-house, and much beyond the rest of the Union. I suppose you heard all that?"

"O, yes! Mrs. Claybank is a four-horse team. But I say, is it usual for gentlemen to punch ladies in the side before a promiscuous assemblage, or is it merely a privilege of relationship?"

"The patriarchs do it to any one, even on a first meeting, if they feel friendly enough. At least Uncle Jacob does; he's a cordial old soul. Nobody takes it amiss from him; but it's not expected of us, so you needn't practise it as a new accomplishment. Well, as you used to ask me when you had taken me out in New York, what are your impressions?"

"Mixed, like the company. We could hardly duplicate the hostess in Gotham. But do you think her guests, taken all in all, are any improvement on Mrs. Magellan's?"

"They are not so far removed from primitive nature, if that's any recommendation. I'm not sure it is."

"You're not much more of a ladies' man than you were, after all. Mrs. Claybank intimates that the girl of the locality is not to your taste. You don't find them more attractive than Miss De Grout, then?"

"I didn't come here for society, Bob. Of course that is like the scenery; with rare exceptions, flat. This is not the place to study character: you've already seen the best of our eccentricities, except my neighbor in the next room; and assuredly you wouldn't come here for culture. We are neither one thing nor the other; we miss alike the picturesqueness of a new border settlement, and the ripeness of an old community that understands itself and can look behind. We have no background, no past; people neither know nor care who were their grandfathers. A town not far off was lately jubilating over its

twenty-fifth anniversary; there's history for you!
The aristocracy here, as far as we have any, is
in theory the 'Old Settlers;' in practice, those
who have made thirty thousand or so. Grocers
and dry-goods men live in the best houses, and
rather look down on doctors and lawyers; nor
is there much to choose in mind and manners,
as I told you. As for the parsons, they are expected to pay not more than a hundred dollars
rent, and to cringe to their employers."

"Why, man, Mrs. Claybank was bragging about
the enlightened toleration and liberalism here, as
against our hidebound bigotry in the East. I
thought your ministers must be fed on Mill and
Darwin, and ladle out the Religion of the Future
every week."

"It wouldn't be safe for them to try it, if they
knew how. Stay over Sunday, and you'll see
what sort of doctrine we get. I don't say the
western spirit isn't in some respects freer than
the eastern; our dominant puritanism has changed
its tone a little with the change of scene and
climate. We are less wedded to old opinions because we know less about them; so the fetters
of theology are relaxed slightly. 'Liberal' is a
fine word, and popular in proportion to its vague-
ness; the tendency is that way, but they don't
know — how should they? There's a man in
Hector who has read parts of Draper's Intellectual Development, and thinks himself an oracle;

Buckle and Lecky he had never heard of, when
I chanced to mention them."

" I say, old boy, do you go to church much ? "

" Sometimes.   I did when I first came, to catch
the tone; I caught it.   Oh, you heard of that
Sunday-school business?   They wanted me to
teach Shorter Catechism, and I couldn't.   Yet you
see, I am still invited out.   That is their liberalism; in New York or New Haven I would have
been sent to Coventry at once — or so Mrs. Claybank probably supposes.   But this is petty detail ;
let's take a larger view.   Our winters and sum-
mers are both severe, lacking the remotest influence from sea or mountains ; not an elevation
of the ground, or body of water worth mentioning
within hundreds of miles.   Well, you know what
that means.   'Depressing,' the natives call it in
July, though the mercury goes no higher than on
the sound.   Depressing !   I should say it was,
and the year round.   Why?   Because the mind
of man follows the face of Nature, and where
she presents no great or lovely objects he will be
a crawling cripple.   Your New York is big and
bad, but the Hudson and the Catskills ought to
save it ; and Baltimore can't go altogether to the
dogs while the Bay is at hand.   A man may be
chained to his desk in those cities, but he knows
there is something glorious not far off, and that
propinquity keeps him up, if he is not a mere
muckworm.   Nature, when she gives a decent

account of herself, is an educator and a spirit-
ual leaven: here, she is barefooted and out at
elbows, fit only to raise crops, and support
wretches who are content with salt pork and the
local paper. A country without trees, hills, and
waterfalls is God-forsaken indeed: what can you
expect of those who live in it? An Adirondac
guide ought to have more mental force and brightness than a graduate of our State University. A
Maine fisherman will give you more points of
character and quaint discourse in an hour than
you will get from the whole population here in a
month. No, I'm not forgetting Mrs. Claybank.
She's only bizarre, not original; but she's of some
value as the concentrated essence of this region:
when you've heard her, you know it all."

"She's an admirable person, Dick, as you say;
but isn't she somewhat disconnected — lack of
mental continuity, you know?"

"Of course. Her speech goes beyond her
thought, and her thought overlaps such basis as
she has for thinking. She picks up a word here
and an idea there, and her active brain pieces
them together anyhow in crazy-quilt fashion,
without waiting to get a pattern, or see what
her materials mean and what relation they bear
to each other. All this is not merely personal,
but typical. Such is our style here: life is short,
and we can't take time to study a subject down
to the ground, or follow out a line of thought.

I like her talk, it contradicts the facts with such naïve simplicity and exemplary confidence. Look at this: we know but two kinds of dimension, vertical and horizontal. Now how can you have any adequate idea of elevation till you've seen a mountain, or of extension but from the sea?"

Here I interrupted his sophistry. "She talks of the illimitable vastness of the prairies ; and so do others. I've heard that often."

"Illimitable bosh. One gets mortally tired of that rot about the prairies; what are they but great fields stretched out *ad nauseam*, with or without fences and cultivation? A lot of land as flat as a floor is no better than so much water ; and who cares for that, out of sight of shore?"

"Why, you've just been saying that the sea was the salt of life, so to speak, as beautiful and precious as the mountains."

"Evidently you've not been at debating society of late, Bob. It's the sea and land together we care about, the sea as seen from the land. We don't want to live on it, not being aquatic animals. Mountains are best, I think, though I'm not so used to them. Where I was brought up, it was as level as here, but we had the water, and plenty of it. Wisconsin and Minnesota have their lakes — not large, but numerous and pretty ; when you see Minnetonka and Fort Snelling, you might fancy yourself in the East. Minnehaha is a real cascade, with some rocks ; it wouldn't be noticed in your state, but it's a great feature, and very creditable. We go there from six states to polish up our intellects, as the richer folks in the larger towns go East, and as you go to Europe. The lower Mississippi may have its points, and it has been settled longer. West, if you go far enough, there is plenty of material. The Rockies and the Pacific slope have their literature already; the South is getting it; New England has had it since Americans began to write. They have traits, as they have landscapes; but such efforts as have been made to immortalize this middle region have failed totally, or succeeded only in the realistic way as strong photographs of the deadly dismal. What great poem or novel ever dealt with a land that had no hills or lakes or forests?"

"You've got me now, though they might be able to answer that at Yale. Then, according to you, all this section has no future at all?"

"O yes, a fourth-rate future. Time will mend it somewhat. I suppose cities of the plain, away from coasts, may amount to something — when they have a history. But in a new country whose natural features are conspicuous by their absence, society is inevitably raw, and men and women in the brown sugar or crude petroleum stage. Still, my neighbors are redeemable. Do you know why I think so? Look at the flowers in their windows, and the trees they have planted

along the streets.   And they have all their pic-
nics on the river."

"Dick, I never supposed you cared so much for
scenery."

"Because I didn't make a fuss over it when I
had it?   Try to live a year or two without it, and
you'll learn what part it plays in life.   But the
wind is tempered to the shorn sheep, and we'll
take in the river to-morrow."

CHAPTER XIV.

UP THE RIVER.

THE Major sat at the bow, and I at the stern, with a bait-pail for each, and Dick to share mine; I trailed a long line behind as we sped up stream. Above the town it widened into marshes, called by natives sloughs, though they bear no resemblance to that into which Bunyan's Pilgrim fell; the water is clear, and some feet deep, they told me, and boys go there for sunfish and baby bass. Aiming at larger game, we kept in mid-channel. "I'm doing my Christian duty, sir," said our leader, "and giving you the chance of the first fish."

Suddenly I felt a tug; the reel whirred. "You've got him," Dick cried. For a moment —this style of procedure being then new to me— I was tempted to drop the rod, and pull in hand over hand like a greenhorn. Subduing this weakness, I reeled in rapidly. Grafton made a dash with the landing-net; a two-pounder came over the side, and lay flopping. "Lake bass," Way commented; "nearly as good as the black; can't tell the difference by the way they pull. Consider yourself initiated, Mr. T."

"Not much science in that," I confessed, as I put on a new bait.

"Can't be, in trolling. If he isn't well hooked at his first plunge, he won't be, and to stop the boat and let you play him might only increase the risk of losing him. Trolling is all chance; but you'll see something that isn't, before long. Aha, you've got another."

So I had, and presently a third; after that, a blank interval.

"Would it pay to go back, and try that ground again?"

"Hardly; a spurt like that never lasts. We might row up and down there all day, and not get another bite. Good beginning, though. Go for the right bank, Boggs: I want to try those bushes."

The Major's gaunt figure stood erect; his eyes were searching a low shore, heavily fringed with brush. At thirty feet distance he made a cast, direct for the largest clump, it seemed. "Missed, by Jove! That's a grandfather. Back water, Boggs; out a little. Steady now."

These instructions were delivered in a voice just audible.

"But, Major," I ventured, "if you saw him he's seen you, and won't come back."

"Saw him, no : I saw his signs, and felt him. Look how he's torn the bait ; but it'll do." He cast again ; the glistening minnow dashed over one twig and dived beneath another. " Pull now —away from shore ! " The rod bent, the line went out, came in, went out to sixty feet or more ; the great fish dashed up stream and down, this way and that. For thirty breathless minutes we sat and watched the struggle between instinct and intelligence, between fins and fingers, the fight for life on one hand, for victory on the other. An idle waste of time, you say ? Try it, and see if not merely the hour, but the day that holds it, is not repaid. A fishing-rod is " a stick with a hook at one end and a fool at the other," is it ? In some cases, perhaps ; but plainly, Doctor Dogmatist Johnson, you were never in a boat with Major Way. Had the pole and reel been in your thick thumbs, your aphorism might have been justified ; but had it once been your privilege to see them in a master's hand when a big bass was straining at the other end of the electric line, you never would have written yourself down such an ass.

At length the net engulfed the victim, and sighs of relief ascended.

" Well, Major," said I, " your first will beat my three."

" About even, I think." He drew a scale from his pocket. " Just over five pounds. One of

eight was caught below the dam last week ; but
this is very fair for up here. Dick, you might
string them in two bunches, and hang over the
side. Now for the head of the island."

He sat down, wiped his brow, and filled his
pipe, while we gazed admiringly, now on him, and
now on his prey, as with wiggling protests it followed our course, tied securely to a thwart.

"What comes next ?" I asked.

"Still-fishing for small bass in a sharp current,
among the branches of a big tree," said Dick.
"You lose an average of two hooks for each fish.
Sometimes the bass are there and sometimes not,
but the snags are reliable."

The town was out of sight now, and the river
had changed its character ; its depth was less,
its banks higher and more thickly wooded. About
these varying shores — here meadow, there apparent forest — it curved and twisted blithesomely,
dividing itself by sandbars and green islets.
Above one of these we paused, and tied to a
protruding branch.

"Take in the fish," said our chief; "too risky
to leave 'em out ; too much current, and far too
much tree. None of us would love this spot if
the bass didn't. Curious tastes they have ; I like
my wood and water best apart, but fish prefer 'em
mixed. Short lines now, and sinkers; and pull
up every minute, or you'll get fast. That's too
far south, young man."

I had thrown cautiously, as I thought, but the bait went careering rapidly down stream. "Where are the fish?" I inquired.

"Underneath, mixed up with the tree; perhaps they've made nests inside. The problem is to find them at home without disturbing their furniture, which we have no use for. Here's one;" and the visitor came swinging over the side. "No nets just now, thanks. These animals combine the habits of the turtle with those of the woodpecker and tree-toad; if they take hold they'll keep it, and if you can disentangle them from the branches you have no trouble to lift them out of the water."

In fifteen minutes we had taken as many bass, a weight of perhaps twenty pounds, and lost but five hooks. "Enough of this; we'd better go while we can with unimpaired self-respect. Now for the cut-off and the croppies. We could sail up there if we had brought the canvas, but with our work it's mostly in the way. A fair mess" — he surveyed the striped sides and shining bellies under foot — "but all one kind, except for black and yellow. We must have a variety. Dick, if the croppies don't bite and we can't raise a pickerel, you'll have to sit on the bank and catch us a dogfish. — You don't know dogfish? Great coarse thing, full of oil and not fit to give to the pigs. The first one Grafton caught broke his pole; he was out with a boy, up the creek,

before he fell in with me. He thought it was
a prize, and dragged it back two miles on foot,
a redhot August day. Then nobody would have
it as a gift : they told him it was poisonous, and
made him take it away and throw it in the river.
Haw, haw ! "

The Major, who had been somewhat glum and
silent at the start, was now happy and even hila-
rious. Dick's spirits too had risen ; he seemed
another man from the lugubrious critic of last
night. It was a heavenly October day, and no
other human beings, nor any signs of their existence, were in sight. We were out of the world,
far from the crowd and scramble, gone back to
primeval paradise — but for the implements we
carried and the victims at our feet. They missed
something in Eden, as Brahmins and vegetarians
do to-day.

" Say, Major," upspoke the oarsman, " yonder's
some ducks. Pity we hain't a gun along. Durned
pooty shot." But on such a day even I was content to have no blood on my hands. Fish have
scarcely any, and do not count ; the lively things
that cleave the air, or walk the earth like us, seem
much nearer to our humanity.

The cut-off is a section of the river, severed
from the main stream by a long and narrow island.
No fields line its banks ; no habitation, or fence,
or domestic animal, or reminder of intrusive man,
is there, but thick woods and tangled vines on

either side, and here and there such wealth of pebbles as in that region you may not see in a week's journey, away from the water. You think there is no beauty in a stone? Sojourn there awhile, and when you escape you will sit up at night, if there be a moon, to see rocks from the car windows.

"I might take a swim here," I suggested. "No danger of meeting ladies?"

"Too cold; that's all. If you were up here every day, you might meet twenty fishermen's boats in the year, and two or three farmers' girls after wild grapes.— Now put her against the bank: we'll fish around that stump, about five feet deep. Use corks here."

I soon learned what a croppy is: as round as a sunfish, but silvery white, and weighing from six ounces to two pounds; not a game fish like the genuine bass, but its broad flat side against the water makes a strong pull, and its tender mouth requires delicate handling, or the larger ones break from the hook: its flesh is soft, but good eating. They came zealously to our call; for half an hour the four lines were busy. Then we strung our spoil over the boat's side, and climbed a high bank for lunch. A soft carpet of moss played chairs and table, yellowing leaves of maple and oak the ceiling, and through abundant windows we had a water view east and north.

"This is glorious," I cried; "worth coming all this way for, Dick, apart from you."

" I told you it was the best thing here," he said ;
"by far the best."

" I go further," Way remarked with solemnity :
"it's the best thing in life. I'm older than you
two : I've seen most parts of the country, and
most ways of living. Some men prefer shooting,
or driving, or dancing; some enjoy grubbing in a
store, or mooning over a book; some like to make
a home, and have wife and children round their
heels. But give me a boat, and a stream like this,
or one of the Wisconsin lakes, and a light wind,
and company of the right sort — here's to you,
gentlemen — and the bass biting, and I've got the
best this planet can give. Fact is, I can't live any
other way. I've tried it. It's hard for me to get
through the winters : I should want to die before
spring, if it wasn't for this ahead."

We were all silent awhile. "If you'll stay a
fortnight, Mr. T., I'll show you all there is on this
part of the river. I can't promise luck like this —
it's above par to-day; but there are other places
we could try, off the main track." I told him I
should like nothing better, but my limit was three
days ; this visit was but a brief respite from business. "Ah yes, business : I never let it interfere with fishing. In the next world perhaps
there will be no business: that would suit Grafton
too."

I must condense the record of that golden day,
so rich in the book of memory, so poor and trivial

on the printed page. The flashing rapids, where we warily cast a long line for tourist pickerel or bass; the peaceful secluded bays, that gave surprised yet tranquil welcome to what might seem the first white men's oar; the bed of reeds in a broad reach of water, from whose border we lured one lonesome perch who must have been pining for his multitudinous kinsfolk far away. "Do you always have as much variety as this?" I asked.

"We can if we want it — of place at least, and exercise: as to the fish, that's as *they* please. But the less we get of them, the more we move about and commune with nature. There are queer nooks you've not seen yet. That's the beauty of it: it's not like sitting on a bank and watching a float all day."

My respectful recollection goes back to the wall-eyed pike, rare bird at that season and in that part of the stream, which the Major's deft hand extracted from a certain rippling by-path; and to sundry big bass — but none to rival the five-pounder — that made free with the hooks of one or two unskilled pretenders, and, pleading previous engagements, resolutely declined to accompany us home. I am not strong in natural history, but I made some observations in that field, aside from the main and more profitable business of the hour. A large sunfish joined our party uninvited, with half his side bare and his red gills exposed. We had no surgery for his case, but, thus horribly

wounded days or weeks before by some pirate of
the shallow waters, he tugged at the hook as
vigorously and returned to his native weeds as
merrily as if he were sound. Another intruder
was a rock or stump bass (a small and despised
variety) crossed in some abnormal way with a
wholly different species.

Far up stream we had landed to stretch our
limbs, and laid our rods on a high bank that over-
hung the deepest hole for miles. Here Boggs
with objurgatory clamor pulled to the surface a
snapper, and kept him there to break loose if he
could; when lo, from the depths appeared another, which followed the prisoner about, pawed
at his shell, and strove to rescue him from his
misplaced attachment. Such domestic affection
in that rank of life seemed unfamiliar enough to
deserve encouragement : the angry oarsman, forced
at length to drag his unwelcome captive ashore,
would have committed unsportsmanlike destruc-
tion, but our intercessions, rising to commands,
restored the turtle, with mouth injured no more
than was inevitable, to liberty and the presumed
embraces of his mate.

As we rapidly sped homeward, the chill of
approaching evening seemed to have touched our
spirits. "Ah, well," said the Major, "everything
must end. Pity one has to sleep in town, and
spend the evenings. It's tame, after this." Dick
nodded a discouraged assent. I, who had a hun-

dred interests in the crowd, had been finding satisfaction too in its momentary remoteness, and could almost sympathize with these misanthropes —the worn veteran who had tried Life and found this sequestered stream the best of it, the dreaming neophyte who thought it not worth the trial. The rower alone was jovial, meditating on a fish supper, and dollars to be gained from his finny wares.

Suddenly our chief roused himself from his abstraction. " Dick, you must show our friend your pet rock bass.— He got off Grafton's hook last year, and swallowed it. Dick takes him in whenever we stop there, for old acquaintance, sake, and sees if he's safe."

We paused at a partly submerged tree, and Dick dropped three feet of line, which came up instantly with a five-inch fish. " See, his throat has grown over that hook to the head of it, and he doesn't mind it at all."

" You don't mean you've had him in your hands before ? "

" Often; he's marked, you see, and less of the steel is visible each week. Next time it will be out of sight. We've watched the process with interest : he grows fat on it."

As we neared the boat-house, our trophies were removed from the water, where they had kept fresh; six heavy strings. "•We'll send a mess to Mrs. Claybank with our compliments, and take specimens to the hotel ; that will leave about forty pounds for Boggs. Not a bad day's work,"

CHAPTER XV.

MR. RUSTLER.

As we settled to our post-prandial pipes, I remarked, "We're in for a quiet evening, I suppose?"

"Unless some of the men you've met drop in — or unless you want to call on any of the ladies. — Well, if you don't, I don't."

"Dick, what's the matter with Way?"

"Old bachelorhood, and ill-health. He couldn't live without the river, as he says—or not here. You see what is before me."

"Not if you take care of yourself: your health appears to be all right thus far. Why did you come here, if you don't like it?"

"I had to go somewhere, and this was suggested. One place is as good as another."

"And a good deal better, as Paddy said. I don't see exactly where your philosophy comes in, my boy."

"I'll show you. 'There is no armor against Fate;' so the old poet sang, and so people be-

lieve. They are mistaken. The world is full of
unmanly howls and earsplitting wailings ; Rachel
mourning for her children, and boys crying over
spilt milk, or whining because they can't have
the moon : it makes very poor music. All this
might be avoided ; only men are so busy trying
to get rich, or to enjoy themselves, that they
neglect to ward off misfortune or prepare to meet
it. Now since, according to all testimony, there
is more misery than happiness abroad, and what
is called happiness is mostly factitious and delusive, not worth the trouble of searching for, the
part of common sense is manifestly to accept the
facts and arrange yourself accordingly. There *is*
an armor against Fate : Indifference."

The last sentence he delivered in his most
impressive manner and with an accent of deep
conviction. So this is his last valuable discovery,
I thought. But I said nothing, and waited to
hear what more he had to urge about so priceless
an addition to our fund of knowledge.

"I made up my mind long ago that much less
profit than is usually supposed comes of human
efforts and ambitions, and that the main stage of
life is really the mind within, not the world without. The most disgusting and humiliating of
emotions I take to be disappointment. I experienced it once or twice in childhood, and that
was enough ; I determined to shut it out. How ?
By not expecting or desiring things. Then there

was the fear of death, which makes one feel like
a coward — ashamed of himself, and most uncom-
fortable. Well, before I was fifteen I had overcome that, by steadily accustoming myself to the
thought; in such a case familiarity removes all
terror. I had plenty of time to think, you know,
and enough to think about, in view of our domestic mishaps — my father's death, and the rest. I
said to myself, it is caring that makes one vul-
nerable. If you love life unduly, you dread to
lose it, and so are held in bondage, as St. Paul
says. If you build castles in Spain, and invest
hope and heart therein, down you go to the depths
when your cloud-capped towers fall. If you anticipate this or that eagerly, as men do with their
amusements and love-affairs and financial ventures
and what not, you merely put yourself in a way
to be hurt. That's clear, isn't it? Now what's
the remedy? Simply this : don't build, don't
anticipate, and above all, don't care. I saw no
wisdom in being torn in two and broken to pieces
by every stroke of ill fortune, such as must come
frequently when one tries to do things and attain
given objects, no matter what; nor yet by the
mere absence of success and prosperity, such as
was my hereditary lot and likely always to attend
me. So I took for my watchword, Indifference.
What does Marcus say? 'Another prays, How
shall I get this thing? Do thou pray, How shall
I not desire it.' That's the point. I used to be

criticised for this at college, you may remember, and there was no use of explaining my position to the boys—they wouldn't have understood it, or would have thought it heresy and schism; but I saved myself a lot of unpleasantness, no doubt. Bardie wanted to see me roused : I didn't. You thought me naturally phlegmatic : it wasn't altogether that. Know thyself is the maxim to start with. In this world a man can't afford to be passionate and eager and anxious ; at least I couldn't. Even affections are expensive and dangerous, and as the natural channels of mine were cut off, I took that as an indication of Providence that I had better not form any artificial ones. It's safer to work one's brain, and live in that — not neglecting the conscience, of course. It was none of my business to force this doctrine on others : we're all made differently, and each must find out for himself what he needs. But this was the medicine for me."

I had listened to this harangue with exemplary patience, feeling, as any one must, how wide of the mark the arrow flew. But here seemed to be an opportunity to point out my poor friend's error, without being too rough with him. " Medicine — what do you want of medicine ? I don't see why you should pose as a sick man. And to people in ordinary health physic is considerably less important than food. What does your theory say to the question of ways and means ? "

So grossly practical a suggestion he dismissed
with his habitual easy contempt. " That's another matter: stick to the one in hand. You
don't see why I should treat myself as a patient?
Well, for instance, how could a civilized man
stand it in a place like this, if he weren't armed
and fortified? I say to myself, with Marcus,
What does it matter whether you are here or
there?

> ' Life is not that which without us we find,
>   Chance, accident merely, — but rather the mind,
>   And the soul which, within us, surviveth these things.'

And that keeps me up, you see."

" I should think a little tolerably congenial society, and some adequate occupation, would do it
better. You're out of place here, Dick : I always
thought it was a false move."

" It's of no use to talk about that. I'm here,
and may as well make the best of it."

" If you would ; but I fear it's not in you to do
it. You're a tender plant and a fragile flower,
Richard, and I'm not sure I hadn't better take
down your sign and carry you back with me."

My friend was offering some feeble assurances
that he was all right, when the door opened and
admitted one of the men I had seen and discussed
the night before : Dick introduced him as the
occupant of an adjoining office. Mr. Rustler was
a heavy and hearty person of twenty-eight or so,

carelessly attired, with a red face and a familiar manner.

"Glad to know you, sir; meant to do the civil thing this mornin', but heard you'd gone fishin'. Grafton can afford that, I s'pose; rest of us have to stay home and catch men, as the 'postle says. Bet you he didn't take two dollars' worth; and I've made five to-day. Been lecturin' him? You look like it, and he needs it. Yes sir, he's a nice boy, Grafton is, but he wants somebody to look after him." The speaker emphasized his remarks by a fraternal thwack administered upon the shoulders of his topic. "We'd do it, some of us, only we don't feel intimate enough; ain't in his set exactly. I was raised on a farm right outside town here, I was."

"I was raised on a farm too," Dick interposed; "so we're in the same set as far as that goes."

"That was way off in Maryland, where folks are lazy and easy-goin'. And then you went to college; that's what's the matter with you. When we heard he was comin' here, some of the boys got scared; thought a prize pumpkin from Yale would take the shine off our native products. But I said to 'em, 'Go slow now. There's only seventeen of us, and four thousand people in town to live off of, besides the farmers. It's a free country. Give the sucker a chance: meet him friendly.' And we did, didn't we? Leastways, most of us. But bless you, he didn't take to our

ways, no more'n a hen to a duckpond. You see,
one has to hustle round lively here, to get on.
I've thought of takin' him into partnership, for
I'm gettin' 'most more'n I can do, and I want
somebody that's up on the law points, as he ought
to be ; why, he's read more books 'n I can shake
a stick at. If he was willin' to be led, now, and
to learn the tricks and follow suit, while I did the
hustlin' and 'tended to the active business, me
and him'd be a smart team."

"Yes," I said, anxious to give the good cause a
boost. " Grafton would make a first-rate office lawyer—under the guidance of an energetic, practical
chief."

Mr. Rustler looked dubious. "Well, I ain't sure.
O, I can do the practical and get up the steam, of
course ; but I'd have to do it for both. You know
office work is mostly bamboozlin', and gettin' round
clients and persuadin' 'em to sail in, and such; and
he'd be no good at that. You're in the profession?
No? Lord, I oughtn't to said that, then. Well, don't
give me away : it's all between friends and in confidence. Here's the way it'd be : some old rooster
comes in, and Grafton hears him through and tells
him he's got no case, or to go home and make it up.
That's his style. No, he might be more use in
court. He makes a good speech, if it was to the
point. He can soar, only he don't soar when you
want him to ; goes off at half-cock about Justice
when he ought to be foolin' the jury. Eloquence

is a good card, but you have to play it at the right
place in the game, not promiscuous, hit or miss,
accordin' as you feel like it. Judges and juries
ain't caught like that; they want to be handled
careful. O, I know he can write; draws up a dam
sight better paper'n I do. But a clerk can do that,
or a student."

"I wasn't aware you had either as yet," Dick
put in slyly.

"No more I haven't, but I will before you do,
my christian friend. You get most of my writin'
now, and it don't fetch you two dollars a week,
does it? I've got more important business. The
trouble with you is, you're too doggoned fine. You
like to wear a clean collar, and cuffs, and feel like
a gentleman. That ain't the way. If you want
to get on at law, you must turn up your sleeves
and go and roll in the gutter a bit."

"I fear I must plead guilty to that indictment,"
said Dick with a pensive smile. "I *do* prefer to
keep clean; I've not been able as yet to acquire a
taste for mud."

"There, he owns it; talks about taste, and prefer-
rin'. You see," exclaimed the practitioner, turning
to me in indignant appeal. "He's too blamed
finicky and high-toned for any use, out here.
Maybe his notions might suit in York, though it
don't sound so from what I read in the papers.
Why, sir, he lost a case last spring, just by not
breakin' up a witness on the other side, when all

depended on it. She was a widow woman too, with nobody much to back her; ignorant and nervous, and scared easy. But he just wouldn't do it; has no idea of bulldozin'."

"But in that case," said Dick gently, "you know she had the rights of it."

"What if she had? What in thunder has that got to do with it? Once you're in a case, all concerns you is your client's interests, and your own of course. Just look at him;"— the visitor turned to me plaintively; "he's got no more notion of practice 'n that."

"Well," said Dick apologetically, "that time I was a junior, suddenly called in with imperfect instructions, and misled as to the leading facts. Had I known that our man was trying to cheat the widow out of her farm, I wouldn't have touched his suit. If I'd been retained on the opposite side, I might have done something."

"Now that's Grafton all over," Rustler vociferated, in tones of much feeling. "Won't take a case unless it suits him; wants to represent only Sunday Schools and Orphan Asylums. A man was up for pig-stealin', and went to him. Did you take the pigs, says he. Yes, says the man, me and Bill Jacks; but they hain't onto Bill's trail, and he and his wife'll swear I was to their place all that night, which I was, 'cept when we went after them pigs. Get out, says Grafton. Now that's no way to do business. He came to

me next — right next door 'tis — and I says, How
much you got? Seven dollars, says he. All right,
says I, and I took the cash, proved the alibi, and
got him off. *That's* business, that is. There's
where Grafton might have been seven dollars
richer if he wasn't so goldarned particular.
Won't touch divorce suits even; and they make
an item in these parts, I tell you. You can see
the unhitched couples in church of a Sunday,
man sittin' in one pew, ex-wife in the next, proud
and smilin' as you please. Yet Grafton thinks
divorce is nasty. Gosh! He's a fine feller, he is;
'most too fine for this world, or this part of it anyway. He ought to staid East, done up in cotton in
a bandbox with blue ribbons. Well, sir, *you*'ve got
horse sense, I see, and maybe you can raise some
influence over him; nobody else can, as I know of.
It's a pity to see him throw himself away like this.
Talk to him some more; and if you can make
him hear reason, why I'm good to step in and
make a man of him." He wrung my hand,
patted Dick avuncularly on the head, and withdrew.

We resumed our chairs, looked at the stove, and
then at each other.

"Well," said Dick, "you see?"

"O, come; they can't all be like that. You don't
mean he's an average sample?"

"No; he's the best of them — for scientific pur-
poses: the others are more commonplace and

varnished. His frankness and directness are his own; but he's justly popular, and a rising man. His trumpet may not be of the finest make, but it gives out no uncertain sound; he is single-minded, and beautifully clearheaded. He knows just what he wants, goes straight at it, and gets it. To acquit a petty thief and earn seven dollars is to him an object to be seriously pursued, a step on the ladder of life. He wisely declines to despise the day of small things. He is a model for men of his sort. But I fear I'm not his sort of man."

"Dick, you're growing cynical, I'm afraid."

"No, not yet; I speak in good faith. If I could see and handle things as he does, how the problem of life would be simplified! Besides, he is good-natured, and rather kindly. He wouldn't oppress the widow and orphan for love of it, nor do any one a mean turn except in the way of business. But much as I admire him as a specimen, I hardly think I could work with him as a partner. Perhaps I am old-fashioned and prejudiced, as he says; but so it is. I can see that his view is the conquering one — I never denied that; but I can't take it, that's all."

"Dick, would it have been any worse to accept the charge of Van Snoozer's brother, or such a post as Mr. De Grout would have offered you, than to take work from such a fellow as Rustler?"

"Yes, for they wanted to help me, whereas he

means only to use me. I can't take benefits in
cold blood ; but out here we show no such delicate consideration, and whatever comes to you is
in the way of business. Matters are simpler
and more manageable : you don't have to be on
guard."

" I never could see much need of being on guard
against my friends — unless when they wanted me
to toe the mark too closely. — You must have a
good deal of time on your hands : what do you do
with it ? "

" Read. I have some books, you know, and I
can borrow a few, though the range here is somewhat limited."

" Try any teaching ? You always were good at
that."

" I might, but none has offered. The law was
an experiment with me, as it is with so many. It
can't hurt one to know a little of it, and when it is
proved that law and I can't pull together, I can try
something else. But it's not time for that yet, and
I'm making ends meet as it is."

This might be, but I was satisfied with neither
the aspects nor the prospects of his case. So I
did some thinking that night, and evolved a plan ;
not much of a plan, just an humble pottering
affair, but if I could get it to work it might
improve the present situation a little. And the
next day I talked up education, and told him he
ought to aim at a professorship, or something of

that kind, in the future. I felt sure he never
would do any good at law, and wished to induce
him to accustom his mind to the idea of looking
a step or two beyond day after to-morrow.

CHAPTER XVI.

A PHANTOM BALL.

ON the last night of my brief stay there was a
phantom ball at the hotel. The giddy youth of
the town encased themselves in sacks or sheets,
in which they resembled Kuklux, or grand inquisi-
tors, or members of the Venetian Council. This
mediæval costume was not obligatory, and Dick
and I, like the sober elders, attended in plain garb
with lineaments unconcealed. The dining-room
was cleared for dancing, and we stood in the
doorway gazing at the performance of the gayer
spirits, wherein the weird and the boisterous were
agreeably joined, when an episode not on the bills
was suddenly introduced. A long-legged gymnast,
prancing about to show his agility, came into violent
contact with the chandelier, *i.e.*, a large kerosene
lamp suspended from the ceiling: down it fell
with a crash, and the floor was ablaze in an instant.
The votaries of Terpsichore jumped out of the
way, and luckily none of their flowing draperies
caught, but the flames presently filled a space as

large as a good-sized table, and mounted four or
five feet in the air. Then ensued such a scene as
untrained humanity is prompt to furnish on the
slightest provocation. Women fled shrieking from
the room and the house : men rushed furiously
hither and thither, and fell over each other in
blind zeal to do they knew not what. A servant
(as we learned afterwards) dragged her empty
trunk laboriously down four pair of stairs, leaving her garments hanging on pegs about her
attic chamber. But the best of the show—though
I did not realize it till later—was right under our
noses. The fire by itself was a pretty sight, and
unusual in the middle of a room ; the sheeted
figures which sprang and howled around it supplied
a combination not precisely paralleled, so far as I
remember, in any opera. Half a dozen of the
dancers, who scorned to fly the scene of danger,
had been reinforced by two or three of the bravest
from without : these hovered on the edge of the
conflagration, shouting aimless orders and encour-
agements to each other and to the ambient air, or
dashing about in wild excitement after ropes, step-
ladders, wash-tubs—whatever could be of no possible use. One snatched a handkerchief (it was
her very best) from a lady who imprudently lingered
at a distance to see what might come next, and
flung it into the devouring element. Another
tore off his coat and therewith beat the flames till
but a scorched rag remained to tell of his self-

abnegating public spirit. A third raced in with a pail of water from the kitchen and inundated his colleagues : fortunately not much of the unharmonizing fluid reached the blazing oil. With their frantic movements, these preservers were in much more peril than the building ; but the Providence which watches over drunkards and madmen protected them. Animated by their exertions, I was stepping forth to offer aid, when Dick seized my arm.

"Keep still, Bob, do. Let the natives conduct this entertainment; you're only a guest. I don't want to be the only sane person left in the premises. Don't burn up your coat : you can't get another to suit you nearer than Chicago. There's nothing to do : don't you see that the fire can't possibly reach the walls? Five dollars will pay for all the damage, except what those donkeys are making. It will be out within two minutes now."

And so it was: the exhibition was over in less time than I spend on the recital, and all that remained of it was a few charred planks in the floor and some singed sheets and bootsoles. The aqueous element had proved more injurious than its rival, and the sufferers retired to change their soaked clothing and lynch the too zealous water brigade of one. The company was collected again from yard and street, from hallways and neighboring houses, and joy was even more unconfined than before its interruption, for the most belated borrower of the county paper was now blest with perfectly fresh news to discuss.

"O Mr. Tipton," cried Mrs. Claybank, "was it really incendiary? And did you catch the guilty man who started it, and put it out yourself, as I hear? Here are two reporters to interview you: but tell me first. They say you were quite the hero of the occasion, and displayed most matchless presence of mind."

"That was Grafton," I replied. "I suppose he and I were the heroes of the occasion, for we stood by the door and looked at the fire till it went out, while others were piling on fresh fuel. I should have joined those misguided men, had not Grafton deterred me. I will not deceive you: he deserves all the honor. When there is nothing to be done, he of all men is the one to seize and point out the fact: his mind is singularly perspicacious in that direction."

"Yes, I should never suspect Mr. Grafton of doing what he ought not; but don't you think, as the Episcopals are so fond of saying in their church, he sometimes leaves undone things it might be well to do?"

"That is possible, madam; but in a world where so much is done that ought to be omitted, is it not better to err by deficiency than by excess? Think of to-night: the mistaken zeal of some of us might have led to the most terrible results. I might be lying a blackened corpse before you, but for the calm wisdom, the heroic self-command, of my young friend. In the hour of peril, the man who keeps his wits about him is the one we recognize as best and bravest, and that's Grafton to a T. I wouldn't tell any one else, but do you know what it was he said, that restrained me from rushing madly toward the flames? He said he didn't want to be the only sane man on hand, it would be so lonesome. Yet that is just what he was."

"I'm sure you talk beautifully, Mr. Tims, and it's an accomplishment so few of our young men possess: so sorry we couldn't induce you to address the literary circle. Yes, I always thought there was something in Mr. Grafton, and I'm sincerely glad to see it come out. If he was the hero —though I suspect your share was larger than you will admit — we ought to do something to recognize the fact. What should it be — a testimonial of some kind?"

"His modesty would shrink from that; he's modest to a fault, you know. *You* can appreciate him, you have such insight into character; but I don't believe most people here do. The thing would be to put him into some way of being quietly useful."

"Why, I asked him to teach in Sabbath School, and —"

"My dear madam, that was his modesty again. He doesn't like to set up for a religious teacher,

and let his light shine.   He's so young, he thinks
it wouldn't be proper: he has the nicest ideas of
propriety — exaggerated sometimes, I admit.   It
would have to be something private, and secular,
or scholastic, if I may use that expression.   I
hardly like to hint at such a thing; he would be
so offended if he knew."

"Any secret is perfectly safe with me," said the
lady eagerly.   "You may speak to me as to your
mother; and anything that is for Mr. Grafton's
good I think I ought to know."

"So you ought: he would tell you if he could
bring himself to talk of it to any one.   You would
hardly suspect it, he is so close about his own
affairs; but he's a great scholar.   Why, he took
the Berkeley scholarship — founded by Bishop
Berkeley, you know, who was so liberal, and wrote
that about the star of empire moving in your direction."

"He did?   And did Bishop Berkeley crown
him, or reward him, or whatever it was, with his
own hand?"

"By deputy, madam; the bishop was prevented
from being there in person.   But Grafton has remarkable gifts as a teacher.   The president and
professors have asked him to take particular
cases in hand, when they themselves had failed to
bring a boy through his classes, and he succeeded.
Fact, I assure you."

"You don't say so!   Why, they ought to have
made him a professor then."

"Too young, and as I said, too modest for his own good. He might have had a nice position if he had staid there; but your free and bracing air attracted him, and, as you remarked, he wisely came out here. Still, his educational candle ought not to be hid under a bushel, and — but these are his private matters, which I hardly ought to mention."

"O, tell me; I must know all about the dear young man. Purely for my own satisfaction, and that I may understand how best to serve him; you must see the necessity of that. I never talk, you know.

"Of course; and he thinks so much of you. Well, you know he's far from rich, and his legal income can't be much yet, there is so much competition. Now I ought not to have said that; it sounds like asking favors for him, and there's nothing he so abhors. He would never forgive me if he were to hear of this conversation of ours."

"I'll not tell him, and you needn't. Yes, there is no doubt of it, he needs some one to look after him; he does not push his interests as he might. Why, my husband has heard of his actually refusing cases that were offered to him."

"None in which Mr. Claybank was concerned, I'm sure — not if Dick knew the fact: he would do anything for you. He did refuse to defend a thief; he will be no party to injustice. His con-

science is not for hire, like some lawyers' : he is
so high-minded. He may have been mistaken
once or twice, and neglected his own interests as
you think, but only from the purest motives."

"That I can well believe. He wouldn't care
for a position in the public schools? Mr. Claybank is a trustee."

"That would interfere with his practice, what
there is of it. I don't want him to cut the law —
not yet. But if there were any boys in town
preparing for college, or the like, and they could
induce Grafton to give them lessons afternoons or
evenings, it would be a great advantage to them ;
he's perfect in classics, and mathematics, and
things generally."

"I see : I will think it over. Yes, there are
my nephews, and the Browns ; and my own son
will soon be old enough. He wouldn't want eastern prices, would he ? "

"O, I think not. You could arrange all that.
Only he mustn't know that I had anything to do
with it : let the idea and the proposition come
from you. And conceal if possible the fact that
you are doing him a kindness : he might take one
from you when he wouldn't from me or anybody
else, but even so it would hurt his feelings. *You*
understand that, though some others might not."

"Certainly I do. Yes, I will arrange it, and
it may prove advantageous on both sides. I'm
obliged to you for suggesting it, Mr. Tippen. So

you go to-morrow ? You must come and see us again. You will, I know : they always do. No one who has once breathed the air of the free and boundless West can be content to stay away from it. Perhaps you will arrange to settle here like your friend ; then you can help me to take care of him. Tackville has a great future, and we should be so glad to have you amongst us."

That night I intimated casually to Dick that there might be a chance of pupils ; Mrs. Claybank had been speaking to me about it. "I told her I thought you might find time for it, and that you were a dabster at such work ; so don't go back on me if they come after you. I don't suppose they pay much, but it will be at least as good as copying law papers." I said nothing about any trouble having been taken, or harmless little stratagems (and possibly fictions) employed, toward the attainment of this humble end, for I knew he would have to be older and wiser before he could understand that these things must be done in such cases, and that when the person most concerned will not do them himself, he simply transfers the requisite intellectual and moral expenditure to his friends, if he has any who care for him enough not to be willing to see him left out in the cold. To my guarded communication Dick replied, rather indifferently, that he was on hand if wanted, and I turned homeward with a somewhat easier mind.

CHAPTER XVII.

FIFTEEN MONTHS LATER.

THE pupils came, and added a few weekly dollars to Grafton's depleted exchequer : he did not dwell on them, nor need I. His infrequent letters had little to say of externals, and less than before of his beloved theories : either he was growing more sensitive to a lack of sympathy with his flights, or the airy regions of abstraction were losing their charm. A busy man makes a poor correspondent, but that could hardly be his case. Days that glide by in placid and uneventful content furnish little nutriment to epistolary zeal ; but the desire to remind others of one's existence dies, when one has nothing cheerful to tell and is too proud to complain. A vigorous spirit, thrown back upon itself, may find a safety-valve in pen and paper ; but when discouragement damps its powers, and it begins to find its efforts vain and to suspect that life is no great boon, it says of its nearest, first, "I will not inflict my dullness on him," and then, "*Cui bono?* he will not care to hear." — Should these and sundry reflections scattered through my pages appear out of character with a healthful mind, remember that I am trying to play biographer, and bound to take the tone and view-point of my subject when I can : if the chronicle be sombre, that is Grafton's fault, not mine.

More than a year passed before I could revisit Tackville, and then the blizzards were blowing and life was all indoors, for with them zero is more frequent than twenty above with us. The river was frozen over, and Major Way wisely gone to Florida. I renewed friendship with Mrs. Claybank, and again drank in the instructive accents of Mr. Rustler; but my business was with Dick. At first he was reticent, almost secretive, as one loath to confess to error or defeat : real life was beginning to claim his attention, and he liked neither the matter of the discourse nor the manner in which it was forced upon him. The few external topics of common interest were soon exhausted, and we sat in silence before the red-hot stove. The room bore signs neither of wealth nor want. There were no tapestries, no Persian carpets, no buhl and ormolu and bijouterie : if there had been, you would probably have heard of them before. As for the plain pine table and bookshelves, the two armchairs and the cuspidore (though I am straining a point to entitle it thus), I decline to expend labor in describing what you

may see in any poor young lawyer's office of your
acquaintance the next time you exchange the
splendors of the metropolis for your native country town.   I know it is the custom to give further
particulars, and if you insist on them I may say
that Richard slept in his office, on an old lounge
which he had purchased for $3.75 at a sale.
When I objected to this arrangement as unsocial
and unsanitary, he said he had wearied of hotel
bedrooms, and found them too bitterly cold in winter.   "I can't afford to be luxurious like you, and
order a fire every night, when I have one going
here.   Anthracite's expensive at this distance, and
our soft coal is fit only for factories.   Besides, I
save a dollar a week this way."   He was still taking his meals at the Occidental House, at a heb-
domadary cost of $4.   Another dollar might be
retrenched by the transfer to a boardinghouse,
but he dreaded the enforced proximity of various
salesladies, schoolma'ams, real estate agents, and
rising tobacconists.   "It's well enough," he observed, "to say good morning to them in the
street, or how d'ye do at a party ; but I don't want
to meet them regularly three times a day, and have
to sit at table till all of them are done.   Rustler
likes it : he can get up and go off when he's
ready, and criticise the food, and chaff the land-
lady ; but I can preserve my identity and my
independence best between this and the hotel.
Lonesome ?   No : I can go out if I want to."

He was occasionally invited to tea, I learned, at
Mrs. Claybank's and some other houses, but no
deduction for this item was made from his board-
account — a fact which indicates his unworldly
nature, never sharp at a bargain. His laundry
bill, averaging fully seventy-five cents a week,
showed his lingering aristocratic tastes; that of
Mr. Rustler, I imagine, was two-thirds less. His
annual outlay for raiment I neglected to inquire;
but he still patronized an eastern tailor, though
less frequently than of old. "You can wear your
clothes out, here," he informed me; "that's one
advantage. As for travel, we rarely go anywhere,
for the places worth going to are all too far off.
Incidentals are almost *nil:* so you see I ought to
be able to make expenses with but a moderate
amount of what our friend next door calls 'hustlin'; he likes that better than I do."

These items I gathered and noted down with
care, having in view the requirements of a realistic age; and I trust you will be satisfied. It has
been previously stated that the young man's form
was tall and well knit, his eyes and hair dark: let
me now add that his nose was straight, his hands
and feet of moderate size, his beard short and a
most beautiful curly brown. For reasons that will
hereafter appear, I am unable to set his photograph against the title-page.

I will own that I was more interested in his
inner man, as it was revealed in our conver-

sations, or rather in his monologues. Had Dick
worn blue spectacles, a throat-fringe, and a wool-
len comforter, I should still have liked, once
or twice a year, to hear him disclose his mental
processes and their singular results. The arguments by which his tenets were supported might
be far from satisfactory, but they were minor
matters, thrown in as it were in memory of our
college days; and I recalled the advice of the
sage to the young Englishman going out to
assume judicial functions in some colony: "Never
give the grounds of your decisions. The conclu-
sions will probably be right, the reasons for them
will almost certainly be wrong." With Grafton,
indeed, the ends he attained were no less open to
criticism than the steps by which he sometimes
professed to reach them. Most men, if they had
heard his views announced, would have thought
him in jest or doubted his sanity; even the few
accustomed to weigh opinions might have wondered at so much brain-cudgelling with no possible
outcome beyond his own mental satisfaction, and
that very limited and dubious in the long run.
His postulates, or the way they were held and
stated, bore an air of peculiar guilelessness, as if
the forming and discussing of them were a man's
main and proper business. He had an unequalled
gift for contemplating Life and receiving no more
personal impression from it than if he were outside its circle: he treated the world as a beetle

which he might pin to a card and examine at his leisure, without expecting it to make any active demonstration in return. At least he had maintained this attitude up to date; but now there were signs of weakening, of feeling or suspecting an assault on his castle of inquisitive indolence. Had he lived in the days of the Sophists, his talent might have brought fame and income, except that he was too honest; now, unhappily, chairs for this kind of cosmology are neither endowed nor popular.

CHAPTER XVIII.

A FOURTH OF JULY ORATION.

WE sat for a time in silence, which I finally broke. "What's the matter, old man? You look as if a summons had been served on you."

"Perhaps it has. I may as well tell you, Bob. The notions we learned in college don't seem to apply in outside life."

"So you're beginning to find that out, eh?"

"I don't mean the ordinary curriculum. The mathematics are useful to engineers, and classics to such as wish to teach them, and logic to those who think so, perhaps. I refer to the great underlying principles. The Socratic idea, you remember, was presented as the starting point of intellectual life, the basis of all study, the inclusive rule for thought and action."

"I remember that you said so. You were wild about it in my last year."

"I thought it was self-evident : I think so still. This is supposed to be a scientific age, and Truth for Truth's sake is the avowed maxim of all science.

Investigate, and note the results; collect facts, and try to infer their laws; see things as they are, and speak and act accordingly. What other standard can there be? What other creed can a man accept, unless he owns himself a muckworm, caring only to cover his back and fill his belly, to live as the beasts live and die as the fool dieth? To worship and follow Truth, and welcome her in all her shapes and voices, is what all decent men profess."

"Profess, I dare say; it's cheaper than practising. We're all to some extent muckworms, Dick—all but you, and you'll have to fall into line before long. Don't be so hot about it; it can be done in creditable moderation. You see, we aim to make the best of both worlds, to serve the spirit without starving the body—or vice versa, perhaps, with most. And so we make a judicious compromise."

"You can't," he said with an air almost of irritation. "There's no compromise here; it's one thing or the other. A man chooses either Truth or lies, and serves God or mammon."

"You put it too broadly. Motives are mixed, and oral or written deliverances, and things generally. Your feet are on mother earth, though your head may be in the clouds—as it is too apt to be. You see, we're obliged to consider temporal needs and occasions as well as the eternal verities. You ought to attend to one without neglecting the other; that's scripture, isn't it? Study so to express your truth that it will be taken without offence; there's a deal in the art of putting things. But go on and spin your yarn; I can preach my little sermon afterwards."

"It's this way. The theory, beautiful and noble as it is, doesn't seem to work when you take it out of doors. Try to act on the Socratic idea, and you get into hot water at once. Put your principles into words, and you're marked as a fool; trace them to their most obvious application, though it be plain as a proposition in Euclid, and you're liable to be a blasphemer — because you're butting against somebody's effete prejudice. You don't want to hurt any one, or get into rows: you think your testimony is as impersonal as that two and three make five, or that Virtue is laudable; but old superstition comes in the way, and its owners — perhaps a host of them — rise and howl, and roar you down. You're called on to state your opinions: they may be those held by all rational men, a matter of rudiments and axioms, or they may be in a debatable ground, a region of controversy. Well, you've formed them honestly, according to the best lights within reach; you can't lie, you say what you think like a gentleman: and then it's as if you had insulted Elisha, and he set his bears on you. Who was it said error of every kind might meet with favor, but the world never did and never would tolerate real Christianity? Enlarge that, put general truth in place of a par-

ticular religion, and I believe it's so. People like
neither hard pan nor frank statements : if you
think a thing out and tell them how it is, they
count you a heathen man and a publican."

I soon learned what specific experiences had
given rise to this large lamentation ; there were
two of them. Home talent being cheaper than
imported, Grafton had been chosen as orator on
the preceding Fourth of July. He had had the
forethought to inquire whether the free expression of individual views on public topics would be
acceptable, and the inviting committee-man, who
was not an active politician and regarded the address as a bare matter of form, told him to say
twenty dollars' worth of what he pleased. There-
upon he had ingenuously assumed the scholar's
and reformer's standpoint, and prepared a trac-
tate on Our Dangers and Our Safety. He denounced corruption, narrow partisanship, the
greed for office, and the arrogant tyranny of
bosses and machines ; pleaded for a broad national
spirit that should look not back but forward ; recalled other landings besides the one at Plymouth
Rock ; announced that the war was over and its
results secure ; quoted from Washington's Farewell Address the passages which deprecate sec-
tional feeling ; commended the sovereignty which
is carried under the hat, and the inclusive patriot-
ism which has "love and tears for the blue, tears
and love for the gray." That doctrine is suffi-

ciently familiar now, but ten years ago it was liable to be considered not only novel but traitorous.

Nobody listened to the effort except the dignitaries on the platform and a few bumpkins who did not mind standing an hour in the sun; but among the former was a legal luminary who after much intriguing had secured a place on a certain State Committee, and cherished legislative yearnings as yet ungratified by a nomination. After the proceedings and as soon as the orator was out of hearing, he rose in wrath, denounced the speech as an outrage, and said it should have been stopped in mid career. The local papers, at whose offices Dick had cultivated no great intimacy, published brief and garbled reports of his discourse, and long editorial antidotes to its poison : he was called an unrepentant rebel and an impudently flagitious detractor from the unsullied majesty of the Party in power.

" Well, old man," I remarked when this tale of woe was concluded, " it's a new thing for you to attach so much importance to what folks say about you ; I suppose they didn't warn you to leave the town, or threaten tar and feathers? Short of physical violence, I wouldn't mind if I were you. And it's six months ago now."

" O, I didn't care for the personal aspect of the case. It did me no great harm ; but I don't like to see Truth spit upon and crucified."

" Now, Dick, you analyzed the boasted liberalism of this region for my benefit when I was here before; you told me what their free thought and openmindedness amounted to. What could you expect, when you sprung on them such a new idea as that the war was over? They don't know that, and they'll not believe it on your authority."

"Bob, what I said was all true and sound. It can be disputed only by blind bigotry; it is accepted by all dispassionate thinkers. I'll get the thing and let you read it." And he began to rummage among his papers.

"O, thank you very much, but I'm content to take your word for it — entirely so. Dispassionate thinkers, I dare say: keep it for an audience of such. As you don't find them hereabouts, why should you incur the odium of a prophet out of season?"

"But the people must be instructed. How are they ever to learn unless somebody tries to teach them? Their newspapers won't do it, and I thought I had a chance to."

" Let those do it who have a following, and can afford to take the risks. Why should you tilt at windmills? You're young, and not widely recognized as a leader yet. And then you're from the wrong side of the line."

"Why do you bring that up? I was but eight when the war broke out, and my people had nothing to do with it. I've not been South for ten years, and have no prejudice at all on that score. I'm not even a Democrat; I don't vote—not seeing much of late years to vote for. The speech was strictly unpartisan. My being originally from a border state has nothing to do with the question."

"Not in the clear white light of Truth, doubtless; but it weighs with these stalwarts, who call any man a rebel that is not of their opinion. The unpartisan character of your humble effort was its worst offence; how should they understand a position they never dreamed of? When an Independent movement comes, the hacks will hate it worse than they do the other party. And you've actually been trying to initiate one all by yourself, and here of all places? Do you really think it was prudent, or modest either, to essay the conversion of the community so suddenly? You can't expect people to be reasonable in politics and religion. It's not peculiar to this town, or to the state. You'll find the same thing in our back counties, where the *Weekly Forum* gives the law."

"Perhaps I ought to have allowed for the force of prejudice. Jeremy Taylor says, 'As well charm a fever asleep with the noise of bells, as make any pretence of reason against that religion old men have entailed on their heirs male so many generations.' One generation has done it in this case: political superstition is as bad as the other, I suppose."

"Worse, for the other is merely a traditional

attachment to theories and forms. Except with the parsons, it bears no close relation to business: the rest have merely the limited glory of being trustees and vestrymen. Whereas in politics, every man has a vote, and pays taxes ; some of them have friends in office, or hope to be postmasters themselves."

"Well, what would you have done in my place?"

"Restricted my eloquence to the safe and approved Spread Eagle ; enlarged on our unprecedented growth and advance, specially in this section, — the vast agricultural resources, the free and boundless prairies, the gorgeous Future knocking at our doors. That would have hit them where they live, and preserved serenity and brotherly feeling."

"Stale and wearisome platitudes, repeated *ad nauseam* in every weekly paper ! Would you have told them nothing they didn't know before?"

"They don't want to hear anything they didn't know before. My child, platitudes, decently clad, are always welcome. The attempt to teach people new tricks and uproot their venerable dogmas implies an offensive assumption of superiority, which they resent of course. You've not yet learned the secret of popular instruction, which is simply to bring forth with a solemn air of deep conviction, and if possible as new discoveries, what your hearers believe already. It's all Arrangement and Style, as the books told you long ago ; the

Invention is merely nominal. Not matter, but manner brings down the house, and carries the audience along. Till you master this art, you cannot become one of the Great and Good; never President, and not even a congressman."

CHAPTER XIX.

AN EXAMINATION.

His second eye-opening experience had been in this way. A department of English was vacant in the High School of one of the larger towns; the duties were entirely within Dick's competency, and friends advised him to apply for the place. He had no difficulty in obtaining sufficient testimonials, but the appointment was made to depend on a competitive examination. This was conducted by the local superintendent of schools, a gentleman who enjoyed the double repute of an active, bustling official and a universal scholar. Seeing that his range included all subjects from kindergarten up, and that he had to be a man of affairs no less than a man of ideas and books, here was a task for the most lucid and comprehensive intellect. So heavy and heterogeneous a load, like those of the mules in New Mexico, could be carried only by the most dextrous and methodical packing, and the packer must possess the secret of his art. Where dates, declensions, and formulas are considered in lieu of pans and picks and bundles of cloth and flour and sugar, Definiteness is plainly that secret. Each point must be exactly placed and sharpened, to each question there must be one precise answer, for each topic an accepted authority whose word is law. If you begin to doubt and inquire and discuss, and admit a possibility of different views or of leaving a subject open, you will make slow progress and never be able to cover the ground. The mind wants positive knowledge and fixed conviction; therefore the laws of thought and language must be as absolute as the tenet that twice five is ten. Before this tribunal Grafton fared somewhat as follows.

"What are the rules for the use of the comma?"

"Each book has a different set, and none of them are wholly satisfactory. Some of the rules generally accepted are open to serious exception. No set can approach exhaustiveness, unless drawn out to wearisome and impracticable length."

The examiner opened his light blue eyes to their widest extent, uplifted his Jovian brow, and inquired with sarcasm, "Would you dispense with rules then?"

"Not altogether. With very young or dull pupils I would follow such as the book contained, whatever it might be — with qualifications, of course. To the more advanced I would explain that an underlying principle is to be borne in mind and applied to differing cases by their own intelligence; and that the comma is not always of equal weight, but represents a sliding scale of pauses of the voice or mind, from the slightest to that indicated by the semicolon."

"You regard punctuation then as optional, unimportant?"

"On the contrary; it is so important, and so generally neglected, that it makes a call on the reflective faculties, and should not be left merely to the memory."

"We will pass that point then. How do you classify prepositions?"

Dick reflected a moment. "In English I see no basis for a classification that shall be of any value. With prepositional phrases it is otherwise."

"Indeed? Have not Professor Drybones and Dr. Hairsplit thought differently?"

"Very possibly. Able and learned men have their whims, by which the rest of us scarcely need be bound. I could classify prepositions in several ways, but none of the results would be worth the labor."

"That may well be," said the examiner sagely; and the youngest committeeman tittered. "You appear to have little respect for divisions, Mr. Grafton, and for rules. May I ask why?"

"Certainly, sir. It is because the undue stress often laid on them misleads the student, who ought to be encouraged to look into the reason and nature of things for himself. Grammatical rules exist merely for convenience' sake, as means toward an end, as more or less dim adumbrations of truth: to take them for the end to be reached, the inmost truth of the matter, is to be misled. Language is but the imperfect instrument of an imperfect agent; but both the mind and this its chief product and tool are flexible, capacious, ever changing, and not to be hemmed in and tied down by formulas."

The superintendent of schools looked from side to side of his long table, but none of his committeemen had anything to suggest. Then, like one threatened with drowning in a metaphysic sea, who grasps at the first solid object within reach, he asked, "What is a complement?"

"A term employed to indicate two very different things, object and attribute. I should tell my pupils to use in either case the word which expressed the fact, and discard the ambiguous and comparatively meaningless 'complement.'"

Mr. Grinder shook his head sadly. "If you please, gentlemen, we will pass from Grammar to Rhetoric. Do you place Imagery among the Qualities of Style?"

"That depends on the point of view. If you choose to put it there, I would not wish to say you were wrong; but I hardly care to settle the matter, not thinking myself a final authority."

"Doubtless not. But you perhaps have an opinion?"

"O yes. I am content to hold by Clearness, Force, and Grace as the main qualities, and to consider Imagery as contributive to any of these in turn, or to all three at once; but I have no wish to dogmatize, for the case does not admit of it. It's not as if you were dealing with rocks and gases."

The examiner's eye brightened; he did not listen to the superfluous close of this statement. He was not an unkindly man at bottom, and had no wish too deeply to disgrace this presumptuous rationalist. Moreover he dearly loved to trot out an authority. "Ahem; gentlemen, I may mention the fact that the eminent Professor Botch on this point agrees with Mr. Grafton."

The committee, who had been looking grave, now pricked up their ears and smiled wisely on each other. All no doubt deeply familiar with the fame and works of Professor Botch, they beamed upon the candidate, as if to say, 'Right for once; this is not so scandalously bad after all.'

But Dick, with his incorrigible candor, refused to accept this advantage. "My dear sir, that by no means proves my position correct. Professor Botch is rather noted for his loose and even wild assertions; see his last book gone over in *The People* two weeks ago. But if he stood much higher than he does for accuracy and sound judgment, still he would have no more right to settle this question than you or I."

The committee looked puzzled, the examiner disgusted. "At this rate we shall settle nothing, I fear. Well, Mr. Grafton, at least you have read Thomson, I presume. Can you give me the dates of his birth and death, and of the appearance of his principal works?"

"No, sir: I do not burden my memory with such details. I know where to find them when needed, and that is sufficient."

"You would have found it advantageous to have them on hand now, sir."

But I have no desire to exhaust the reader's patience, and my topic is not Grammar, but Grafton. He replied to succeeding queries in the same unprecedented manner, as if the object in view were the ascertainment of general Truth, and not the securing of a particular appointment.

"Well," I remarked, when he had concluded his narrative, "so that's your idea of the way to conduct your end of an examination. And yet you didn't get the berth? That is strange, now. Do you think you took the best road to attain your end?"

"I was there to answer his questions, and show what I knew and thought, so far as opportunity offered. It was plain from the start that I had no chance for the place, his views and mine were so antipodal. He wanted some little martinet, who had Truth all cut and dried and done up in brown paper parcels weighing so much apiece. At that rate, his ideal school ought to be easily realized. Yet they say he's a very efficient man."

"And that's more than you will be, Richard, till you acquire the virtue of Adaptability. You must have that to be Available. Having tried for this place, you should have kept on trying to the bitter end."

"Why, what could I do, after the turn things took, but bear my testimony?"

"Kept it in your pocket till called for, which was not on that occasion. It wasn't an open debate, nor were you there on equal terms. Why should you defy and antagonize one whose good will and word you were seeking?"

"I wasn't seeking to rise by falsehood. If a man says that black is white, or that we are in the thirteenth century, am I to agree with him?"

"Some would, and wisely: you might at least keep still and not contradict him. When you're after a place in his gift, it's better to seem not to know, and accept his corrections, than do that. He expects you to be meek and deferential, not to fly at him like the rugged Russian bear, the armed rhinoceros, or the Hyrcan tiger. That's no way to treat your superiors."

"Grinder is not my superior in anything but

years. If I were the examiner, I could break him to pieces as easily as he did me."

"Very likely; but that's neither here nor there. You will insist on intrinsic valuations, which are of no account except for our private satisfaction. The world cares only for the outside, and judges by that. When you get to be Somebody, you can ride your hobbies in public, and lay down the law — within judicious limits. You'll know how to do it then, and Greatness has its privileges. But to mount the first rounds of the ladder you must show your smooth side, and say and do what is expected of you, and swear by the prevalent deities. You profess to venerate Facts, yet you wont show a decent respect to those that lie closest round you, even when their sharp edges press you hard, and perhaps cut you. They are mundane, I admit, not celestial; but the millennium hasn't arrived yet, and while you are in Babylon it's as well to obey Babylonish laws and comply with established usages."

CHAPTER XX.

JOURNALISTIC PROSPECTS.

WE sat up late and undisturbed that evening, listening in intervals of talk to the roaring blasts without. The night was blue and white, to the vision all snow and moon and sky, to ear and flesh somewhat too boisterous. I had thought of a sleighride, but not in this temperature, nor amid drifts eight feet deep. And indeed, there was work to be done indoors. I do not love to be harsh with a fellow-creature, but the time had come for very open dealings with my misguided friend. The crust of his self-indulgent indifferentism needed to be broken, and his spirit roused to grapple with the tasks of life. So free a critic could not object to be criticised in turn : he must bear the plain speech he loved and practised. To say truth, he would always listen fairly to another's view, however it might rasp his own ; I will do him that justice. So I girded myself for an assault upon his citadel, and the conversation ensued which is recorded in the first chapter of this history. I have put it there because it reveals the very inmost of Grafton's mind; by turning back the reader will see him in his habit as he lived, without concealment or disguise — not that these were ever much in his way: less frankness would have made him fatter — and with all his imperfections on his head. So long as his battle was to be fought, as he needed anything from the world, no one should have learned from me the depth of his unwisdom; but the revelation cannot hurt him now.

Next morning Dick came in from the postoffice, as I sat dolefully before his stove with a cigar and last week's local paper. His face was rosy from the cold, and wore an amused smile. "Well, old man, you thought I made an unmitigated ass of myself in that examination at Miletus, didn't you?"

"About that — though the expression is your own. But I'm not infallible, and we live to learn. You haven't got the place, surely?"

"O no; that was filled a month ago. But I had two votes, and one of the brightest of the committee, the editor of a leading paper there, listened rather closely to the display of Grinder's learning and my imbecility. He took me to dinner afterwards, was very civil, and asked me if I had ever thought of journalism. He was not in love with the superintendent, I thought."

"And this, as a mere beggarly external, was not

worth mentioning in your report to me, eh? What did you say to the man?"

"It had no essential connection with what we were talking of last night. I told him editing had never come my way yet, but I was willing to think of it should occasion arise. He said nothing definite then ; seemed merely to be sounding me. But now he writes that he can make a vacancy for me if I care to take it."

"Will it be worth your while?'

"It may. The pay is rather more than I make here: it is a much larger town, and I've had about enough of this. I should attend to reporting cases in court, and educational and literary matters : he wants to make a specialty of them."

While we were discussing the prospect Mr. Rustler entered, and was taken into our counsels.

"It'd leave only nineteen of us," he said meditatively," and an even number looks handsomer. Still, if it's for his betterment — I don't know who I should get to do my copyin', but I wont ask him to stay for that. If he'd 've shook himself, now, and put on steam, and gone in with me, as you and me wanted him to — but he just wouldn't. I been clean out o' patience with him, specially since that Fourth of July business."

"Why, Rustler," Dick interposed, "you owned to me, privately, that I was right, in the abstract."

"Dash the abstract. Those notions 'll be all

right next generation, or might be now in Boston :
but you ain't in Boston, and what's the use of
preachin' to posterity? As the man said, what'd
posterity ever do for you? What you want to be
ahead of your time for? If you'd been runnin'
for constable, you wouldn't 've raised one vote in
ten, after that speech. No, sir, he wont ever do
no good here, that's a fact ; and perhaps makin' a
new start in another place 'll sort of shake him up.
Then he's the kind of cuss that works better by
the day 'n by the job; fact, and blamed little to his
credit. I'd a darned sight rather work for myself ;
but he's not got the sand to take contracts. Put
him on a salary, and he'll feel bound to earn it ;
he's got that sort of a slow, down-east spirit in
him. Leave that out, and it'll be nigh about the
same as here, I s'pect. You've got to hustle in
editin', same as in law, if you want to get ahead.
You wont see him set the Mississippi afire; no,
sir. But if it's nice clean work, so's to suit him,
he may do a bit better 'n he's done here. Law-
reportin', is it? O, he can see the points of a
case, once others have carried it through. I'd
rather have him report my cases 'n work 'em up or
argue 'em — a dam sight rather. But all the
law Jandyke can put in his paper wont keep
Grafton busy more 'n four days in a month, and
how's he to earn his meals rest of the time?
Lookin' sharp after Grinder, and comin' down
on him once a quarter or so, wont fill up. Book-

reviewin', eh? Yes, he can tell the women which novels is fit for 'em to read — and write his own poetry for the obituaries, likely. Charge extra for that, don't they? Might be a good lay, that. No? Then I'm darned if I can see how you'll make a business or a livin' out of all these drippin's together."

"Come, Rustler," said Dick, perversely delighted, "don't be so discouraging. You oughtn't to look with scorn on a sister profession, you know."

"The sister profession, youngster, is made up mostly of two branches you're noways fit to navigate. That is, the writin' part. Politics you daresn't touch, or the fat 'd be in the fire as 'twas with us last summer. Catch me recommendin' you to orate another Fourth of July! And as for local news, how 're you to know whose squash 's taken prizes at County Fair, or what girls from the rural parts are visitin' at Miss Duck's, or which policeman· caught the last burglar? Th' other papers 'd get the facts down a month before you'd hear of 'em. As to business, I don't s'pose Jandyke 'd trust you with that, if his head's halfways level. Don't let him send you out to dun subscribers or tout for new ads., or you wont keep the place a week. You get a nice new desk, and have it railed in, and sit there with a nice new scissors and the Eastern papers. Once in a while you might go to a high-toned concert, or a select

family circle kind of play, and write that up, but
no minstrels or such — nothin' common.   I hate
to have you go to Miletus anyway : it's a big town,
and your morals may get hurt.   Reckon I'll have
to move down there and protect 'em."

When he was gone Dick said, " Do you know
what I should most regret in leaving this ? "

" Rustler, rather than Mrs. Claybank ?   Why ? "

" She palls on you before long.   But he's so
racy and virile and suggestive.   He paints things
in a good broad glare, with no sidelights or shad-
ings.   You rarely get such a full-front view of
yourself, with the sun in your eyes."   And the
subject of this unflattering portrait sat and laughed
till the tears came.   This was one of his peculiari-
ties, that, however hard the jest or the argument
might hit him, he was always ready to recognize
and rejoice in a point well made.   Truth in his
view gained and lost nothing by having a personal
edge ; his egoism was curiously free from vulgar
vanity.   In his way, poor boy, he was as consistent
as man born of woman may be.

His practice, then in its third year, showed no
signs of increasing; his copying was mere journeyman's work.   His pupils were nearly ready for
college, and others might not come to take their
place, for that small town supplied few materials
for a permanent ' connection ' of this kind.   All told,
his income could not equal the six hundred a year
offered by the *Boomerang*.   I went with him to

Miletus, which was certainly a great improvement on Tackville. It could show handsome business blocks, stores worthy of Broadway, and residences such as you may see about Central Park. A great river flowed at its feet : it was on a main line of travel, and several hours nearer the East. "You will be less out of the world here, my boy ; it is more like civilization," I had to admit, as I took the cars. Mr. Jandyke seemed a fair man, and all was satisfactorily arranged. In the early spring Grafton gave his last lessons, said a cordial farewell to Mrs. Claybank, and turned his back on the scene of his first adult venture. His departure, I believe, was sincerely regretted by a few, but left no aching void in the local body politic.

CHAPTER XXI.

MILESIAN OPPORTUNITIES.

OF Grafton's new experience no detailed account
need be given. One third-class inland town is
much like another, and editorial life in these has
been sufficiently depicted in the work entitled
" Seth's Brother's Wife." Dick's case, however,
differed from that of Fairchild in several particulars. His tasks were in good degree separated
and defined ; it was not his way to expend much
time or cash in the unhallowed precincts of the
beer-saloon ; and he did not rise in his profession.

In truth, it was always easier to tell what he
did not do than what he did. He still wore the
air of being undesirous to make or receive any
strong impression, of keeping aloof from life.
Like Theodore Winthrop, he was 'proud of his
individuality, and resisted all the world's attempts
to merge him in the mass.' That may answer
when one's tree can bear uncommon fruit ; till
justified by such a crop, the world cares not a
brass sixpence for your individuality, and thinks you

— if it deigns to notice your case at all — a ninny
to build a house of self-complacence on so narrow
and sandy a foundation.   In Grafton's case the
attempts at merging, never numerous, were now
wholly intermitted.   Miletus enshrined some very
good society — so good that, as with Seth afore-
mentioned, it was out of reach of an obscure
subeditor.   Or rather the sub, if endowed with
Dick's bearing and education and with a resolute
ambition, might perchance in time have been
privileged to ring those exclusive door-bells, gaze
admiringly on the treasures of art and upholstery
within, and on dancing nights even to enfold the
West Hill's daughters in partial and reverent
embrace.   But of ambition of any sort, as long ago
stated, Dick had not enough to float him; and
why should Wealth and Fashion note the existence
of a poor young scribbler who has not spirit
enough to approach on bended knee and crave the
boon of kissing their sacred feet?

If either the human or the artistic sensibilities
had been more strongly developed in him, he
might have found a pure or throbbing joy in the
widening of his horizon; for Main Street, on any
clear afternoon, could afford spectacles such as
had rarely been presented to his organs during
the last three and a half years.   When one has
been in banishment a while — in the mountains
after big game, or on the plains cattle-raising, or
penned by exigencies of business in some remote

nook of the coal or oil regions, looking up dull
but auriferous details of some great producing
interest — how it stirs the blood to feel the pavement under foot again, and to behold fairy forms
approach, garbed in the latest marvels of Pinkfern
and Mme. Belletête ! A halo seems to encircle
them ; you wonder if they have not wings. They
are a celestial vision, the noblest joint product of
art and nature : if custom only allowed it, you
would like to fall down and burn incense. When
you have been in town a few days, and are taken
to call on these same sirens, the divinity has
mostly rubbed off, and their talk is probably
human and insipid enough ; but when you first get
back from a month's yachting, or a sojourn in the
Wayback Woods, you feel as if you were in an
improved Mohammedan paradise, ennobled by a
highly superior and spiritualized race of houris,
who have souls finer than ours, and are not to be
touched on any account, but only gazed upon
adoringly. That is, on the street ; the right
streets I mean, of course, and at the right hours :
it is somehow different indoors, on a closer and
continued view. O, shade of N. P. Willis, you
spent your life and most of your soul, in days
when they applied to it the text, *Adhæsit pavi-
mento*, over this kind of thing, but you never
exhausted the subject, nor even did justice to
it, whether in your glittering prose or your
rippling verse. To feel the enchantment at its

fullest, you should make your leap from the desert into some city where you have little or no acquaintance, say Cincinnati or Baltimore. On my native heath, where I know many of the ladies, the charm does not work so well. But the poet's mind was tottering on its throne when he wrote that line about Beauty when unadorned being adorned the most : the sex knows very much better.

I never could instil these orthodox sentiments into Grafton, who in some respects, it pains me to own, was dull and deficient. I will not say that he cared absolutely nothing for feminine faces, forms, and costumes ; but he looked on them coldly, as if they were hung in a gallery and he were no collector. " I'm not a nabob," he would say ; " I can't afford expensive tastes." In this he was below the level of Mr. Haggard's savages (in ' She '), who venerated their wives, though addicted to the blameworthy practice of removing them when they grew troublesome. As Tennyson says of King Arthur, the right thing is to love one woman and cleave to her ; and till the time comes for that, you can distribute your homage promiscuously. Arrange the programme as you please, always preserving the unsullied purity without which man is unfit to approach Woman; but indifference to the better half of humanity is a crime many degrees worse than having no music in you. It is against nature, and

he who is guilty of it must have a shameful hollow
in his head where the bump of reverence ought
to be.   As a rule I never trust that kind of man ;
if he has not courage enough for secret, dark, and
midnight wickedness, he will usually begin as a
cold-blooded sneak, and end as a miser, appropri-
ately starving in grimy solitude.   Dick was an
exception to this law, as to most : I used to wonder how, lacking the saving grace of gyneolatry
(or perhaps it would be as well to say in plain
English, Woman-worship) he could amount to as
much as he did.

With so much society in range, he had less
than before.   In a small place like Tackville
everybody knows everybody else, and a young
man who is not positively bearish perforce takes
part in the moderate round of festivities : in Miletus there was room for class distinctions, and it
was possible not to speak to your neighbor on the
street.   I suppose he felt the finer atmosphere
in his languid way, but thought it no loss to be
exempt from social obligations.   For the rest, it
was not work he objected to, but the looking for
it ; his position had the humble advantages of
prescribed duties, a monthly stipend, and no
office-rent to pay.   But its chief attraction in his
eyes was that it gave him without cost the periodicals and some of the new books, with occasion
to read them ; to be paid for following his own
tastes was thus far to solve the problem of

existence. The invention of printing has been a boon to the lazy and unsocial, in that it assists them to take Life at second hand. Without leaving slippers and easy-chair, one may know what is going on in the street and across the oceans: you may dine at the Russian ambassador's, and note all the types of home and foreign character, yet spare the fatigue of putting on your dress coat and company manners. "Yes," said Dick, when I made a visit of inspection the following spring, "this sort of thing is less of a bore than pupils or law business. People are less uninteresting in books than they usually are in flesh and blood, and less obtrusive; you can get away from them when you please. Others do the jostling and move the scenery, and you simply observe their activities, note their points, and say what you think of the show. It's more amusing to be spectator than performer."

"You don't find it exciting, then? Do you like your work?"

"It's well enough, but in no way thrilling. If I were to get excited over it, nobody else would."

"Then you're not strongly drawn to literature, after all?"

"I don't delude myself into the notion that I'm making literature because I write on literary topics. I'm only a hanger-on, a sort of camp-follower. What I do is mere skimmings; even I don't care to remember it, and why should any one else?"

"Still, I should think you'd want to do your best, while you're at it."

"I do. Not an ideal best, but the best I can now and here, the best the occasion calls for. What I mean is that the circumstances are not stimulating. Newspaper criticism goes for nothing, unless in one or two of the New York and Boston dailies. And out here, who expects it? Jandyke flies too high: I doubt if it pays him to keep up my department."

"Well, don't saw off the limb you're perched on. That's his affair to determine, not yours."

"Yes, he doesn't ask me for advice. While he keeps faith with me, I will with him, of course. If he wants this work, I do it well enough for the purpose; but what does it amount to? What would it amount to, if I were Hazlitt and Taine and Sainte-Beuve rolled into one?"

"More than you think, perhaps. You might be discovered and transplanted to bloom in a richer soil and more genial climate."

"O, I don't know that I'm particularly worth discovering. This is mere prentice work, and very possibly I shall never do anything better."

"You don't believe that, you know; not a word of it. So you mean to be an author? Well, they say in that trade one has to work up from the foot of the ladder."

"I've begun a rung higher, and omitted reporting. Yes, if I had an ambition it would be to make books — by and by, when I'm older, and know enough."

"You might be practising now. You have some spare time, haven't you?"

"Yes; not so much as I had at Tackville, but several hours a day. Want to come here and study? I'll coach you at reduced rates."

"Don't you write anything beside what you put in the *Boomerang?* Novels, and stuff for the magazines? Most people do, I'm told."

"Far more than is wanted. I marvel at the cheek of those who think themselves fit to instruct the universe as soon as they are out of school. You and I are mere boys, Bob, though we've been loose several years now — and you've seen more than I. Our minds are not mature enough yet to do anything permanent; we want a lot more experience. How should I write a novel — what would I put in it? I can comment and analyze, perhaps, but not invent; I have no constructive imagination that I'm aware of. And I've had no adventures : nothing ever happens to me. What have I seen or heard that's worth recording?"

"That's because you keep yourself shut up so, and practise your benumbing old theory of Indifference. If you would go out like other fellows, and take an interest in events and persons more recent than Socrates, things would happen, and you might collect plenty of literary material.

Then you'd have a stock in trade, and be ready to open shop, you see."

"Thank you : I've no fancy to put my fingers in the fire, that I may be able to tell how they were burned. Do that yourself, if you like."

"Well, you might look into your heart and write, as somebody advised."

"That seems to be as empty as the view out-side. What have I ever had to fill it ? I might have had, you say ? It may be bad taste, but I don't admire mock rhapsodies, and engagements made only to be broken, and playing with what ought to be serious. Very possibly I'm prudish and out of date ; but I can't claim the privileges of genius. I'm not a Byron or a Burns or a Goethe, to get up a new love-affair each month."

"One in a year or two would be enough — or even less. You could be perfectly sincere in them, and exquisitely high-minded ; you would, I know. It would be most instructive to see you, and especially so to yourself. You could note down all the symptoms, and analyze the mental processes : it would quite make a man of you. Well, if you wont think of that, can't you at least string rhymes together about the Moon, and the Return of Spring, and such ? The monthlies allow extra rates for poetry ; it páys better than prose — when you can get it in. You might even thrash the Socratic Idea into metrical shape. Truth and

Youth — Beauty and Duty — Miletus and Epictetus : why, I can do it myself."

"Robert, to stop your eternal catechising, I will throw modesty to the dogs. You keep on insisting that I should do this or that, till I'm forced in self-defence to show you what I have done." He opened a drawer and took out some manuscripts.

CHAPTER XXII.

DROPPING INTO POETRY.

I<small>F</small> I had suspected what was in that drawer, I would not have sailed so near the wind and tempted Fate thus rashly.

"You have only yourself to blame for this," he remarked. "To slake your thirst for useless knowledge, and assuage your somewhat blind and random hortatory zeal, I'm going to read you these."

"Take a short one, Dick; a very little one will do. I'm a homeopath, you know. Excuse me if I spoke unadvisedly, not knowing how you spent the midnight hours: I didn't mean to provoke you to this extent."

He grinned malignantly, selected what I believe was the worst one of the lot, and with less than is decent of blushing and stammering began to read.

> " Life is a land of dreams
> We cannot render real, though we try
>   With many bitter tears, and schemes
> That call on effort and philosophy.

> Between the fool and wise
> What is there? what between the mean and great?
> For many prosper without eyes,
> And others' seeing is their grief's estate.
> What due distinction reigns
> Between Nobility in rags, and Vice
> That is not worth the jailer's chains?
> Is the world senseless, or are we too nice?"

" Pause right there," I cried. "The world may be senseless, but there's no doubt whatever about our being too nice — a blanked sight, as Rustler would say. What's the good of those conundrums? They don't pay for *that* kind of thing: you couldn't even print it in the *Boomerang*, except at advertising rates — not if you value your present berth."

"You're off the track, Bob," the bard said coolly. "These humble effusions are not in the market. I don't expect to make anything by them. They're merely to get my hand in and see what I can do, which is very little as yet; simply practice, as you said just now."

"Then why not practise on something sensible? They say the Chinese beggars sit in the streets of Pekin with their bones protruding, and howl just like that thing you read. You're not particularly hard up just now, so far as I see; and wailing, tuneful or not, hasn't usually been in your line."

"No, I trust not. You have a literal mind, Bob. Those verses simply represent a mood, and exaggerate it, no doubt. We're all liable to be downcast and lachrymose at times, in idle moments; if we were not, there would be less alleged poetry. The closing stanzas of that are the best, but I'll spare your feelings, since you take it so hard. Here's one that may suit you better." He turned over the leaves, and I again resigned myself, though really this was pushing Friendship too far.

" These hopes and dreams of mine shall live,
   Though none on earth should share them,
Though Fate delay her crowns to give
   To those who yet shall wear them.
Though Time with slow methodic tread
   And silent step moves by me,
I feel the garland round my head,
   The hours of glory nigh me !

It is not time, ungalled by tears,
   That stamps the wrinkles keenly,
For some might live a thousand years,
   Yet wear their age serenely;
But something in the feeling breast
   That gnaws its fleshly prison,
That yearns too bitterly for rest
   And sees too bright a vision.

And so its light is clouded here
   And broken is its singing,
Though caught from that diviner sphere
   Toward which the soul is winging.
And ever as it journeys on
   The darkness clings beside it,
Till Death beholds the victory won
   That Life so long denied it."

" Yes, that is not as bad as the other. I've seen things in print that were not much better than that, really. If you were to turn it over in your mind again, and bring it out in a different shape, digested and compressed — The double rhyme is a good deal for you to undertake, don't you think? 'Prison' and 'vision' wont do at all. But what's all this about hopes and dreams, and crowns, too? Are you really after something, and have you concealed the fact all this time? What are your hopes and dreams, anyway?"

" Probably I only dreamed that I had any. That's the outcome of another mood, no more important than the first. Sometimes, you know, it seems as if Life might conceivably be of some account, if circumstances could be wholly changed. And when you write verses you have to project yourself into a poetical frame of mind, and make the most of limited and perishable emotional materials; that's why it looks so much more serious on paper. Every one has fancies of that kind, I presume — except densely practical men like you. I'd like to see you try to go beyond your Duty and Beauty."

It was plain to me that these lyric efforts meant more than their parent cared to acknowledge, and I was grieved and disgusted by them, especially by the first. But it was not my cue to encourage this downward course, or give even such sympathy as lies in apparent comprehension to questionings that could end in nothing but paralysis, and lamentations which Grafton had always been too manly to utter in his own proper person and in simple prose.   His case had been bad enough, but if it were to be complicated with poetical woes and yearnings, I should begin to despair.

CHAPTER XXIII.

HOMESICK.

I SAT thinking what to say next, when he took up his parable, opening as it seemed a new subject. "Bob, I can see now where I made a mistake."

"If it was one only, you were wiser than most of us. I've made dozens, and so have you, old man — a string of them, in sad succession."

"This was long ago, when I was too young to understand. I ought to have kept the old place."

"Down there in Maryland? Why, you always said you hated farming."

"So I did ; but I might have learned enough of it to manage what was left of the estate. One has to make some sacrifices, and I might better have sacrificed my tastes than my home ; I'm never likely to have another. Even if I had reserved merely the house and a few acres, it would have been something. Birds are plenty there in season, and fish the year round ; with a gun and a rod I could have kept myself alive, and been independent."

"But I thought the whole went for debts, and to take you through college."

"It might have been managed differently, if my guardian had taken the trouble to think for me. As I look at it now, it seems scandalous to have gone through my patrimony as I did. What was the use of those twenty months at law? And the course that won my B.A. might have been abridged. A year or two in the north, to shake off my rusticity and get a plan of study, and I could have done the rest at home, and be a Grafton still."

"You are a Grafton still, my boy. The name and the blood don't depend on the soil."

"You can't understand it, Bob: northerners never do, at least those who camp out in cities. You are a migratory race, we are stationary. When your people for six generations have lived on their own land, you are identified with it, rooted there — and to be torn up by the roots is bad for you. How much fun was made of the Virginian 'sacred soil'! Yet that was no mere big talking; the words had a real meaning. The ground may be poor, worn out, dear at three dollars an acre, but that's not the point. Where your fathers are buried and you have played in childhood, where your earliest associations are, reaching back from the days when you began to think and feel, as far as your family history goes — that's sacred soil, and he who has it should stand by it, not let it go to strangers as I did. It was no better than sacrilege."

He laid down his pipe, joined his hands behind his head, and stared at the ceiling, as if he saw the old roof-tree there. I hastened to oppose his antediluvian reflections with some of the wisdom of this world.

"My dear Dick, all that is utterly unpractical, and you know it. We can't be idling about the rural parts, worshipping old clapboards and grave-stones. We've got to be up and doing, as the poet says; adding to the resources of this great and glorious land, and making our individual piles. What did you use to say yourself? It matters little where you live, so it's to some useful purpose — to fulfil the end of your being, and get on in life."

"You never heard me say that last part of it. And as far as that goes, only a small fraction of us do get on in life; the vast majority appear only to get off. What's the use of my trailing pain-fully over half the continent to make a failure? I could have done that as well at Grafton Manor, as those before me did."

"Exactly; that's about all you or they could do there. I want you to make a success, whether here or in the East. You have the brains for it, and the grit, if you would only make a rational use of them."

"We define 'rational' differently, Bob. I can't

join in this everlasting hymn to the few who have made their million. How did they do it? By narrowing and sharpening the mind to a hatchet edge, indurating the conscience, deadening the heart, and sinking the soul. What did they do with it? Left it to their sons to spend in gambling-hells and places worse yet. It's better to dwindle and snuff out as we did on the Chesapeake."

"We're not all as bad as that, Dick. Look at Mr. De Grout. My father wasn't a millionaire, but he belonged to the class you're condemning. You don't mean him."

"No, no, Bob." He grasped my hand, and we sat a minute or two in silence. This was a tender spot, for my parents had died while I was abroad, about the time Dick finished his law at Hector; he had been in our house more than once, and met Christian treatment there.

Presently we shook ourselves: men are not fond of sentiment, at least not of wasting it on one another. "How long have you had these notions about the old place, Dick?"

"They came too late to act on, of course. Only since I've been in the West, to speak of; but they grew on me every day."

"That's a pity, for, as you say, you can't act on them; and if you could, what on earth would you do down there?"

"Escape from the crowd — from the noise and

dust of the struggle for existence; from the pressure of base needs and the contact of baser
motives; from standards that I can't accept, and
aspirations that degrade, and a routine that appears
to me as objectless as the life I would lead appears
to you. The Manor, half-ruined as no doubt it is,
would be a haven of refuge, and more. You can't
understand how wood and earth and water can be
to a man as a mother or a wife. If I still owned
the place, it might even be a motive to work, so
that I could free the acres, repair the house, and
ultimately go back there to stay."

"Well then, work, make a fortune, and buy
it in."

"No sir. The tie is broken, don't you see? If
I could do it, which I can't, I should spoil what
there is of me in the process, and not be fit to live
there. Careless unthrift might be at home at the
Manor, — it was, for generations, to my sorrow,
but never dishonor, never a spirit soiled by huck-
stering."

I stared at him; here was heredity with a ven-
geance, the foolishness of the fathers reproduced
in their descendant. I had thought for years that
I knew this man to his foundation : could he, with
all his northern culture, with his cool analytic
temper, thus suddenly revert to ancestral traits,
and blaze up at nothing like an antique landlocked
cavalier? If his heart had been touched at last,
or his honor — but there was no cause whatever

for excitement, and he had never talked in this strain before. It was all moonshine about the Manor; at least he had displayed no undue affection for it while at college, when the recollection of it lay much closer than now. Had his reason fallen into some depth lately opened in his nature? Had that nature put forth new tendrils of sensibility, which reached out for something to twine around, and finding no nearer or more available object, seized wildly on this revised and glorified idea of the Old Home? That must be the secret of his explosion, I was driven to conclude. So I said, "Old man, that's very morbid, and wholly unjust, as you owned just now: in both qualities it's unlike you. You've been living for ten years on friendly terms with hucksters — me, for instance; why should you fly at our humble pursuits like this?"

The volcano appeared to have been exhausted by its solitary outburst, and had become a peaceable mountain again. I might quote that text about a mild answer disarming wrath, but there was no wrath to be disarmed in this case, unless against himself or some less tangible adversary, such as Things in General.

He smiled. "True as Tupper, Bob, and I meant no reflection on you or anybody; only you run me pretty hard, and the worst of it is, there's some sense in what you say. My position is quite indefensible, no doubt, in your eyes, and not much

to brag of in my own ; such as it is, I'll try to
explain it. The bump of locality used to figure
on all phrenological charts. It's a poor word, but
it indicates a real part or passion of our nature ;
see The Old Oaken Bucket, Gray's Ode on Eton,
and so forth. You can't form these attachments
except in the country. Who cares for a city
house or streets ? They serve only mechanical
uses ; no hallowed associations cluster round them.
And the basis for the feeling is laid in very early
life ; beyond that, it's mainly retrospective. The
boy feels it after he has left home ; while he was
there, being there seemed a matter of course. It
may make a poor showing on cold analysis ; but it's
something powerful and precious. O yes, distance
lends enchantment ; it's in the region of imagination and sentiment, scorned of the practical. But
these more ethereal faculties belong to our finer
part ; in this gross and shifting American life
they are being blunted and lost. No use for
them ? There you're mistaken. You see, a man
needs ties and an anchorage. Most of you have
these supplied somehow by nature for a while, and
when you are older, you find them in your business and domestic relations. Found your own
family, make your own fortune, build your own
house ; that's the modern idea. It's not mine ;
my roots go too far into the past. A house you
build for yourself is merely for the body, good to
eat and sleep in ; the soul takes no shelter there.

I ought to have lived as my father did, a pastoral recluse ; it's all I'm fit for.   Ask Jandyke, and he'll tell you that I make no progress, and never will. Whether it be law, or teaching, or writing, I bear my part in a routine in which I see no point or profit, except that it pays my board bill.   I can't help questioning the value of my own work, and that of most.   What does it all amount to ? "

"Dick, you make it worse than it is.   We thought a good deal of you at Yale; the De Grouts, and Van Snoozer, and some others.   Mrs. Claybank told me they were more than satisfied with the progress of those boys you coached at Tackville.   Rustler said you could do something at law if you would ; he wanted you for a partner, you know.   And I dare say some people care for what you write now in the *Boomerang* — as long as you let poetry alone.   You shoot the arrow ; you can't tell where it hits.   You sow the seed, and then you don't wait to see the crop, but jump to the conclusion that it will be no good.   If you could have more faith now, and take an interest in things — "

"That's just what I can't do.   When I do my best, and it comes to nothing, am I to lie about it, and delude myself into the notion that it's something fine ?   Is it your fault if you're so constituted that you can't help seeing things as they are, with no halo about them ?   I didn't make them so, nor ordain these limitations and incongruities and hindrances. — I can go on in this way as I am, indefinitely, I suppose, and keep my head above water, and not growl audibly except when you come and poke me up; but as I told you, I've no anchorage. I belonged to the old ship Grafton Manor: she was supposed to be foundering, and I stupidly left her, and went off alone in a cockleshell. So here I am adrift, without chart or compass, or any particular port to make for. That's the state of the case, and I don't see how it's to be mended."

I sat meditating. "Dick, if I could buy back the Manor —"

"Then it would be yours, and an extremely poor investment. No gain by that, since it wouldn't be mine and never will. I'm not a beggar yet, old man. While I have health, and a tolerable conscience, and a fair sort of fourth-rate brain — good enough for journeyman's work of the disregarded kinds, though not fit, as Rustler says, for taking contracts — I'll hardly need to come on my friends. It's not your funeral, dear boy: you're all right, a man of the time. I'm not, unluckily; but I presume my case might be worse."

CHAPTER XXIV.

MR. JANDYKE'S VIEWS.

THE next day I privately interviewed Mr. Jandyke, and found him a very fair man for an editor, and quite sufficiently frank. He knew who I was, and naturally said things to me he would not to a subordinate. "I have no fault to find with Mr. Grafton," he remarked, with dignity; "not the slightest. He has done the work for which I engaged him, and most creditably. His legal reports are clear and accurate, and have in several cases won recognition in high quarters. He might return to practice with fair prospects, if — if he cared for it; but he does not, as you must be aware. Literature seems more to his taste; his criticisms are far beyond anything ever before attempted in Miletus. In this respect he has entirely met my requirements, and even given tone to the paper, I may say. There has been no such chance as I thought there might be to chip into our school management; but his educational views are sound and progressive, and forcibly put

on occasion. In fact, from the vigor with which
they were expressed at that examination — I'm
leaking now, but I see you know all about it — and
from the way he stood up for his own notions
against Grinder, I was perhaps led to form
expectations which have not been realized. He
is not so combative as I supposed; his zeal
appears to be for theories, not for interests.
Let him alone, and he's meek as Moses. Not
that I complain: any disappointment I may have
felt was my private affair, not affecting the
contract. He has kept that to the letter, and
blamelessly; still — you know how things are,
Mr. T. There's always something beyond the
contract expected of a man; and that's where
Grafton falls short. I don't mean anything you
can put your finger on: he's faithful and reliable,
and wholly free from the loose habits which
sometimes discredit the profession in its younger
members. He never neglects his work — but his
heart doesn't seem to be in it. He has plenty of
mental margin, I think, but he keeps it to himself;
we don't get the benefit of it. I'm sorry, for
he's the loser in the end, necessarily, and I like
him. Some men, with such an opening as this,
would have forged ahead — made themselves
indispensable to the paper in other ways, or found
outside channels of usefulness. There's plenty
of room in Miletus for those who push; but that's
not Grafton, you know. He has made very few

acquaintances beyond the office; seems content
with his own company — and when a man feels
that way, nobody wants to intrude, unless there's
something to be made off of him.   With all his
quietness, there's a sort of lordly air about him,
as if he hadn't been born to this sort of thing.
Came of old stock, did he, and raised on a plantation?   Well, that accounts for it ; rather hampers
him, too.   A most estimable gentleman, sir ; gives
you the idea that he ought to be rich, if he isn't.
I've felt that his present post wasn't adequate ;
with his talents and attainments, he should
command something better — but it's not so easy
to see exactly where, unless in a country college,
or some good quiet library.   I think he'd do better
East ; they take more stock in ancestry and manners there.   Here in the West, sir, we all have to
come to bed rock, and keep wide awake and stirring.
To tell you the truth, I have some thoughts of
selling out and going to Chicago ; that's the
place for a live man, sir.   I should probably have
no use for Grafton there, and my successor might
not appreciate his services here as I do ; few
would, in fact.   I've not mentioned it to him, for
nothing is settled yet.   I'd be sorry to lose him
while I run the *Boomerang*, but don't wish to stand
in his light, in view of these possibilities, if anything else offers ; and he ought to be East, as I
said.   His experience here will be money in his
pocket, if he likes to go on with this kind of

work ; and I'll be glad to certify to his ability and character as shown under me."

An idea struck me. "If you wouldn't mind writing a line now, Mr. Jandyke, to say what he's done here and how he did it, I may be able to use it for him." The editor graciously complied, and I went home with the paper in my pocket.

BOOK THIRD.

THE OAKLANDS EPISODE.

CHAPTER XXV.

BACK TO GOTHAM.

THERE is plenty of literary work to be done in New York, from pennyalining up. True, more than a sufficient number of people are always ready to do it, and additional thousands to come in and try; but still there should be room for a young fellow with a facile pen, a modicum of experience, economic habits, and no incumbrances. A three-story brain and esoteric views may be dubious advantages to such a one, or even handicaps in beginning the race, and I knew that Dick would be imbecile to make his way in a strange city — Chicago or St. Louis would be vastly worse for him than Tackville; but with some sort of position secured, and a few friends to invite him to dinner and look after him in case of accidents, I thought he might in time become a moderately useful member of society. So I sought some acquaintances who were familiar with the trade that depends on manufactures of ink and paper, showed them Mr. Jandyke's testimonial, and prevailed on them to bestir themselves on Grafton's behalf. Not to burden my page with details which he who benefited by them never deigned to inquire into, the end was that inducements were offered — that is the polite way of putting it, though his new employers thought such amenities unnecessary — which brought the wanderer back to the Atlantic coast in early summer.

He appeared glad of the change. "This is your doing, I suppose," he said. "I've submitted to your guidance at last, you see."

"I hope it hasn't involved too great a sacrifice. Was it hard to tear yourself away from the free and boundless West? You think you wont pine for the prairies?"

"Not I. You know why I went there, and why I stayed so long; it has been merely a five-years' camping out. There may be more for me to do here; but I don't love big cities, aud it seems absurd for me to live in Gotham. Why, my room-rent will cost four dollars a week more than it did in Miletus."

"What if it does? You can earn an extra two hundred a year. It's rather funny for you to be grudging small outlays, Dick."

"It's rather necessary for me to live within my small income; I wish my father had thought so. Expenses will mount up, I'm afraid, meals and all."

"You'll soon learn the ropes; lots of fellows

can show you.   We expect you to dinner Sundays, and three times a week at least.   The De Grouts want you, too."

"O no, Bob; the less of that the better.   You'll not see me often, for I'll have to work hard now. The difference is as great as it was six years ago ; greater, because I have nothing to show, and then there was a possibility I might.   I don't mind you, but I don't want to be mixed up with others."

"Do you propose to be a hermit-crab, here in the great heart of the metropolis, amid the teeming millions?   That's not the way to do it.   If you're going to write, you've got to gather materials, and keep your eyes open ; to mix with society, continue your observations, and see what's going on.   You can't stay in a corner by yourself."

"I shall meet men like myself, no doubt, who are at the same kind of work ; they can tell me most.   For the other sort, it wont do ; you know my way is best — for me."

The shrinking pride of a reduced gentleman — whether the reduction was practised on his own person or those of his progenitors — is not exactly an object for contempt, misplaced and unremunerative as it may be.   I have known a poor student to decline a supper like Chatterton in the play, though his would-be helpers had contrived their best to coat the pill.   Perhaps he was right : he had his soul to save, his self-respect to keep

alive under pressing difficulties, in his own way.
That was more important than the body, and he
was the only judge of how to do it. Probably what
stood in place of conscience told him it was better
to go hungry than to receive what was at bottom
charity, however delicately offered. So it was
with Grafton, except that he had thus far been in
no very near danger of literal starvation, and had
progressed far enough mentally to accept any
kindness that came in the shape of work — if he
did not see your hand in it too plainly.

I noted with regret that he had learned no further wisdom; but he did not succeed in wholly
evading the De Grouts. They were curious
people, and even their high position did not shield
them from the reproach of eccentricity. Generations of increasing wealth had not taught them
to measure men only or chiefly by the dollar
standard. The mother cherished intimacies with
several persons who were wholly out of society;
and the daughter, with the parental approval and
uncalled-for curtness, had refused one of the great-
est matches in New York, because of certain tales
which I need not here repeat. For the cardinal
virtues and for benefits once conferred they had
an equal and antique regard; and according to
them my luckless friend had in his uncalculating
and aimless way been a benefactor. I had been
careful to warn them of Dick's expected advent,
and the son Clinton, now a correct junior partner,

caught him at my house before he had been twenty-four hours in town. From what pitfalls and gaping jaws this youth had been rescued long before I never precisely heard; but he met his alleged rescuer, on his own account with that demonstrative regard for which college fellowship gives excuse in after years (on the infrequent occasions when it is wanted), and with more than cordiality on that of the family. They were at their country place on the Hudson, he explained, and there desired Dick to join them.

" In fact, you're to go up with me this afternoon ; I'm sent for that express purpose, and you can't get out of it. The governor doesn't like to be crossed, as I know by sad experience in the past : I never try it now, and you'd better not. You're an old friend whom we've not seen for an age ; they want you at once, for a week at least. O, you can begin business when you come back ; take a little pure air first. You used to be a rare hand to pull a fellow out of a hole ; don't push me into one now. I'll get a wigging if I don't bring you."

Grafton hemmed and hawed, but could not escape without ungraciousness. He had arrived ahead of time, and was not to report for duty till the following week : his only real reason for eluding this urgent friendship, as too embarrassingly advantageous, scarcely admitted of open statement. So he compromised on the next day, which was an unlucky Friday, and committed himself to his old pupil's care with many misgivings, intending to return early Monday morning.

CHAPTER XXVI.

IN THE GLEN.

HE stayed longer than he had meant to, detained by circumstances not under his control. The most tame and decorous natures probably hide a lurking love for the unusual, the romantic, and more unheroic men than Dick have been thrust into a hero's part. He had said to me, neither in boasting nor lamentation, but I thought with a half conscious tone of regret, that no adventures ever fell to his lot. Fate now determined to make amends for this neglect, in a way that should mingle sweet with bitter. Going no further than it did at the moment, most men of Grafton's age and condition would willingly have had this episode for their own, and seen it lengthened by an appropriate sequel.

It was not my privilege to partake of the fatted calf spread for the prodigal at Oaklands, so I will not pretend to tell you what terms of endearment the host and hostess lavished upon him, nor how many wines were on the table. They were tem-

perate people, and I judge that Clinton under his
father's eye assuaged thirst in moderation. But
for what happened the next day I do not depend
on the newspapers, which gave but garbled accounts. A party was made up to explore a glen
some miles from the house, and Miss Edith was
committed to Dick's care. I am sure he did not
seek the honor, for he never had any sense about
such matters ; he would rather talk to an old lady
or to some destitute wallflower than to an attractive girl, especially if she had five or six figures
to her credit. But this time it was all arranged,
and he could not help himself.

He might have felt safe enough with her, for
she was twenty-three now, and as stately as her
mother; but then she was very handsome, with
a classic profile and an exquisitely turned neck,
and eyes that could go through you on occasion
and make you feel queer and disagreeable. I
never saw them perform this exercise, but it was
said they operated thus upon Gander when he
proposed to her, and on several men who had
made unadvised efforts to establish a footing.
"Dem it," De Shyster once observed at the
club, "what does she mean by it ? I merely
remarked that her eyes were like the stars of
heaven on a dark blue night, and if a feller had
'em to shine on his lonely path right along it
would be good for him, you know ; and then she
up and glared at me." I do not believe she glared

at Grafton during their ride, and he certainly gave
her no occasion for so doing. He probably left
her to support most of the conversation, and gave
his mind to the horse, an animal with whose traits
he was unfamiliar; but he managed to keep the
road, and what occurred afterwards was really not
his fault. Arrived at their destination, the party
broke up into pairs, as is usual on such expedi-
tions; there was a waterfall to see, and what
not.

At this point it would be the correct thing to
describe the scenery, which must have gratified
Dick, he had been so long without any to speak
of; but most of us know such resorts by heart,
and one of them is about like another. The lady
and her reluctant cavalier were going along the
customary narrow path above the regulation precipice, when she, being of a venturesome and
enterprising turn and little afflicted with nerves,
stepped to the edge to look down. "Take care,"
said the prudent Richard; "that's dangerous."
The words were hardly out of his mouth when a
stone gave way beneath her foot, and over she
went. He made a desperate clutch at her and
got his right arm about her waist, but there was
nothing for his left hand to hold on by, not even
a twig or a projecting rock. One shriek resounded
through the glen, and was followed by an awful
silence. Those who were nearest ran up horror-
stricken, and the boldest peered over the verge:

the two bodies lay motionless, not at the bottom
of the ravine, but on a little ledge, barely long
enough to receive them (indeed Dick's feet hung
over) ten feet below the path. He was underneath, and she, as soon appeared, entirely protected from the rocks by his subrecumbent frame:
he being the heavier and keeping tight hold, they
had reversed positions in the air and struck the
ground in that desirable though unbecoming attitude. The distance was just enough to swing
around in, and a good jumper might have taken
the leap with little risk ; but coming down on his
back with a hundred and thirty pounds on top of
him knocked the breath pretty well out of this
unwilling athlete, and he lay as if dead. Edith
had simply fainted from the horror of the fall ;
which, if a lady must tumble over cliffs, is the
most rational thing she can do after so reprehensible a first step.

It was not easy to approach them, but some of
the men did it by going well around and climbing
up from the bed of the stream on hands and
knees. When they reached the shelf, after five
anxious minutes, Edith was kneeling —there was
just room for that — with a very white face but
all her wits about her; one hand was on Dick's
heart, the other behind his head. I knew several
men who would willingly have been in Grafton's
place then, and taken his chances of recovery and
of what might come after.

"He's alive," she said to her brother, whose hat now appeared at the level of the ledge, while the rest of him was groping for a foothold on the cliff's side. "Send for help and for a doctor, quick."

"How are you, Edith? Can you walk? We must get you out of this first."

"No. I can go where you do, but I shall stay here till he is removed, of course."

Young De Grout found a scanty footing higher up, raised his arms and body to his sister's side, and proceeded to fumble over the prostrate shape. "No bones seem to be broken, but it's a devil of a place to get him out of. Excuse me, Mrs. Tomkyns, I didn't see you were there." The female contingent of the party, fortunately not numerous, was now on the path above, whence ejaculations of sympathy and awe descended. "You'd better go back, ladies; we'll have to haul him up just where you are. Thanks, no, we don't need you on this spot; it's not well adapted for gatherings, and you couldn't very conveniently get here, nor up again. Look out there, Smithers" — to a gentleman who stumbled half-way down, and dislodged a quantity of shale, which went clattering into the brook: "we don't want any more accidents just now. Call the darkies, please, and send for reinforcements. Hi, Cicero" — as the coachman's staring face was seen above — "run to the nearest house. get all the ropes they have, and a few men if you can. Send one on a fast horse, or with Polly and the buggy, for Dr. Jakes. Come back at once with the ropes; mind, now. Anything else, sis?"

It may have been early training, inherited capability, or both, but those two young people ordered all that was done, while others, who had but a general human interest in the matter, pottered about, offered impossible advice, and were of no use at all. After a woful half-hour, Dick opened his eyes with a groan, which he cut short on beholding the ministering spirit by his side. She had been pouring brandy down his throat and doing what else the case admitted: it was not a good spot to get supplies to, but her brother had a flask in his pocket.

"You're not hurt?" Dick asked, faintly. "Then it's all right." He attempted to rise, but fell back.

"Easy now, old man," said Clinton. "I'm doctor, till a better comes. You keep still, and do as you're bid."

The long and short of it was that this commander trussed him with ropes, and the men above pulled him up; he was able to use his hands enough to keep from rubbing against the cliff in his ascent. Arrived there, he tried to walk, but found it impossible, so they carried him along the path, which was ill suited to such exercises. Seeing him safely started, Edith with her brother's aid clambered down the ravine, and mounted in a less impregnable part of it. As soon as they got home, Clinton, fearing internal injuries, telegraphed to his father, to their family physician, and to me as Dick's next friend and presumed executor, and we all reached Oaklands before dark. By this time it was tolerably well settled that the patient was in no great danger; but though little blood was shed and no bones fractured, his rear was one mass of bruises from neck to ankles, and his head and arms were pretty well scratched. The eminent professional man from New York approved the local practitioner's treatment (they always do, I believe), and said the invalid must be kept quiet and undisturbed that night; everything depended upon that.

CHAPTER XXVII.

EMBARRASSING.

I WILL say for Miss Edith that she appeared much ashamed and disgusted: her usual serenity had vanished at finding herself responsible for such a catastrophe. "It is a wretched business," she said very frankly, "all but Mr. Grafton's part of it. He saved my life, I suppose, or near it, and at the risk of his own. But one doesn't like to be under such obligations to anybody, even to him. I wish he had let me fall off by myself, if I had to do such a stupid thing. I don't see what possessed me. Now I presume you and he and the rest will think I'm in the habit of posing for tragic melo-drama. It's perfectly sickening."

"Well," said I, somewhat dismayed, for this was not the mental condition I desired to see in her, "it wasn't exactly his fault, you know: he didn't mean to offend you. And he's the last man to presume on a mere accident, or indeed ever allude to it. I'm awfully sorry you have all this bother with him just now: I'd take him away to-night if he was fit; I know he'd rather go, and not be a burden here. You see he just happened to be on hand, and he really couldn't help it."

"O, thank you," she flashed back; "I don't need to be reminded that it was all my fault. Do you think that makes it any pleasanter? We insisted on the man's coming here, whether he would or not, and before he had time to turn round and see how New York had changed during his long absence; and then the first thing I must go and pull him over a precipice. Fine hospitality this is; much as if Clifton were to ask you to dinner and then spring at you from behind the door with a club. I wish he would pay his own debts: this is what comes of getting into scrapes at college."

I actually did not know what to say: I was afraid to look at her, lest I should encounter one of those demolishing glances I had heard of. But she did not go into hysterics, and presently she calmed down a little. "As you are in Mr. Grafton's confidence, I wish you would explain to him that I do not make a practice of falling off heights and requiring gentlemen to jump after me. I never did it before, and can promise solemnly that I never will again."

Dick on his side was equally out of humor; I have rarely known him so nearly to approach profane language. "This is a beastly mess, Bob. The doctor says I can't get out of here in a week.

Confound it, I wish I had staid with you, as I wanted to."

"Richard, this is an unhallowed frame of mind. Would you rather have attended Miss Edith's funeral than lie in bed a day or two? You ought to be glad to bear a few bruises for the sake of saving such a girl as that."

"That's all bosh. At least, I would rather take the hurts than let her or any woman have them, of course; but there wasn't any saving. We just turned a somerset in the air like two fools, and came down on a shelf of rock; a fine figure we must have cut. There was no sense in it at all."

"Anyway, she says you probably saved her life."

"I didn't. It was only a little way down, and if she had a taste for going off just there she might have done it alone with hardly any risk. But with my pulling her about, and our joint weight, it became more dangerous. Yet I couldn't let her go by herself, you see, if only for the name of it. I had no time to think, and it would have done no good if I'd had an hour, unless to persuade her to keep away from the edge. The doctor calls it a lucky accident, but I call it a dismally ridiculous one."

"She's hugely vexed about that, and about getting you in the scrape; wanted me to assure you she didn't do it on purpose, and isn't in the habit of such. But others take a different view; they think you did a big thing, like Curtius and Theseus and all those historical preservers. Prepare to see your gallantry blazoned in the papers, and to be coddled as a wounded hero."

This prospect increased his irritation, and he was inveighing against his predicament and things at large, when the doctor came in and looked sharply at him, and then at me. "Here, this wont do. I thought you had more sense, Mr. T.; don't you see he's feverish? No more conversation to-night, Mr. Grafton; take this dose, and go to sleep." And he bundled me out of the room.

It was not an enjoyable evening, for every one was excited and nervous. Mrs. De Grout had been overcome by the news of her daughter's danger and deliverance, and her husband was worried over Grafton's injuries. Clinton and I went out, ostensibly to look over the stables, and he said, "You want to see where that thing happened, don't you? Well, we'll get up at sunrise, and either ride or drive, as you prefer. I'll lend you some old clothes and heavy boots, for it will be wet, and we'll have to climb around. I want to make some observations."

"All right. But what do you start so early for?"

"So that we can do it on the quiet, and be back and dressed as usual before breakfast. To-morrow's Sunday, you know, and mother might object."

I agreed, and we turned in early. I had offered to sit up with Grafton, but they would not hear of it; said there was a reliable manservant in the next room to watch, and the doctor within call.

I shuddered when I beheld the place of the catastrophe; but for that little shelf, they would have gone down sixty feet, bumping over rocks two-thirds of the way. "See this break in the edge?" said Clinton; "here's where the ground gave way under Edith. He stood where you are. Now look down — all fours first, or we may go over, too. By Jove, I thought so!"

What he thought you will soon learn. We had brought pencils and paper and some ropes; we surveyed the ground, which was adapted neither to architectural nor agricultural uses, and made some measurements, returning in time to assist at family prayers. Mr. De Grout was strong on the doctrine of every man being a priest in his own household: he alluded in affecting terms to the events of yesterday, and I gathered from his petition that our patient was better, which proved to be the case. After a while he went to church, but all the others begged off. Thanks to repose and arnica, Dick's condition was so far improved that the doctor said he might be taken downstairs; as soon as he had seen this done, Galen departed for his city rounds, enjoining prudence and patience. His reproof to me the night before meant nothing but professional pompousness; they always make the most of their cases, except when these are serious, and then you die before they give you notice to prepare.

CHAPTER XXVIII.

CLINTON EXPLAINS.

WE arranged the invalid in state on a lounge, and gathered round him. After the requisite civilities had been administered, Clinton coughed to attract attention. "Ahem. As this is a day set apart from secular cares for praise, instruction, and inward improvement, it will be well to review a recent occurrence, that each person present may the better comprehend his or her reasons for thanksgiving or penitence, and the relation in which she or he stands to other members of this select circle, with the resulting duties of gratitude, respect, affection, or possibly the contrary."

He paused impressively; his mother looked at him in surprise, his sister spoke. "We understand all that well enough; do let Mr. Grafton alone."

"I shall commit no such injustice," the orator resumed; "if the country at large neglects his fame, this humble hearthstone shall cherish it. You needn't stop me, mother; I'm coming to the point now. The hand of Providence has brought him here, from far away in the wild and wondrous West, where his muscles have been toughened and his soul uplifted to deeds of derring-do. You see, when a young woman will go about falling over precipices, it's important to have on hand a big, strong, brave man who can at least mitigate the consequences and break the fall."

If Galen had stayed, it was not I he would have had to rebuke this time. His patient was very red, and so wrought upon that he even forgot to choose expressions suitable to the presence of ladies. "Let up on that, Clint. I can't thwack you as I used to, and it's mean to take advantage of my helplessness. Drop it, do, or I'll go back to bed.'"

"You can't. Father's out, and the doctor's gone, so I'm in charge. What you want is cheerful and improving conversation : keep still, and you'll get it."

Edith frowned at her brother, and then sighed and appeared to resign herself to the inevitable : I suppose she knew what he was capable of, and when he was beyond control. The mother made a feeble effort. "You must not annoy our friend, Clinton. And are you sure what you have to say befits the time ? "

"Positively. Annoy him ? No ; it's just the tonic he needs, the gentle stimulant to put him on his feet again. He must get used to the sound of his own praises. The illustrated papers will no doubt send artists here to-morrow, to sketch the ravine and the ledge, and take portraits of the principal actors. I shall give them my last photo, mother — the one you said was my best ; they can print me from that. You'd better do your hair up to-night, sister ; they may come by the early train. Grafton looks most interesting as he is, but I'm not sure we oughtn't to put a patch on his manly brow, for increased effect. He shows no traces of his leap except a poetic pallor, which the artists wont be able to catch ; he differs from the ancient warriors in this, that his wounds are not in front."

There was another pause ; Edith looked bored, Dick embarrassed, and Mrs. De Grout very grave. "I think we ought not to speak lightly of so serious a topic, my son ; least of all you, for whom Mr. Grafton did so much, long ago. I cannot talk of what he has done for us now. But for him —" Her voice broke, tears came into her eyes.

Dick too was much distressed. "My dear madam, you exaggerate enormously ; indeed you do. The thing is not worth a second thought. I've given more trouble than I've done good ; in fact, I was rather in the way. As I told Bob here, last night, as soon as I saw him, if Miss Edith had been alone, she might have escaped harm altogether, and merely had to climb down the rest of the way ; and then she wouldn't have been bothered with me. At worst she would have got a few scratches, as I did."

The sense of justice which is so strong in a few women here impelled Edith to touch a distasteful subject. "You forget what prevented my receiving any injury at all. And in supposing the other case, you exaggerate, whether mother did just now or not. If I had fallen exactly as you did, I should have been hurt, but less than you were, for I would have had no weight upon me." Her mounting color belied the coldness of her voice, but could not check her testimony. I looked at her in silent admiration. Most men would have envied that obtuse icicle Dick, who merely turned his head away.

Clinton now claimed another hearing. "Sister, your conduct is shameless. After bringing all this trouble upon us, and causing your gallant rescuer to be plastered from head to foot and laid on his back, where he never was before since infancy except in the peaceful hours assigned to slumber, you calmly split hairs over his prowess, and would fix to an ounce the weight of his services. I mentioned penitence as one exercise appropriate to the day; that was for your benefit. The rest of us have done nothing to be ashamed of, but you ought to put on sackcloth and ashes. The very least you can do is to register a solemn vow, here in the presence of the victim of your propensity and of this goodly company, not to fall over any more precipices."

"She's done that already," I hastened to depose.

"She promised me that, last night, out of her own head, without any asking. So you might be easy with her now, if she *is* your sister."

"Indeed," said the mother, "I trust this will teach you a lesson, Edith. And you too, Clinton ; you are generally far more reckless than she. One cannot be too careful in such places. My dear, you might have lost your precious life, and destroyed, too, that of one to whom we owed so much before. Your father would scarcely have forgiven you, you could never have pardoned yourself, if Mr. Grafton had been seriously hurt in saving you."

"My dear lady," Dick interposed, "enough and far too much has been said about this trivial incident. I thought I had shown you that there was no saving, and no service worth mentioning. Of course I should have been glad to be of some use, but I can't flatter myself that I was. If you're going to hold her responsible for the mishap, she would very likely have done better without me."

"There's where you're out, young man," said Clinton, dropping the ragged remnant of his pulpit tone. "Without you she would have struck the edge of the shelf in passing, and gone clear to the bottom ; that's a nice thing to think of, isn't it ? Where she stood on the path was just above the north end of that ledge ; you were at her left, say two feet south. You pulled her toward you, and changed the direction of the fall enough to land on the shelf instead of going further. See?"

"I don't see how you know more about it than I do, since I took part in the performance, and you weren't in sight at the time. Nobody was but Mrs. Tomkyns and the man with her, if I remember."

Thus spoke the invalid, rather hotly; but Edith looked pale, and nodded, as if to confirm at least so much of the narrative as dealt with their relative positions. Her mother chimed in. "Yes, my son, how can you be so sure of this?"

He put a bold face on it. "Only because I was there this morning before you were up. Having no distressed damsels and wounded heroes to haul over the cliff, Tim and I took notes like a couple of surveyors. If you don't believe me, I'll take you and Edith there to-morrow; but not Grafton — he's had enough of the place."

"So have I," said his sister. "I wonder that you could go there: I never want to see it again."

"Clinton!" broke in his mother severely; "you went there on the Sabbath?"

"It was a work of necessity and mercy, mother; both together, as you should be the first to perceive. It was necessary to understand just where we stood, and what we all had to give thanks for; and so we undertook this investigation, not after Edith's pennyweight method, nor in Grafton's way of barren suppositions — you always were too

much of a theorist, Dick ; it is the one fault linked
to so many virtues — but like two experienced and
clear-headed men of the world." He bowed to
me, and to himself. "This is the up and down of
it : he saved your daughter, madam, and my sister
— not that she deserved it ; and though in so doing he didn't risk his own life as much as would
have been the case if he had adopted her style and
place of falling without revision, still that wasn't
his fault, for he hadn't opportunity to examine the
ground as fully as we've done since ; so we'll overlook that blemish. Our preserver, accept my
blessing ; here's my hand, with my heart in it.
This séance is now concluded ; Tim, let's go out
and smoke."

I wondered a little at this boy's coolness in over-
riding his elders, as all of us were except Edith,
and she but a year his junior ; and presently I
asked him, "What did you run them so hard for?"

"Why," said he, "this kind of thing is apt to be
stiff unless you give it the right tone. Mother
would have slopped all over Dick if I'd let her, and
he and sis both feel awkward. I don't wonder at
that ; they must have looked like precious fools,
tumbling about in each other's arms." He looked
over his shoulder to see if the windows were
closed, and burst into a peal of irreverent (and, as
I thought, ill-judged) laughter. "There's nothing
like free discussion, in a sensible matter-of-fact
style, to remove undue solemnity and any little em-

barrassment that may exist, and make everybody
feel easy and comfortable ; as you'll see. Besides,
we all think the world of Dick, only he's so deuc-
edly formal and offish, because we've got spondulix
and he hasn't. Now this thing, with these touches
I've just given it, ought to make him feel like one
of the family. That's what was needed, to get rid
of all constraint and be 'omelike and haffable, as
the Britishers say. Only I had to do it while dad
was out, or he'd have stopped it. He wanted to
reach just this point, to domesticate Dick with us ;
but bless you, he'd never accomplish it in his
Grand Monarch style, nor let me try mine. Now
it'll be all right : church is a good thing, sometimes."

I had my doubts whether Clinton's management was exactly the right thing, either for his
sister or for Grafton ; but I was on his premises,
and had no right to meddle in his domestic matters. His talents were promising, his motives
excellent, and youthful light-heartedness will excuse much ; but I was not sure it would please
me to be gone over in that way, supposing I had
been practising acrobatic feats in the woods with
a young lady, and been painfully battered in consequence ; especially if I were poor and proud
and unattached and delicate-minded like Dick,
and she were a beauty and an heiress and all
the rest of it. In that case I think I would
have preferred not to talk about the business

at all when the girl was by (unless she insisted
on so doing), and certainly not to have sermons
preached upon it in the manner of the once celebrated Dow junior.   All efforts toward the ascertainment of truth are laudable, but that easy
freedom of handling, with its occasional approaches to levity (as Mrs. De Grout hinted) is
not suited to all topics, nor yet to all tempera-
ments.   The boy meant well, but I question
whether he did any good, even for the moment.
I could not stay to see how his method worked
beyond that, for Dick did not need me, and home
matters did.

Clinton and I went down Monday morning,
and called on the head of the firm that was to
employ Grafton.   He knew our names, and received us blandly ; had seen the accident in the
papers, and rejoiced to know that so gallant (and
so well befriended) a gymnast had escaped serious
injury ; told a story or two that might be supposed to bear on the case in hand ; chuckled and
ha-haed, and appeared much pleased that one of
his young men should be staying at Oaklands
and enjoying adventures with the millionaire's
daughter ; offered to show us over his establishment in person, and favored us with several
circulars and prospectuses ; assured us that there
should be no difficulty about Dick's work, which
could be carried by others as heretofore till he
was fit to begin it.   "Our business is increasing

daily, we are crowded to the utmost of our great capacity; but in such a case a point may be strained. Let him complete his cure under such — er — happy auspices, and come to us reinvigorated. Our firm, sir, can afford to be liberal. It is not every day that we are privileged to contribute, I may say, the means of preserving one of the city's loveliest fair ones, and rendering a service to so honored a family as that of Mr. De Grout. Ahem; gentlemen, you understand that Mr. Grafton's stipend begins from to-day, as if he had entered on his duties as expected. No thanks; it is a pleasure, and such is the character of this house."

"By Jove," said Clinton as we went out, "I believe the old cock would like to send the governor a bill 'for services in saving life of daughter.'"

"He can't," the irreverent youth was reminded, "because Dick did it on Saturday, when he was his own man: he belongs to Lybert & Co. only from this morning."

"That's so, and it's lucky. But the firm mean to take credit for the rescue anyway."

"Well, it turns out all right for Dick; this thing happening at your place has given him a big send-off. They think he must be quite a little man because he's a friend of yours. Perhaps they'll raise his wages." But Mr. Lybert's appreciation stopped short of that point.

CHAPTER XXIX.

IT WOULD NOT DO.

Not to trifle with the reader, I will say at once that this hopeful beginning of a romance came to nothing at all. It was disappointing; from the viewpoint of poetical justice and spheric melody it might be called odious, and even low; but that is the way things go in real life, especially with such a fellow as Grafton. He was made much of at Oaklands for a week, and then returned to the city, somewhat stiff in the joints and slow in his motions, and began his new work. If he had been anything of a business man, with half an eye to the main chance, he might to-day be a partner in a great firm (I do not mean of publishers), and possibly in more senses than one. But the truth is, his friends found they could do nothing with him or for him. Clinton used to drag him up the Hudson on Saturdays through that summer, and after the family came back in the fall they deluged him with invitations to dinner; but he would go there only when civility absolutely required it, and

I presume they at last reluctantly concluded that friendship was deformed, being all on one side.

A year later I took him to task for this con-duct. "Dick, do you think you've treated the De Grouts well?"

"Perhaps not. But if so, I couldn't help it, as you know perfectly."

"What have you got against them? Don't you like their style?"

"Eminently; to me they were kindness per-sonified. They are just the sort of people I would choose for my closest friends — if I could meet them on equal terms."

"Why can't you meet them on equal terms? Because they pay more taxes than you do?"

"Because I don't see two dollars where they turn over a thousand, if you want the coarse fact. We're not in Arcadia, and that makes a very real difference."

"But if they can overlook that, you might."

"It's just the other way. If positions were reversed, I could afford to ignore it, and would be glad to; as it is, they can, but I can't."

"You make too much account of money — far more than they do. All this quixotry is merely inverted wealth-worship."

"Let it stay inverted then, so honor keeps on top."

He was keen enough when put on the defensive about a definite matter; but his tone was not so repellent as of old. He had seen a little more (though not much) of the world by this time, and was doing tolerably well for him, that is, making expenses and a few dollars over; and I suppose that kept his spirits up. Finding him thus amenable, I ventured a step further. "I'd like to ask you another question, Dick, if you don't mind."

"Ask as many as you like, old man. From you I have no guilty secrets."

"Do you think you behaved exactly right to Miss Edith?"

He stared at me. "What do you mean now?"

"Well, there were rumors, you know."

"I didn't start them, nor did she, I judge. The best way to stop them was to keep away from there."

"Did it never seem to you that — that she — "

"No, it didn't. She's not that kind of girl, and I trust I'm not the kind of cad to think such things. I don't wonder you're ashamed to put it into words."

"Still, you seem to know pretty well what I mean."

He flushed: it was an ingenuous habit he retained long past the proper age for it. But he parried the stroke neatly. "I know what you mean, because I know you. You like to go over and through and around and beneath and behind a question, and to settle how it might have been under totally different conditions; whereas I am content to determine on the apparent facts. You are forever overworking your brain to conjure up not merely what might or should be, but the impossible and absurd. In this case it's indelicate, improper — a — a sort of sacrilege." (Oho, I said to myself; so he was hit hard after all.) "Why should she have thought twice of me? She's seen lots of fellows in her own walk of life just as good as I, and possibly much better."

"No doubt. But she might not think so; women are so peculiar. It was worth inquiring into. Suppose, now, she had cared for you?"

"Why then, she'd soon have gotten bravely over it. You ought to have more respect for her than to suppose such things, Bob."

"I would have had enough respect for her to ask if she had any further use for me, if I'd been in your place, before I sheered off. You are the most insensate animal, Richard."

"I should be if I had done what you suggest. A thousand reasons forbade it."

"The thousand black cats, as usual, resolve themselves into ours and the neighbor's. You were not rich, and you had saved her life; that's about all."

"And isn't that enough? I don't care to spend strength in demonstrating an axiom. The thing was impossible."

"Dick, you're an anachronism. You would have made a good hermit in the Middle Ages.

Most men have in them certain chords which respond when properly struck; but you were never guilty of any such weakness, were you? Miss Edith is called a very charming girl, and you were brought rather closely in contact with her — very closely, in fact. I thought at one time that you were a little — just a little — touched in that quarter; but evidently I was mistaken."

I knew this would draw him out, for he could not bear a misstatement of facts. Concealment he would submit to and even practice in a private and delicate matter, so long as it involved no falsehood; but (when no ladies were by) if you said, 'This thing is white,' he would speak up and say, 'No, it is black,' even if it cost him a dinner or his prospects in life.

He emitted several rings of smoke, watched them ascend to the ceiling, and drummed a martial air with his fingers on the table. Then he remarked slowly and judicially, "I'm not fond of unnecessary lying, Bob, and it's not clear that any is necessary here, seeing it's only you. The thing is not worth talking about, but it's all over now, and since you are so curious, I may admit that I'm not quite so cold-blooded as you pretend to think. That young lady is all you say, and I know it better than you, or perhaps than most. But to be conscious of such a feeling in the germ was of course to shut down on it, since no good could come of it."

"Ah, indeed. And if somebody had left you a million or so about that time, what then ? "

"In that case I should probably have — been inclined to cultivate the acquaintance. But as things were with me, it wouldn't do — it wouldn't do at all."

"I can't see why, if she and her family were willing. They thought a heap of you, and encouraged you in every way; and then there was your great-grandmother, or her aunt's first husband's sister, whichever it was, that intermarried with them before. Besides, you had done them a great service — "

"Or they thought I had, which was the same thing so far. Well, would you have had me go up and say, 'Here, I want to be paid for that : give me your daughter, and a furnished house on the avenue, and so much a year to keep it with'? If you can imagine a man acting like that, I can't."

"He needn't use those expressions, nor be so peremptory. Take a part you can dress — say that of Lady Geraldine's lover. You stand around awhile, and look poetic and haughty and yet tender; then some day when it comes handy you say, ' List, fairest, to my doleful moan ; This bosom beats for thee alone ' — that sort of thing. Tell her you haven't the least idea she'd ever care for you, and wouldn't dream of asking it, but you thought she ought to know that your heart lies bleeding at her feet : that when you came near dying for her on

those rocks, that was nothing at all, you'd be glad
to do it over any number of times if it would do
her any good — you don't take any stock in that
tumble, but only mention it as a sample of your
capacity: that in the highly improbable event of
her responding in kind and meaning business, you
would have to make a much greater sacrifice,
seeing you value your pride more than life and
happiness; but that, while a purely platonic arrangement would meet your views best, you
wouldn't stand on that in case she thinks otherwise — you wish her to understand clearly that
you're at her service in any shape she prefers.
That, now, would be quite in character for you,
and well adapted to the circumstances.   It does
the disinterested and magnanimous to a T., and
yet it's practical.   No girl could ask for any better
than that."

"I fear it would go better in verse than in prose,
Bob.   Such a flight is beyond my humble powers.
Keep your recipe for somebody who can use it.
I suppose you'll never let me hear the last of that
confounded accident."

"Then the lady's feelings are to go for no more
than yours, and any views she might have in the
matter to be completely disregarded?"

"Certainly, if you insist on your absurd supposition.   Modest women don't have views in such
matters till they're asked, nor feelings, to speak
of.   And haven't you been preaching to me all

these years that not views and feelings, but facts, govern our lives? In this case it's true. Between Miss Edith and myself a great gulf is fixed. A poor girl may marry a rich man without shame, because in Nature's order the man is the provider and supporter; but when the reverse occurs, the finger of scorn is justly pointed at the man forever after. And worse than that are the stings and arrows of outraged self-respect. He must bear a lowly mind indeed who sells himself for cash, or even for love. I'm not so poor as that. Let Fitness rule, though Cupid fly."

"Dick, I'm disappointed in you. I thought you went it for chivalry, but this is mere selfishness. You're only thinking how to keep right with yourself."

"That comes first, of course; if a man doesn't attend to that, who else can do it for him? We're all selfish, but we're not all content to be honorably so. The skin is nearer than the shirt, and I never professed to be a sentimentalist. But I wouldn't say 'only.' I would stand by a friend if I had the ability, like you and the De Grouts. And if I were to make acquaintance with the tender passion, I might go as far in it as most, within bounds of reason and decency. But I never could cry amen to all that slop of Byron and Moore.

'I know not, I care not, if guilt's in thy heart;
I but know that I love thee, whatever thou art.'

That's immoral mush, fit for lunatics.   The seven-
teenth century men understood these things
better.

> 'I could not love thee, dear, so much,
> Loved I not honor more.'

That's the idea.   And so long as I can't go into
love-affairs honorably, I shall keep out of them."

"That sounds fine, but man was not made for
solitude.   You shut yourself up tight in a cave
of egoism, and contemplate, I'll not say your own
perfections, but your principles, till everything
else looks small.   If you own to selfishness, why
not be selfish to some purpose, like others ?   Why
sacrifice yourself to these finedrawn fancies?"

"I'm not sacrificing myself, Bob ; that's the
lingo of your accepted system, which puts the
cart before the horse.   My income, or the income
I haven't, is not myself : I should sacrifice myself
if I gained money by unworthy means.   'What
shall it profit a man,' you know.   Whether I have
a remarkably good time, or no better time than
I've had so far, is not vital to the question of
myself.   Whether I make my way and my
mark, or continue in total obscurity, is not of
primary importance either.   If it looks priggish
I can't help it ; I've no yearning to lay down the
laws for others, but I see what it is for me, and
I'd sacrifice any number of external chances to
preserve my soul, my standards, my individuality."

"That's what one hears in church, and no doubt it's all right — in theory at least. But you're not asked to accept the wages of unrighteousness, or to love anybody with guilt in her heart. On the contrary, all you can bring against her is that she has money. But that's not her fault, nor yours. You don't want her for her money. You'd rather you had it yourself, and she not have any — "

"O no I wouldn't. I'm not so envious as that; I don't want to rob her. You've got me mixed up with somebody else now."

"Well, you know what I mean. Here's a good girl, pure and sweet, and as highminded as yourself — "

"She's not here, Bob, and she never will be. But if she were, and if she had condescended to such foolish fancies as you credit her with, she would say I was right, that I must forego her to save myself. Yes, sir, I know her well enough for that."

I saw it was of no use. "Well, Dick, I fear you'll never make your fortune."

"Probably not ; but I don't think I shall ever sink into the pensioner of my father-in-law, or the husband of my wife."

BOOK FOURTH.

IN HARNESS.

CHAPTER XXX.

MR. PRANCE.

GRAFTON's duties were somewhat motley and multifarious. The establishment of Lybert & Co. was a vast manufactory, where brainwork of all degrees prepared for and underlaid the toil of many score of hands. He had nothing to do with the type-setting, nor with the filling of orders at retail or wholesale; but he corrected proof, furnished book-notices and items as at Miletus, and occasionally sat in judgment on manuscripts to see if they were worth printing. Not that any of these momentous functions was wholly intrusted to him; the publications of the great house, and still more the products of genius or learning which aspired to be taken into that category, whether in a permanent or periodical form, were numerous enough to claim the attention of more skilled laborers than I should want to feed or oversee. These gatekeepers of Literature were more or less carefully graded, and only long service, or high pretensions, could reach the posts

of command. The method by which their tasks
were divided (for method there of necessity was,
and rigidly maintained) was veiled in mystery to
the newcomer, and the mere contact of so much
symmetric thinking fatigued his rural brain. So
rapidly was he initiated, so much was taken for
granted as already within his ken, that he felt as
if whirled through some vast congestion of novel
machinery.   His superiors were many, and he
knew not as yet in what relation they stood to one
another. If he asked for instructions, the curt
answers resolved themselves into a single formula,
Do what you are told, and leave the rest. The
motto, He that does the Will shall know of the
doctrine, appeared qualified by the warning, What
is that to thee? In pity for his bewilderment,
or more probably by the rule of the place, they
assigned him at first to kinds of work with which
he was familiar ; but when the incoming mails and
express packages claimed his assistance in sorting
their contents, awe and perplexity filled his soul.
Yet though his labors were in great part mechanical, he could not affect to despise them, for the
material they dealt with concerned itself with
ideas, and only mediately with dollars.   What
solid bundles of thought, what dried flowers and
preserved fruits of research, were passing hourly
through his hands — science, divinity, travel, history, all the way down to fiction ! The building
in which he spent his days was a warehouse of

intellect, the pages he helped prepare formed journals of civilization. He respected the reigning silence, the intent air of so many mintmasters and coiners of the brain.

"You'll get used to it in time, youngster," said elderly Mr. Prance one day. "Meanwhile, if you can't take it easy, take it as easy as you can."

Mr. Prance was a dignitary of grade unknown to the novice, with an observant eye which at times emitted humorous gleams; to him, more freely than to the rest, Dick turned when in quest of information. They were going out to lunch, and he ventured on a leading question.

"I wish you would tell me who edits the fortnightly."

"Who edits it? Why, the editor. He's a most valuable man; he never blunders, or gets sick, or goes off for a vacation; and he never dies, because he's plural. There are several of him; I'm one, and you're another."

"But who controls or manages it? Who's the head?"

"Lybert & Co., of course; they're head of everything here. We all look up to them, as the planets to the sun. Didn't you know that?"

"Do you mean to say there's no responsible editor?"

"We're all responsible. Neglect orders, or make any mistakes, and you'll think you're in Utah, with the all-seeing eye staring at you from the rocks. O, I forgot, you came from the West ; you mean the fighting editor. We're not like that ; we print nothing that can offend, and it's seldom that anybody comes in to complain : when he does, we refer him to the porters. Bear that in mind."

"But I don't see —"

"You will in time. You're young yet, and have much to learn. But why this exclusive interest in the fortnightly? Are you attached to that ? "

"That's what I'd like to know. I seem to be hanging on the edge of various things."

"Just so ; we all are. Didn't you read the proof of the Illustrated — the advertisements at least — and punctuate the heavy article on Hygrometry in the last Quarterly? Did it very well, too. Yes, and you corrected the mythology in the *Puerile Delight,* and saw to the logarithms in the *Modern Mechanician,* and supplied offhand those points about literary females for the *Glass of Fashion* when they were a quarter of a column short and in a hurry. That's right, my son ; always be ready when you're wanted. But do you know about Kalmuck musical instruments, and the secret history of the treaty of Utrecht, and the founding of Perdue University, and the style of topboots A. D. 1300 ? No? Then look them up ; they may be needed. We are paid to know everything, and when we don't it is laid on the last recruit. I have most of the other points myself, and could prompt you ; but you must learn to rely on your own resources, and none of us have those I mentioned."

"You like your little joke, Mr. Prance," said Dick, half offended, and not knowing exactly how to take this quizzical elder.

"Who, I? Not at all. When I get any new jokes I keep them for the funny columns ; we pay extra for those, as for poetry, when bad enough — that is, when strictly adapted to popular apprehension. That is why all our men are so silent and serious : they are saving up their good things, and trying to invent others, in training for the charge of the Humorous Department ; it is the most lucrative place we have. But the incumbents never live long, the brain-work is so exhausting. Apart from that, no levity is tolerated in the shop. What I wish to show you is that we are all parts of one vast and I may say glorious system, revolving around in our several orbits, but in perfect harmony, and together enlightening the universe — yes, sir, no less. You are an editor of all these invaluable publications ; so am I ; so are most of us. What more useful, more noble calling? Let that be an incentive to you to avoid the temptations of the metropolis, to labor diligently, and above all to seek no public recognition, to shun the siren Fame. The personal element is suppressed here, except in the books and the signed articles, which are all done outside. What we write is editorial

and nameless, and thus the more impressive. I
went once on business to see Bolland, the conduc-
tor of *Filmer's*, and shamelessly acknowledged as
such.   He pointed out a young man seated in the
office, and whispered, 'That's the assistant editor
of the *Indian Ocean*.' I thought something would
happen to those men ; and mark you, within five
short years Bolland died, and the other is now a
greenbacker in Congress.   Let this be a warning
to you.   It was a bad beginning when you fell out
of the haymow with that girl, and got your name
in the papers.   O, wasn't it a haymow ?   Well, an
apple tree then.   But as that had no connection
with your work here, you may be able to live it
down, if you eschew all thoughts of authorship."

They had finished their lunch, and were reënter-
ing the great building on Lore Street.   "'Sh, now :
not a word of what I've been telling you, or we'll
both be discharged.   When you need any more
points, give me a hint, and I'll explain to you, out
of office hours."

This erratic monitor aroused Grafton's curiosity,
which he saw no means of satisfying just then.
But a few days after a colleague of his own age
or less joined him at the nooning, and cheerfully
answered a casual query.   "Prance ?   O, he's a
queer old cock.   Used to have money, they say,
and lost it ; wrote some books an age ago, but they
didn't sell, so he got disappointed and cranky.
What does he do in the shop ?   Dashed if I

know; loafs round and pecks at things generally,
I guess, same as you do. Got a pretty daughter
though. I made an excuse to call there one night
— way off in East Sixteenth Street it is; but he
saw through my little game and sent me off in
short order, so I didn't see the girl at all. Wont
have any absinthe? Where in hades were you
raised? That's what I come here for." Dick was
not drawn to this comrade, who affected very loud
checks and a flaming necktie, and whose manners
had by no means that repose which stamps the
caste of Vere de Vere. The youth, as he afterwards learned, was employed in the mailing department, and did not properly belong to the editorial
brotherhood at all.

When he had been at work nearly a month, he
was called into the inner sanctum by one of the
chief managers (as he supposed) of the periodicals,
who said, "Mr. Jones is sick to-day, and I must
ask you to look over these," indicating somewhat
less than a bushel of manuscripts. Dick gazed
at the pile with respect, and suggested that he
would prefer to carry them to his lodgings, which
was assented to with an air of faint surprise.

"When do you want them again?" he asked.

The editor looked at him queerly, he thought,
and replied, "I don't know that I want them at
all. You can probably attend to them; only note
such as are accompanied by return postage, and
keep separate from the rest."

His pride in this more elevated task dampened
by uncertainty as to what was expected of him,
he attacked the bundles zealously, and kept at
them through half the night.   Many of the intending contributions were either intrinsically
worthless, or plainly unfitted to the use for which
they were offered; others were dubious; a dozen
stories, some essays and sketches, and a few
copies of verse, he thought might be 'available.'
These he presented next morning to his superior,
who received them with visible reluctance.

" What are these for ? "

" For one or other of our publications, sir ; it
is hardly in my province to determine which.
But I can report more definitely if you desire."

" O no.   Did it strike you that you had enough
here to fill two weeklies and half a quarterly ? "

" I don't urge them all for admission, sir.
About these two there can be no doubt, in my
opinion, and probably little concerning these
verses and this paper on education, which might
do best for the Review ; the rest are for further
consideration.   My judgment was not meant to
be final, I presume."

" H'm ; not on a question of acceptance, certainly.   You're not looking very bright to-day,
Mr. Grafton."

" I sat over these till three, sir, and then was
not half way through the lot."

The editor stared.   " If you propose to spend

so much time over half a day's mail, I fear you will never get through your duties."

Dick flushed. "You may remember that I have had no instructions as to this part of my work. You told me to look the manuscripts over; I supposed that meant to examine them. Doubtless I shall be able to do it more rapidly when I have had more practice."

The editor fanned himself, and looked very weary: it was a hot July day, though but ten A.M. "You had better talk to Mr. Prance; I am very busy. Take these things to him; don't leave them here. — Just one word: remember Talleyrand's advice."

Dick took Mr. Prance aside, and briefly stated his case. The veteran shook with silent laughter. "What, you read 'em? That'll never do. But we can't talk it over now. Come to my place to-night, at nine, or later if you have girls or theatres first. No? Exemplary youth. Well, at nine — not earlier."

CHAPTER XXXI.

EDITING MADE EASY.

MR. PRANCE occupied the second floor of a small house in an unfashionable neighborhood. The door was opened by a bare-armed maid of Teutonic appearance, who told the visitor to go upstairs to the front room. Feeling his way thither through the darkness, he was bidden to enter and sit down. The host was at a desk in his shirt-sleeves, writing furiously. "Take care of yourself for two minutes," he said, "and then I'll attend to you." Dick looked about him; the disorderly room was full of a workman's litter. Books were on the tables, the chairs, the floors, as well as on two of the walls; everywhere newspapers, pamphlets, proofs, and 'copy.' The furniture was solid and far from new; there were a few good pictures, and one, of an attractive woman in the costume of twenty-five years before, hung above the desk. Presently the writer threw down his pen and turned his long lean frame and grizzled locks toward Dick.

"Either you're early or I'm late. Here's the devil now." A grimy boy entered, grinned, received some sheets on which the ink was barely dry, and departed. "No, you're not disturbing me; I'm free now. You see, I don't work for Lybert only. I leave the shop at four and go to the *Battle-Axe* office; come home to dinner, and write for two hours or so. Been looking at the books? Sad survivals of the past, except these tools for constant use. I had a library once, but it went long ago, with most possessions of youth." He glanced at the portrait, and, Dick thought, suppressed a sigh. "Now about your business. You needn't have brought that truck." He glanced contemptuously at an armful of selected MSS. "I see you're warm. There's a little balcony back, where we can get what air there is. Take off your coat if you like. No? Then I'll put on this jacket in your honor. Here's Persian tobacco, and a choice of pipes; I can't afford cigars. Better light up here."

He turned down the gas, led the way through one or two dark rooms, opened a window level with the floor, struck a match, and found two chairs. The dainty white bed, the feminine devices strewed about, bespoke an absentee. "There's no other way through," said the host. "My daughter's away, but I wouldn't let every one in here; not that fellow Snide, for instance." Dick remembered the youth of the absinthe and the scarlet tie. "Met him? Like him? No, or you wouldn't be yourself. I can tell a gentleman when I see him, and it isn't altogether by the clothes. You'll find all sorts in this town, and in our line of business. Precious poor business it is too; but you've chosen it, and I suppose you want to stay in it awhile, so you've got to learn how to handle contributions."

The balcony afforded just room enough to tilt your chair back and deposit your feet upon the railing; a reprehensible practice, in which Grafton seldom indulged. It was a quiet place for that part of the noisy city: the stars were shining, and the streets and their traffic out of sight. "We've got eight feet of back yard here; an unusual privilege."

The old gentleman seemed to have left his sarcasms down town, and to meet his visitor in a mood of human brotherhood. Dick was emboldened to open the budget of his troubles. "What did Mr. Perkins mean by referring me to Talleyrand?"

"Why, he saw you were too conscientious. It's a frailty that leans to virtue's side, and when you've outgrown it, you'll make better stuff than if you began carelessly; but it's apt to be troublesome while it lasts. No zeal, except for your employers. You're not here in the interest of authors, or of the public, or of literature, but simply of Lybert & Co. Ever hear what the manager of the Independent Wesleyan Board of Publication said when somebody proposed to him to reprint their early documents? 'We don't care a button for the fame of John Wesley, or of Charles Wesley, or any other man : we care only for what will sell.' Minister he was too, and stood for a religious house. He put it with unnecessary coarseness — brutal frankness like that rarely pays, except in Bismarck ; it's best to smooth things over — but he stated the principle. Intrinsic merit is neither here nor there : market value is what concerns every publisher and every editor."

"I understand that," said Dick ; "but the *Delight* and the quarterly and the rest are made up of contributions, mainly. These are sent in good faith, I suppose, and to be taken ditto. If we don't examine them, how can we tell which to accept ? "

" My dear boy, contributions are of two classes. We get all we want by contract with known and privileged writers ; those that come unsolicited from people we never heard of are of no account."

" But then we ought to give notice that stran-gers are not admitted."

" That wouldn't do ; too undemocratic and exclu-sive. Appearances must be preserved. We can't protect ourselves against these tons of truck that come in by mail ; but we needn't spend our days and nights on 'em. If the writers enclose return stamps, we can send back their stuff, though we never promise that ; it's a mere courtesy. By the way, you've got your stack of rejected addresses yet ? "

" Yes ; I waited for further instructions."

" Don't send any of 'em off for a month. That keeps up the proprieties, shows that our time is valuable, and lets the anxious scribes think, if they like, that we've read their bantlings carefully, after your style." Mr. Prance took his pipe from his mouth, and gave way to merriment.

" I didn't read all of them through ; some I could see were worthless, just by dipping into them here and there. If we don't do that much, it seems to me the writers are hardly treated."

" A writer has no rights — except the favored few ; that's the office maxim. They are a guilty and obtrusive tribe, the natural foes of editors : the thing to do with them is to suppress them ; politely, of course, but firmly. Dismiss from your mind any lingering sympathy with them, if you want to get on at the shop. They've been stung by Io's gadfly, and their mania is to waste ink and spoil paper, and then send the result to us. There's no time for dipping into their evil concoctions : we're not paid for that, unless Jones. Do you know what he gets ? Six dollars a week. He can do nothing else, except read proof indifferently, but he's a good skipper. He can wade through a hundred of these burdens of Tyre, or say two thousand pages, in a day, and that's our average. He takes them as they come in, and they're never heard of again ; he knows too much to hand any of 'em to Perkins. You can understand now how Perkins felt when you took him that stack this morning; I think he was lenient with you." The iron-gray moustache again shook with mirth. "Perhaps Jones reads 'em sometimes; he can if he likes to sit up nights. But it takes a good deal of time, and management, and a sense of order, which Jones happily possesses, to handle a hundred papers a day, of all sorts and sizes — most of 'em in a dozen or more loose pieces — and keep two-thirds of 'em a month, and then send 'em to the right owners with our circular. *You* can't go into that sort of business ; your time's too valuable."

"I'm sorry, for I should like to do just this, if I were allowed."

The veteran bestowed a glance of pity on his junior. "You wouldn't, if you'd seen a little more of it; it's a dreadful job. Sentimental farmers' daughters, who've been one term at boarding school, send you their ideas of life and men as they might be. Ouida's a fool to these ; you've no conception, till you strike them, how gorgeous heroes, and palaces, and passions can be. Widows, who can write no more than the dead, tell you how they've got nine small children to keep from starvation, and wont you please find a place for this first effort, and they may do better next time.

Leading members of the Podunk Debating Society
have observed with approval your endeavors to
raise the standard of poetry, and enclose a little
thing which was hailed with enthusiasm at the last
meeting ; all their friends say it's just what you
want. And evil-minded old parsons in the back
country weigh you down with dreadful lectures
on temperance and citizenship. This kind always
want their rant back, under the delusion that they
can get it in elsewhere : the widows seldom think
of that. My boy, I've been there — long ago. It's
far worse now."

Dick allowed one remorseful throb to the alleged
widows : they might have planted unwisely, but
they had looked for some small harvest, and it
seemed hard for them to lose even the seed corn.
"Then, if a writer forgets the stamps, his produc-
tion is absolutely lost and thrown away ?"

"O no ; it's worth a cent and a half a pound.
The firm has a paper mill, you know. They offered to allow Jones the waste as his perquisites,
but he was fool enough to prefer a salary. I judge
he repents that mistake now. All this is confidential, of course."

"Is there no way of stopping this flood of offer-
ings ?"

"None. Were we to attempt the ill-judged
charity of requiring certificates of moral character
and a high-school education from new contributors,
or announcing that none but trained writers need

apply, we should scare away only those who might perhaps do good work. The ignorant, the incapable, the hopeless cranks, would keep on just the same."

"What does one in Jones' position do to these persistent scribblers, who wont take No for an answer? Can't they be warned off somehow?"

"Jones doesn't know one from another. With our method, you might see a name fifty times and not remember it. Should you chance to recognize a professional bore, you might hold his piece two months, and then three, and finally lose the next. That ought to be sufficient notice, if he has any sense. But many of 'em haven't. They're anxious to get into type at any cost, and think they're Thackerays and George Eliots in disguise."

"Yes, but with this system the real Thackerays and George Eliots are liable to be suppressed. How is a new man who has anything in him to get started? There must be some good substance in this deluge of trash."

"Of course. Bolland used to say the trouble was not so much in the flood of trash as in the flood of really good matter; but then he was a popular author. The chances are against the sucking Thackerays: I mean, they are such rare birds that we can't afford to be looking for them among the crows and sparrows. You see, of every fifty contributions we receive, forty will be useless for any purpose, and whatever the other ten may be, we haven't room for more than one of them, and no time to see which it is. Now are you satisfied ?' "

"Between ourselves, no. Those ten possibilities, or at least the one writer of merit, has some human rights, the office maxim to the contrary notwithstanding. I can't see that we are doing our duty by him, or by the public, which wants him detected and brought to the front."

" My dear boy, Clough has answered that.

> 'The Summum Pulchrum rests in heaven above:
> Do thou, as best thou mayst, thy duty do.'

You're not editing an ideal magazine on your own account : if you were, it would soon go to everlasting smash. The young writers of merit must take their chance. Once they've shown what they can do and got their names up, they may have all the space they want and most favored nation terms."

"I can't see how they are to do it, so long as we confound them with the mob. They can't get anything printed, you say, till they've made their mark, and how can they make their mark except in print ? What ghost of a chance have they while we refuse to look at their writings?"

" Somebody else may — though it's not likely. Let them begin on the country papers and work up, like Artemus and Mark and Petroleum V.; that's the way now, unless one has money and friends. Or if they're of superfine fibre, and allow themselves to be driven off the track by disgust or starvation, the world can wag on without them somehow. It's their funeral, not yours."

"I know, and I'm not quite ready to be buried yet. As you say, I am powerless to help; but somebody ought to discriminate. Every magazine in the land professes to long for fresh, bright matter from new sources, and hold out both arms to budding genius."

"Of course. If any responsible party will guarantee us that Brown or Blue is going to be paying stock, we'll invest in them fast enough. But how the deuce can we tell beforehand? We can't sift all these tons of sand in search of a stray diamond or two."

"It comes to this, Mr. Prance; let some one else discover and label the best writers, and we'll let them in. I thought the discovering was what we were for, in part."

"Well, you were a green tree; you'll ripen in time. Exploration is too expensive for us; we haven't the force for it. It's cheaper and safer to stick to the old approved hands. Did you ever know a publication — except the *Shakerly*, which pays nothing — to invite contributors?"

"No. But how did the old approved hands get to be such? How does any one come to be known, at this rate?"

"Some by the newspapers, as aforesaid; some

by hiring a hall, that is, spending a few hundreds and sacrificing a first book to secure an audience : some by having friends at court : some by pure persistence, or pure luck, or a combination of the two.   If it's in them, it'll come out ; if they have any call to write, they'll keep on writing — at least that's the supposition.   We're not responsible for their discouragements, or for any temporary injustice that may be done.   We've got — that is, our employers have — to sell our publications, and you and I and Perkins and the rest are paid to keep up the standard."

"But do we keep it up with truck like Wegler's last story, and Boom's dissertation on Infinity ?   I thought they rang very false."

"O, the concern's not gotten up for you and me.   Nobody wants to read the whole magazine, and nobody wades through that swamp of Boom's, but it looks well to have a few heavy articles : they carry an air of profundity, and give us a reputation as all-round men, knowing about all there is to be known, and able to tackle any subject in the heavens above or the earth below or the waters beneath, though we generally deign to be intelligible and entertaining.   That kind of name pays better in the long run than a merely literary or a merely popular one.   Boom got only half rates for that thing, of course.   As to Wegler, he's running out, you know ; but he can travel a year or two yet on his old passes.   It's not intrinsic excellence we're after, but the public taste, and the dear public wants names. They look to see who's written a thing before they read it, and if we brought out a number blazing with new Turgeneffs and unaccredited Tennysons, the circulation would fall off. How many do you suppose judge for themselves? Nine out of ten readers want a fingerpost. Of course a man who's made a name may lose it by being too greedy and careless; but it takes a long time, longer than it does to make it. However, that's not the point; you want me to talk to my text, for your private edification and guidance. Between the brew that's always on top and in demand, and the dregs that go into the gutter, is an intermediate class; things from men that have been personally introduced or are of some standing, and so mustn't be offended: you don't want their stuff, but you must be civil about it. I hope Perkins wont give you any such without notification; it might get you into a scrape. In fact, I'll see that he doesn't."

"Much obliged, I'm sure. What must I do in such a case?"

"Write to the author, giving the reason for rejection; something half complimentary, so as to let him down easy. Say the dialogue is very bright and sparkling, but the action hardly rapid enough: or you're deeply impressed by the imagination and feeling of his piece, but it's long, and

you're awfully pressed for space or nothing would
prevent your accepting his admirable sketch but the
fact that you've just booked one on the same subject.   You can ring any number of changes on these
tunes, and it's not often necessary.   Always sign
'Editors,' plural — never individually, of course.
Twenty years ago, and even ten, such letters were
sent more commonly, if not in most cases.   Some
of the smaller magazines still make a pretence
of doing that, but it's a mere formula, like our
printed circulars, except that they return thanks
for the opportunity of examining the nuisances;
we're above that particular humbug.   I've heard
of cases, too, in which those concerns actually
looked at a strange MS. enough to form an idea
of what was in it: Priest came to light in that
fashion, and perhaps Hawser and Braddock.   It
must be very exceptional, even with them.   I suppose some new hand like you had the strange
fancy to take a bagful of papers along on his
vacation, and put these in with a favorable report
when the chief was in a good humor after dinner.
Even so, I don't see how they can afford the time.
Of course, there are just as good fish in the sea as
ever came out of it; but we can't go fishing for
them — not here: perhaps they can in Boston and
Philadelphia.   Now as to these reams of spoiled
foolscap, send 'em back for the guilty authors to
wear on cold nights — after a month, mind — or
sell 'em to the ragman.   O yes, amuse yourself

with 'em evenings and Sundays, if you like, and grow old before your time ; but remember, it's a bad habit, and it's not business.   And above all, don't bother Perkins.   I'll see you again soon."

CHAPTER XXXII.

AN·UNDOMESTIC INTERIOR.

ALTHOUGH Grafton did not then realize the full
measure of his indebtedness to Mr. Prance, he
was strongly attracted by the outspoken old man.
What he heard had not delighted him, but he saw
it was laid down not as abstractly excellent but
as actually existent if not inevitable; as fact, not
theory; as a rule for his conduct, and by no means
as food for his soul. And he was beginning to distinguish between these two sorts of truth; to learn
that though man may not live by bread alone, his
baser part cannot live on ideals at all. He had no
wish to imperil his position by coming into absurd
conflict with the rules and ideas of his superiors:
if scamped work was insisted on, he was not responsible for the scamping. If the eminent and
variegated publications of Lybert & Co. awoke
delusive hopes in a myriad bosoms of the scribbling
tribe, that was not his doing, and really he could
not expect the great house to alter its policy at the
bidding of a newly imported and inexperienced

subordinate. It was not so much the quality of the work you had to do as the spirit in which you did it that credited or discredited you ; and if his tasks were not quite what he had expected, he could but discharge them as well as circumstances would allow. As long as no positive dishonesty was required — and Mr. Prance must have been joking about those humbugging letters to rejected but respected contributors ; at any rate, they were seldom needed. In such a case he would be taken sick like Jones, or avoid the job somehow. He would not go direct against conscience, even in such a trivial matter ; but he could not again tax the patience of his friends to find a new place in which he might earn his bread. Did he not remember that poor Maryland minister who used to say with such beautiful faith, ' The Lord will provide'; and then the neighbors, knowing that the mealbag was empty and not likely to be replenished by any active efforts of that trustful parent, would bring in provisions, lest the wolf should devour the unprotected colony of little Red Ridinghoods. No, he could not play that part — though he had no wife or children to suffer, thank Heaven. He must, he would be practical : he would bend his pride, and submit to fate, and do the duties that lay nearest, though they were nothing to boast of, and seemed to result in no more than keeping him decently clad and out of debt. It was horribly hot and lonesome here in town, with his few friends away; and it was so peaceful and homelike at Oaklands. If only — O yes; if, and if, and if. If fancies were diamonds, then knaves would be kings, and beggars could go on horseback. If one's ancestors had exercised common foresight, or if oneself had any 'faculty,' why then we would be out of this coil. At this point, as he owned to me long afterwards, he dropped into an inexpensive house of refreshment, and imbibed a B. and S. It was a most unusual indulgence for him, but he needed invigoration, and felt as if something would happen if he did not get it just then.

He went home; it was but an unpretentious chamber, such as shelters ten thousand impecunious bachelors in Babylon the Great, near the roof of a fifth-rate mansion in a 'long unlovely street' well away from Murray Hill. He climbed the stairs slowly, and sat down with that faithful consoler, his pipe; it was an old meerschaum that had stood by him from college days. He did not tax its fidelity by too constant usage, but relieved it with humbler substitutes of brier and red clay; but when he wanted to do any special thinking, or draw into himself away from an ungenial world, this was his chosen comrade. Herein, says worthy Adam Clarke, consists the ungodliness of tobacco; men claim to find in that profane weed solace in their troubles which should be sought only from the Spirit. *Per contra*, it was a pious man before the commentator's time who found in his long 'churchwarden' the model for a future spouse, such as should 'never burn to thwart his will, never burn to use him ill,' but by turns soothe and stimulate, and 'often, when his thoughts were low, send them where they ought to go.' In our secular age men take comfort where they can get it, and Grafton's criminality, if such, was not of the grossly sensual kind.

As he pursued his meditations under this gentle influence, it became clearer that he must distinguish between his recent instructions and their giver. Mr. Prance preserved what most early lose, a mental margin. He could put a case forcibly, yet keep himself outside it ; he knew the exigencies of business, but was not wholly swallowed up thereby. Through the severe official voice spoke the practised critic of life at large, who accepted his own doings and belongings as part of a not too admirable scheme of things, and coddled no narrow prejudice on their behalf as being his. 'So it is, and we can't mend it' ; this was the burden of his testimony. He talked from the head, not the heart, as one who might have found the latter organ troublesome ; but if the substance of his communication seemed harsh, there was kindness in its purpose.

Dick could not drive the poor would-be authors from his head, with their ill-starred armadas that were lost at sea, or came back bruised and empty, and nothing to show for the expenses of the trip.

They were not his affair at all; but he was an unthrifty manager, whose brain-force expended itself far too largely in speculations on abstract Fitness, and how things ought to be in a conceivable universe. So much waste, such misdirected or unutilized energy, afflicted him like a personal misfortune. All over the land were homes or garrets, and some of them bare of plenishing, lighted now by a flickering candle of hope, to go out when these misbegotten manuscripts came back with that infernal circular. It would be bad enough if they were all born of blundering imbecility; but, however young at the trade, he had seen, and Prance admitted, that this was not so. There might be men and women cabined, cribbed, confined by the blind routine of circumstances, who felt their wings sprouting and heard Apollo's faint far-off call, but were chained to the ox like Pegasus, set to plough stony fields or haul manure, and harnessed down so that they could not soar. And some of these were crying to him for help; but he too was tied and powerless. It was in literature then as in everything else — unless one's whole nature went to money-grubbing. `

> "What hand and brain went ever paired?
> What heart alike conceived and dared?
> What act proved all its thought had been?
> What will but felt the fleshly screen?"

Yes, there must still be foiled Chattertons, minds
that the world needed but knew not, souls thirst-
ing for their proper work but condemned to drop
short of the goal, or survive to be hedgers and
ditchers.   What was it for, this confused and
cruel medley?   What did it mean, the dark vast
roll of failures and of woes?   It was very pretty
to preach about suffering and being strong,
about patience having her perfect work, about
ripening under trials.   All that might be if one
saw an end within reach, held a clue to the
labyrinth.   One could be patient and steadfast
if there were any visible cause to fight for; but

> "Neither battle I see, nor arraying, nor King in Israel,
>   Only infinite jumble and mess and dislocation,
>   Backed by a solemn appeal, 'For God's sake do not stir,
>   there!'"

That was about it; Clough understood.   When
you wanted to make an effort toward mending
things ever so little, no matter where or how, they
would not let you, and probably considered you
presumptuous and profane: if you kept on trying,
you would be pilloried or starved.   How could
'Well done' be said at last — supposing there was
anybody to say it — when one had no chance to
do anything?   Just earning one's bread and
cheese, and helping to oil the machinery by which
the firm grew rich, was not *doing*, it was only
pretending.   Such seemed the way all around;
a set of children playing at this and that, and

making believe it was real and important. Your life might be a lie, your whole work unsound and poisonous, and then the Bishop in your, funeral sermon would praise your persistent energy, and set you up as an example to the young. Energy! One could be energetic for substances, but not for shams. The building materials approved and used seemed no better than wood, hay, stubble; where was the gold, the silver, the precious stones that could withstand the fire? Where the large and noble aim, the hold on reality, the sincere and simple truth? Gone out of fashion long ago; driven to the graveyard or the poorhouse with those who cared for them. Ah well, he had been through this wood a hundred times, and always came out at the same place — nowhere. Better go to bed now, or he might be late at the shop to-morrow.

CHAPTER XXXIII.

AT DINNER WITH MR. LEAF.

GRAFTON expected to hear no more of his selections ; but a few days later Mr. Prance came to him and asked where he took his dinners, and whether he were engaged for that evening. He answered that he never had engagements unless on Sundays, and dined anywhere, at restaurants about town. The older man said he was in the same boat just then, and invited his junior to call at the *Battle-Axe* office at half-past five. As they rode up town (Dick usually walked both ways, for reasons sanitary and financial), it appeared that they were going to encounter a circle of artists.

"But I know almost nothing about art," Dick objected.

"You're not required to ; they don't want to talk shop. They are very good fellows, and generally meet at dinner for company's sake : I often join them when I'm alone at home. They look up places that give the most and best — victuals and drink and style — for fifty to seventy-five cents."

" Not kept by natives, I suppose. I fed *more Americano* in the West, and now I try to get a change."

" Certainly ; foreigners understand these things much better than we, when economy is an object. Few of these men can afford more than a dollar a day for food, and yet they like a glass of wine and a touch of Paris or Vienna or Florence : they favor an Italian place this month. You see, we get enough of our own trade in working hours, if they don't. These painters come the nearest of what's left now to the old Bohemia : they take a man on his merits, no questions asked as to what you're worth or what you've done, and you feel at home at once. It's the most thorough realization of democratic equality to be found in America, among people who know something and amount to something. General society in Baltimore has, or had, a little of this openness, but in no northern city that I've heard of."

They entered an eating-house on Third Avenue; it was small but neat, and nearly full at that early hour. Several gentlemen hailed Prance jovially, and made room at one of the tables ; most of their names seemed familiar to Dick as he was introduced. As a waiter brought in the claret, " Hold on," said one of the artists : "let us have the Neapolitan instead, in your big jug.

He's got that lately, and it's not meant for outsiders : you'll see the difference." Six courses
were produced successively, each a single dish ;
the macaroni was beyond competition. An average appetite need ask for nothing more, unless
in the way of dessert. The talk ranged from
Siberia to Texas, and from the last *People* to the
last prizefight : the newcomer was accepted as
one of themselves, and felt as if among friends.
Cigars were lit, but long before they were finished
Prance said he must be off.

"It's an unchristian habit," one of the others
remarked, "this working at night. I hope you're
not going to train Mr. Grafton to it."

"He should have belonged to your order,"
Prance replied. "You votaries of the ideal can
take life easily ; we slaves of stern reality have no
hours to spare."

When they were in the street he went on,
"Some whom you'd be apt to meet there earlier
or later are out of town : these fellows are stalled
here now."

"Why, I thought Purple and Indigo had a good
deal of reputation."

"So they have in a way, but not a way that
brings much income with it. What you've seen of
theirs were merely potboilers — in our papers and
the like. They paint very well, but it's not every
season that they can sell pictures enough to take
them to the Adirondacs or the Maine coast. Their

studios are rented by the year, and they sleep there, whereas they would have to pay for lodging as well as board in the country. If last year's sketches give out, they'll go a little way up the Hudson or into Jersey in October. Then they're used to this kind of living, and to each other's company : they go out hardly more than you and I. Yes, they make little more than we, and with us it's less precarious — as long as we keep our places."

"But Mr. Leaf surely is a man of note. I was surprised to meet him in such a place."

"O, he goes anywhere with the boys. You might have been surprised to meet Kirk, or Lagerland, or Persimmons: those aristocrats of the brush are at their palatial villas now, and never dine in Third Avenue nor mix with you and me. Yes, Leaf has a national and you might say a European fame, but it's largely in the past, and orders are not plenty with him at present. He's stiff in his notions, though not in his manners ; at near seventy he's the youngest of that set, and a royal good fellow. The purest democrat I know : he resents any show of deference to his age, or his talents, or his repute ; it's manhood suffrage with him, or nothing. He's worth your knowing further ; no man in New York more so. Drop in at his studio when you have a spare hour, as he suggested."

"O, that was a mere form of courtesy, I imagine."

"These men don't use forms of courtesy, my lad — not for form's sake. What they say they mean, and Leaf especially. He'll be as glad to see you as if you were a millionaire; more so, for he hates men of money, and takes you for a man of mind. Go look at his Shakspeare head, and draw him out on the Sonnets. He's a rare talker, and always has time and will to entertain a friend."

"I should think he'd be in demand socially, with his face, and celebrity, and attainments, and peculiar charm of manner — at lion-hunting houses, you know."

"They couldn't get him if they tried, and they've forgotten his existence, if they ever knew of it. He's out of date, as I told you."

"Has he lost his skill? He doesn't look it, nor talk as if he were failing."

"Not a bit of it, but he's lost his prestige somehow. He's his own man, and holds to his own ideas, which is not the way to be a favorite. His success was won by original talent, and lost by original character — independence. The stream has flowed past him, and he doesn't care. He's been everywhere in his day, and known everybody; now he's done with life, in some respects. Except for a few visitors, and these younger brothers of the craft he meets at dinner, he lives like a hermit."

"What you say sounds like a virulent satire —not on him, but on a community that could neglect him and let him drop out of sight."

' "Very likely: such is life in New York, and I judge elsewhere too."

"But I thought if you once made a success, it would last —as long as you deserved it."

"Not much. You've got to keep on making it; to study the arts of pleasing and advertising, and keep yourself right with the public. You should hear Flanigan talk; he says most of what sells is not art at all, but junk, and he'd rather go out whitewashing, or borrow of everybody he knows (which he does, by the way, and never pays), than conform to prevailing canons. A man may begin right, as Leaf did, and make a hit; then presently they want him to caricature himself, which Leaf wouldn't do, and drop him because he wont. To real men, oftener than to shams, success comes by caprice, and goes the same way: the sham can generally hold it when he's once got it. Leaf might as well have died ten years ago. I care for few, but he'd be one if there were no other. When I go anywhere I go to see him. If you're bashful about it I'll take you, late some night. Here's my corner, and there are other things I want to talk to you about. Come round at nine, or say half-past, will you?"

CHAPTER XXXIV.

BUSINESS SECRETS.

WHEN they were again seated on the little balcony, Mr. Prance said with a guilty air, "You wouldn't have expected it of me, nor I either, but I've actually looked over those things you picked out of the dust-heap — the ones you were sure about. I wanted to see what your judgment was worth ; and by George, it's sound. That stuff will go in — sooner or later, somewhere or other, and the writers' names are ticketed on our white list. I've kept the addresses for you, in case you should want to be remembered in their prayers. Two of them were never heard of before, and one is a man who has long been trying, without success till now ; very likely, as you say, because he had no chance. So you may have laid the foundation of their fortunes. But what's more to the purpose is this ; I've seen Perkins, and you're out of that scrape — though it was a near thing, and you mustn't get into another. I've talked with Lybert too, and told them both that you have what is rather uncommon, a good nose — the power of really sifting MSS., and an instinct for what's worth preserving; and that if they should ever want to modify our system, and institute a more careful examination of what comes in from un-privileged quarters, you might be valuable. At first they hooted at the idea; then after awhile they admitted that it might possibly be worth considering as among the contingencies of the remote future. So you're comparatively in their good books; though I don't want you to touch Jones' work again, if it can be avoided — not as things are now. And you needn't think what I said to you the other night was all gammon, for most of it was true, and sounder than advice gen-erally is. Coming in lately from outside, you might take it as the mere *ex parte* opinion of an old fogy who knew nothing outside the shop."

"I'm not quite such a fool as that, Mr. Prance. I defer to your ability and infinitely greater expe-rience, of course. I appreciate your kindness, and the obvious weight of sincerity in most things you say — except when you amuse yourself with guy-ing a new hand."

"What I said then had as much truth in it as the rest, if you knew how to take it. I never talk seriously to a man till I've sized him up. Respect for one's elders is so nearly one of the lost arts that I'm agreeably surprised when I meet it, and perhaps this has put me off my base in your

favor. Well, you're not to have Jones' place now ;
the office would have to be revolutionized to make
it worth your while, and that will hardly occur in
my time. But you may be called in as a Reader,
to go through stuff offered for publication in permanent form."

"So that is considered higher work than handling the shorter contributions ? "

" Yes, for these are meant to be really looked at
more or less — sometimes, at any rate. A book is
supposed to be a bigger thing than a magazine
article, though it finds fewer readers in almost
every case, and in four out of five doesn't pay
expenses."

" I don't see how publishers make money then.
Who bears the loss ? "

" The author, if the house is sharp, and its Reader
has made the right report. Who do you suppose
pays for all these volumes of verse, for instance ?
A young fellow came in from the woods shortly
before you arrived, to see about his first venture.
' How many copies of these do you want struck
off ?' we asked him. ' I don't know ; about fifteen
hundred would do, I fancy,' says he. ' Better say
a hundred and fifty,' says the firm ; ' that'll be
plenty for you and your friends, and the few critics
who care to cut you up, and leave some for the
mill. You don't want to sink over two hundred
dollars on this foolishness, do you ?' You see
Lybert doesn't care for that kind of business ;

there's no great profit in it, and no credit at all —
it makes him look like a mere manufacturer.   The
houses of highest tone profess to eschew this line
of operations, and accept nothing not specially
approved, even at the writer's risk; though most
of the learned and technical books, and lots of
which you wouldn't think it, really come out on
those terms."

"Then one has to pay for the privilege of
putting the fruit of his researches, or his imagin-
ings, before the world?"

"Of course; how else? — unless his name, or
his subject, or his handling of it, or all together,
are sure to sell largely, which can seldom be.
Bookmaking has grown so out of bounds that it
has come to be a bore and a nuisance and a pest.
Poetry's a mere drug, which nobody wants to take.
You remember the old saw, —

> ' Swans sing before they die; 'twere no bad thing
> Did certain persons die before they sing.'

Well, that's nearly all of them; and prose is not
much better.   I can't see what Job and Solomon
knew about it, but our enemies are making books
forever and without end.   In fact, writers as a
class are the foes of mankind, and will soon be so
regarded."

By this time Dick knew the old gentleman well
enough to take some moderate liberties.   "And
yet you get your living by them, Mr. Prance."

"As the policeman does by the criminal classes ; that's all. I get my living by standing guard against their encroachments, and protecting the community from them as far as possible."

"I don't believe the writers generally understand this, nor the public. They think the governing idea of the literary market is free trade, including not only pirated reprints, but every fellow's having his own chance. By what you say, it's severe protection, with a strong leaning to monopolies. It looks as if we and the few scores or hundreds whom we print made a close corporation, determined to exclude competitors, and keep the supply just what it is."

"That's the case exactly, Grafton, except that the supply is always increasing perforce, and it's our business to prevent its increasing too fast. Writers die and go to their reward, and their works do follow them — if they haven't gone before. Books that were popular yesterday are out of date and demand to-morrow, but far too many come in their place : we stand in the way, and put on prohibitory duties, or as near as may be. When you come to be a Reader, remember that you're in the custom-house to prevent smuggling. I hope you have no yearnings toward authorship ?"

"Not after what you tell me. Perhaps I had, in a vague way, at one time ; but if they were not dead before now, they would hardly survive these admonitions."

"They would be the ruin of you; Grafton if such desires ever rise again, tear them out by the roots and fling them far from you. Take me for a warning, if you will: I've borne a share in the guilt and in the punishment. It's a painful subject, but long ago I wrote several books, and I've never recovered from the effects. It gives a fatally wrong direction to one's mind. It's a bad thing to be mixed up with literature at all, even as we are, in this comparatively useful way of warding off inflictions from the public. If we had not taken the itch, though in this modified form, we might have come to some good end, in soap, or stocks, or salt fish, or boots and shoes. You needn't smile, my poor young friend; if you've not learned your lesson yet, you will in time. Do you think even Lybert is happy? No, sir. True, he's made near a million; but he sees others who began at the same time and went into something really necessary to the welfare of mankind, such as whiskey, or tobacco, or Wall Street, or explosive compounds, and are now worth ten times as much. No, in his heart he's not content with the book trade."

"You may gibe at our betters, Mr. Prance, if you like; but don't try to persuade me that you think moneymaking the end of man, for I know better."

"Yes, youth is always self-confident and bumptious, but age is cautious and doubtful. I'm sure

I don't know what the end of man is; do you?
But they don't pay us for our opinions — except
when we have to sit in judgment on a manuscript,
which, as I said, is a bad business."

CHAPTER XXXV.

BOOKS, 'READERS,' AND WRITERS.

DICK began to doubt whether such instructions as the veteran might deliver in his present mood were to be taken literally; these utterances, however improving, were not strictly to the point. "Still, you say that is likely to be my business to some extent. How shall I go about it?"

"The first thing is to settle what not to do; that is always the most important. I've been trying to impress on you the necessity of writing nothing (except in a small way as called for) and avoiding all literary acquaintance. If you attempt to ring in your own productions or those of your friends, you will soon be under the ban: even Perkins has to be careful about that. Confine yourself absolutely to MSS. committed to you at the shop in the regular way, and don't dream of increasing the number."

"That, of course. I presume they wouldn't give me anything in divinity, or the fine arts, or other fields I'm not familiar with?"

"Why not? You could tell how they were likely to impress the general public. You know Jerrold said he never read a book before reviewing it, it prejudiced him so. The same truth applies to a too minute or profound knowledge of a subject at large. School books, and treatises on pyrotechnics and perfumery, when examined at all, might go to an expert. But in what will be apt to come to you chiefly, cases in which you have to judge not of alleged facts, but simply of thought and style, your trouble will be the other way, from excess, not defect."

"In me? How do you mean?"

"You're not sufficiently woodenheaded. You'll be looking for merits, when you're wanted to find defects. You'll not be easily able to get Goldsmith's maxim out of your head, that life and not blamelessness is the desideratum. We don't go by that. A thing may be full of juice, and yet not suited to us at all; whereas if it's simply strong and original, you'd be apt to recommend it."

"Why, certainly. We want strength and originality, don't we?"

"Not if they have the defects of their qualities, as they usually will. We want Propriety. It matters comparatively little about stimulating thought or rousing emotion, provided we print nothing to start a blush on the cheek of innocence, or disturb the conventional calm of accepted standards. Successful preachers, you know, pick out the dullest man in the audience, and aim their discourse at him: those who knew something before they came, and haven't patience to hear the rudiments laid level to the meanest apprehension, can go home — they are but a small minority. The average mind is commonplace: a writer who would be popular must address that, and a Reader must see that he does."

"But this would exclude our best, as Cravatton, and Jacobs, and Miss Lambson, and Mrs. Firett. They did not make their way by commonplace dulness: either in style or situations, in narrative or analysis, they give us something new, and freely handled. So did the great masters of the last generation; so —"

"O yes, of course. You're talking of those already known; they can do what they please, and their books don't come to you for approval. I speak of new writers, whose effort to cross the line is an intrusion to be resented. That makes all the difference in the world. They've not established their right to be heard, and the presumption is against them. So, when you once get your hand in, you will bring to their pages a weary and reluctant mind, corresponding to that of the jaded critic or the fatigued though unprofessional wader through ten novels a week; that's the right point of view. You're dealing with trespassers, remember: if they attempt to be funny, they are vulgar; if they pretend to individuality, that is also an impertinence. As mere beginners their duty is to respect precedents and follow the beaten paths in serious humility. It wont do for you to report favorably on anything that is not imitatively customary and decorously conservative. Nothing is more offensive than a striving after originality, and nothing more tiresome than mechanical and perfunctory humor."

"But suppose the humor is natural and the originality genuine? What right have I to stick to a rigid assumption of the contrary?"

"You *must* assume it: it's *a priori* probable, and will in most cases be true. The favorable supposition is against the doctrine of chances, and the whole body of our rules and precedents. All we expect of a first novel is to tell us when and where John Henry Jackson was born, the color of his hair and eyes, and the details of his adventures in love, war, and politics, with his ultimate success in unmasking the villain and discovering his grandfather's will. Let this be set forth in good plain English, such as is taught in any of our colleges and academies, with no rude obtrusion of his own ideas on the writer's part. Should he succeed, he can sprinkle these over his later works without irreverence; we'll bear them then."

"But I might reject a book which takes a line of its own, and so fails to conform to this very moderate standard, and then some other house risks it, and it makes a marked success. What then?"

"That doesn't matter : the firm wont recollect that it was offered to them, and you needn't tell. Practically you are always safe in rejecting; in accepting the danger lies.   Never forget that you are set to guard the firm against losses, and the public, in some small degree, against the waste of its precious time."

"But how can I tell whether a book will sell or not?   You say yourself that it is all guesswork. The only point I can pronounce upon is intrinsic merit, literary character.   Some books don't succeed that ought to, and *vice versâ.*"

"Make your report according to what you find —on the lines just indicated; and in a case of doubt (which is almost always, except with a marketable reputation, and that doesn't concern you) advise publication, if at all, at the author's risk. He seldom has any money, so it comes to the same thing.   When you reject, write him a few civil lines in the firm's name, saying that his work has merit but is not quite in our line, and you would advise his sending it to the Sunday School Union ; or that the story is rather too slight, and you regret your inability to persuade yourselves that it is expedient to put it in cold type before a callous world ; or that in the present terribly depressed condition of the fiction market the counsel of your literary advisers (that's you) is adverse to the probability of securing for the book such favorable attention from the critics and the public as you consider important for a volume bearing your (that's our) imprint. You can enlarge on the injury done to home literature by cheap reprints; that's perfectly true. And always sling in a little style on these occasions; it shows 'em that we can write, whether they can or not."

"All this is very hard on the young authors, I must say : they seem to be friendless and defence-less. Is there no brotherly feeling among the guild?"

"There used to be, when writers were compara-tively few and life less rapid; but now the profes-sion's crowded, the pace stiff, and it's each for himself and the devil take the hindmost. Any fraternity has to guard its doors and keep out the riffraff; and you know what human nature is. If you and I got into the car at the last crossing, we grudge to make room for those who enter at the next; if we're off for the summer and registered yesterday, we look down on to-day's arrivals and feel that they have no business to be so close on our heels. Why can't they stay at home or go somewhere else, and let us have a good quiet time? At least they needn't expect us to show them around, and point out the paths and views, and explain the rules of the place; let them find out for themselves, as we did. You see there's a strong and general impression that the hotel, or the conveyance, or whatever it may be, is full, and in this case it's only too well founded. Litera-

ture's a trade like anything else. A successful
author must be methodical to get through his
work, and his time's worth so much an hour ; he
can't waste it on poor scrubs who want to be
taught, first how to write, and then how to sell
their scribblings. Most of these aspirants are
lame ducks anyway, and it's best to regard them
all as such till one out of a thousand has proved
himself an exception."

"You don't hold this hidebound selfishness
essential to success, do you?"

"I hold that one may break his heart over
other's woes, or starve himself to feed the hungry,
and get small thanks for it in this world ; how it
is in the next I can't say, never having been there.
Charity must be organized to be effective. If I
were to go into philanthropy I should want to be
paid for it.

" And yet you are taking some pains to post me,
and keep me out of scrapes, and get me started
right."

"We were talking of authors ; I'm out of that
branch since the fifties, and if you go into it I'll
disown you. But you needn't suspect me of dis-
interestedness. I like to hear myself talk, after
nine P. M., and you're a good listener. Then
when my daughter's away so long I get lonesome,
and you're much the same sort of innocent donkey
that I was at your age. Besides, you may be of
use some day ; any good you get by me I expect
to take out of you with inte rest."

" I hope you will. You speak of the old days when beginners found some sympathy and encouragement. Was that in Willis' time ? "

" Nat had a mania for playing godfather. He was wild to catch recruits, bring them to the front, and predict their coming greatness — so long as they weren't his sister Sara. He had a good eye for points too ; he would have been the chief for you, and you the lieutenant for him. Poor Nat, he's forgotten already, or remembered only as a worse fellow than he was. Bayard Taylor was another with a heart open to all comers, corresponding with every small poet in the land ; if he'd had a paper of his own, he might have been a better duenna even than Willis. These two burned the candle at both ends, and died in their prime, when meaner men could have lived in peace to eighty. Too much heart ! Taylor spent himself on others ; it doesn't pay. Ever hear what a certain statesman said of him ? ' Nothing in him, positively nothing.' Such is fame. We're wiser now ; we look to number one, and save up health and dollars. Remember that, youngster, and be a man of your own era."

Mr. Prance's countenance was nearly as grim as his monitions ; but Dick suspected an ironic vein, and taking them *cum grano*, was less dismayed by this definition of his duties than he might have been a week before.

CHAPTER XXXVI.

MISS LOUISE.

But for his new friend's advice, it is doubtful whether Grafton could have held his place three months; at least that was his matured opinion later. Thanks to the hints and guidance of one who had been long behind the scenes, and grown from something near enough for sympathy to what Dick was into that in substance which Dick now saw he must become, he managed to steer between the Scylla of his preconceived notions and the Charybdis of mundane demoralization and unmitigated practicality. He became an expert in inspecting MSS. as well as a dextrous trimmer of notices and literary items : not more than once did Mr. Perkins need to say, " This is too long, Mr. Grafton. We do not require so much elaboration : just the main points, hit off incisively, so that he who runs may read ; with snap, you know, and a little flourish." The accomplished editor-in-chief (for if this awful function did not belong to Mr. Perkins, then whose was it ?) relaxed the languid remoteness of his manner, and grew almost confidential; it was understood that the recruit had passed his entrance examinations, and could be trusted at least a yard or two out of sight. That he was in love with his duties would be too much to say, but he knew they suited him better probably than any others within his reach : he had put his hand to the plough, and admitted no thought of turning back. Developing under pressure the faculty of rapid and methodical labor, he was able to increase his tasks, and with them his earnings : in time he was inducted at the *Battle-Axe* office, and assumed some minor occupations there. But this is anticipating.

Throughout that first summer he saw much of Mr. Prance, and often dined with the veteran and his artist friends. He spent more than one leisure hour in the studios, and listened to Mr. Leaf's laudations of the Shakspeare Sonnets and diatribes against the hermetic interpretation thereof. The talk of the younger painters refreshed his home and foreign geography ; he drank in Flanigan's vituperative comments on contemporary art, and went home poorer by the price of the satirist's next breakfast.

Among these acquaintances he learned something of Mr. Prance's past. "That man has a history," they stated, "though he wont talk about it." He had begun with what were considered brilliant talents and prospects ; had travelled abroad, married early, and put forth a volume of verse, a novel, and some essays which made a noise in their day. " You'll find them mentioned in the cyclopædias and histories," said Mr. Leaf, "but they're long out of print. He might as well have died twenty years ago : he and I are fossils, survivals of the unfittest. He's taken life harder than I ; he looks over sixty, and he's scarcely fifty-five. There was good stuff in his books, but luck was against him." A course of luxurious and hospitable living was cut short by the total loss of his property, through the dishonesty or carelessness of agents whom he trusted and friends for whom he had endorsed ; the death of two children was followed by that of his wife, and at thirty-six he was left with an infant daughter. " But for her he would have gone to the dogs or underground, I believe ; only that responsibility kept him up. If I had had his load to carry I should have fallen beneath it. There are things nearer than money, that are harder to lose." So he had taken shelter in the outworks of literature, and lived ever since by labors more or less editorial. " You can't call him a hack, his leaders are too strong for that ; but he does them as he might lay pavement or cobble shoes." They had no relatives but some remote cousins on a New Hampshire farm, to whom the daughter was always sent in summer. " She wouldn't leave her father but that he insists : however little might come in, he has put by a hundred every year since she was eight to get her away from town in July and August. She's a nice quiet girl, but it's a narrow life, and very different from what he would like for her. It's this contrast with the past that makes him gruff, but he's gold inside — his sort stands the fire. A generation ago there was no more gallant and jovial fellow in New York than he. They used to entertain magnificently: it was one of the best houses. Popular was no name for him ; but after the crash he hid from sight, and of course was soon forgotten."

The old artist's beautiful eyes were moist. "Well, well, he's borne up under it, and there's no need for us to break down. I'm glad he's taken this fancy to you ; he leads far too solitary a life."

Dick had a Chinese reverence for age, and the spectacle of these graybeards summing each other up in almost the same terms struck him as pathetic rather than humorous.

One evening in early September he mounted to the second floor on East Sixteenth Street, where he knew himself a welcome visitor. For once his host was not alone ; a slight fair girl answered to his knock. He noticed her no more than courtesy required, found an errand in some circumstance of his work, and cut short his call with an apology for disturbing the reunion of parent and child. He was not in the humor for

feminine society then, and possibly had as much
of it as he cared for in his half compulsory Sundays at Oaklands. For the next week or two he
avoided Mr. Prance's rooms, and when he went
again, the girl presently arose and withdrew.
This coldness between the young people seemed
to oppress the older man, but his invitations were
not urgent, and Dick remembered how jealously
he guarded his daughter.

At last, on a lovely October night, goaded by
the fear of seeming ungrateful and neglectful, he
sallied forth, and was discomfited at finding Miss
Louise alone in the den. "Father is out, for a
wonder," she said, "but he'll be back soon. No;
sit down, please," for Dick was nervously saying
that his business was not pressing, and he would
not intrude ; "he wants to see you, I know, and
— and I want to talk to you a little."

She blushed, and he was conscious of some
alarm : he was not much accustomed to young
ladies, and his attitude toward this one was complicated by his relations with her father. Yet
there could be no great danger in that ingenuous
face, that rippling light-brown hair, those honest
blue eyes timidly raised to his. I am not going
to describe Miss Prance any further : she was
well enough, but nothing to look at beside — or
after — Edith De Grout.

"Mr. Grafton," she went on, " I'm afraid I have
driven you away."

"O no," he stammered, "not at all. But the last time I was here I seemed to drive you away."

"I didn't want to disturb you. But the time before that—the first time, you remember—you went away almost as soon as you came in ; and you know you would have stayed till eleven or twelve if I hadn't been here."

"That's not so certain," Dick answered more confidently, "for sometimes your father sends me off by ten, when he's very tired ; and that time I knew he wanted to see you."

"And this time I know he wants to see you, as I told you. He has so few friends—that is, so few that he cares about and likes to have come. I never stay in here when it will interfere with his visitors, and you're almost the only one. I'll go away now if you'll promise to wait for him."

"O, that wont do at all ; I couldn't think of it. But you see, Miss Prance, I know your father's very particular about you, and doesn't like to have everybody coming here ; and as a stranger—"

"But you're not a stranger ; as if I didn't know all about you, from his letters through the summer! He writes me regularly twice a week, you know, when I'm away. And you're not everybody, but somebody very particular, and not at all fond of ladies ; so I couldn't blame you, though I did want to see you and explain that you must come here just the same, and I would try to keep out of the room."

"And do you suppose I would be welcome here when I drove you out? No; if I come you will have to go on just as if I were not here."

"O, I can be very quiet, and not interrupt; and I do love to hear papa talk. But if I come in you must do just as you would if I were away."

So they patched up a *modus vivendi*, on the basis of ignoring each other, before Mr. Prance entered — he being in the mind of each the chief person to be considered ; and from that time the conferences on literature from a more or less mercantile point of view were continued in presence of an auditor, but with no great disturbance from that cause. Dick's thoughts did not run to young women, and this one was sufficiently harmless. Though near twenty and brought up in New York, she knew little of the world and its wiles. Her father had managed to send her to private schools, and she had acquired a tolerable taste for books; she was of a retiring disposition, and happily content with few resources ; her friends and her amusements were far from numerous. How a girl manages to get through the week, in almost total solitude till evening, with only her limited housekeeping and three rooms and her father's shelves for occupation, I really do not know. No doubt there are thousands in Babylon as narrowly cooped in as she, kept by instincts and traditions from mingling with the grossness round them, and hopelessly

cut off from society either extensive or select.
Louise had at least her father's company at breakfast and dinner (he never sought his artist friends
and the Italian restaurant when she was at home)
and after nine P.M. ; and while he wrote she could
sit in the den and sew or read. For two months
each year city grime and dust were exchanged for
the rural sights and enlivening breezes of a mountain farm ; and then she made her own gowns —
a practice which I am told combines enjoyable
employment with economy, for any young person
who has a knack that way and not much cash
to spare. Thus fortified, she somehow escaped
devouring ennui and desire for flirtations with
the grocer's boy on the corner. The wind is
tempered to our bareness, and Heaven has endowed the more helpless sex with a mighty fund
of patience.

In time Grafton grew reconciled to this appen-
dage to his Mentor, and came to regard her as an
inoffensive fellow creature who had been assigned
some small supernumerary part on the by no
means crowded boards of his unsensational drama.
It even occurred to him to contribute mild assuage-
ments to her loneliness now and then. I am sure
he never furnished her with flowers or caramels,
for these are costly luxuries ; but sometimes when
he had tickets from the *Battle-Axe* he would take
her to a play or other scene of delight, and the
following spring they might be observed on fine

Sundays in the Park, or at Coney Island before the crowd began to go.   Mr. Prance viewed these proceedings with tolerance, rather glad that the poor child should have some little entertainment, and troubled his head with no fear of the consequences.   He was not addicted to playing Providence in other than a negative way, and Grafton was wholly to be trusted and perfectly ineligible.

CHAPTER XXXVII.

EXIGENCIES OF LITERATURE.

Dick's account of Mr. Prance aroused my curiosity, and I asked him to introduce me at the den. The sage gave a reluctant consent, and sometimes, when my wife was out of town, I was admitted to partake the feast of reason. As soon as I knew the old gentleman well enough, I ventured to compliment him on his influence over my friend. "You have done him all the good in the world; really, you have made quite a little man of him. He always needed somebody to look after him and keep him straight, and he never would listen to me, because I'm not much older than he is."

The host and his daughter looked as if they thought that my advice would have had but limited value under any circumstances, and Dick came to my assistance. "You see, Bob, you and I are very differently situated; our spheres are wide apart. But Mr. Prance and myself are in the same line of business, and — and have other things in common." (He meant poverty, but it was not manners to say so.) "So he has kindly given me the great benefit of his experience, and of his example. An ounce of that, you know, is worth a ton of mere preaching like yours."

"Yes," said the old man, "I could help Grafton to solve some of his problems, because I had done the same sums for myself long before. There was a time when I held it degradation to touch any work that did not square with my liking, and gave taste and temperament the name of principle. I was fastidious and self-indulgent, and must do things in my own way or not at all."

"That's Grafton to a T.," said I. "As I've often told him, laziness was his trouble."

"O no," said the young lady; "I'm sure he's not lazy at all. Why, he works almost as hard as you, doesn't he, papa?"

"It *is* a kind of laziness," her father resumed; "not precisely either intellectual or physical indolence, but allied to them as being emotional or moral — temperamental, we might say. As such it is well enough for the dilettante whose nest is feathered, but quite incompatible with active exertion. When one has dinner to get and rent to pay, he must cast his finer sense and sorer shame aside, as Newman says. Necessity is the mother not only of useful inventions but of ethical discoveries. I found I could do without a throb things of which the bare idea would have been

shocking in salad days — if it had been conceivable then."

"I'm sure, papa," the girl again put in, "you
never did anything that wasn't honorable and
highminded."

"Highmindedness, my dear, is a quality not
commended in Scripture, which speaks reprovingly
of 'traitors, heady, highminded, lovers of pleasures,'
and so on. Perhaps that's what I was before you
came, omitting the element of treason. We're apt
to glorify our condition, and erect our pride into
a virtue. But I got bravely over that. One year
I reported the meetings of Council, and the next
wrote free trade arguments for one paper, and
protectionist for another."

"You did?" Grafton exclaimed; "and at the
same time? Wasn't that a pill to take?"

"If so, it was gilded, and the coating made
it palatable. At your age, I felt as you do ; now,
I justify the course, and would pursue it again
on occasion. It all depends on the point of view,
and those of abstract and practical morality are
quite different. Why should not a journalist take
either side at will, as they do in debating societies
and at the bar? You ought to be familiar with
that, Grafton."

"Yes, but I never liked it ; it didn't seem
right."

"He never would take a retainer," I thought
fit to testify, "except from the angel Gabriel, or

unless he had chapter and verse for it. As a colleague told him in my presence, he was too blamed particular. Excuse me, Miss Prance."

"I think he was just right," she remarked beamingly.

"Too right for this world, which is the same as being wrong," the father corrected. "Except by you two babes, it is universally agreed that in law all sides and all cases should have a hearing ; why not elsewhere, especially in newspapers ? "

"O, well," said Dick, "the lawyer is hired."

"So are we. Any other arguments for the negative ? "

"Yes," his junior persisted. "The advocate is not required to speak from his own private opinion, but according to the exigencies of his client ; whereas journalism is supposed to be serious."

"The devil it is!" the old man broke forth. "I beg your pardon, Louie. You ought to close your ears when we talk this way : I shall have to send you off if this youngster keeps on contra-dicting me. — I thought I had cured you of that delusion, Grafton. Serious ! So you thought it was serious, did you ? " He shook with laughter.

Miss Louise, who had been looking anxious, emitted a softer peal. "There, you see he was only joking." She looked confidently at Dick, and appealingly at me.

"Not exactly," said her father, with a somewhat

awkward air, and his tone was almost apologetic :
"if there's any joke here, you must lay it at
the door of the great god Pan. He's a terrible
joker, and his jests, like those of full-private
James, are sometimes in doubtful taste. What
can we do, except conform to the laws of the
universe — or of this planet, which is all we know
of the cosmos? If our conforming is not agreeable to the higher law, the fault lies with 'the
guilty goddess of our harmful deeds, who did not
better for our life provide than public means,
which public manners breeds.' That's often so,
but this is hardly a case in point, as I will show
you. It seems a little *outré* to you, that I should
take both sides at the same time, does it? On
the contrary, it's an excellent way to get at the
whole truth, and avoid narrowness. The tariff
question, like most others, does not lie in a nut-
shell, and is not as plain as that two and two
make four. There is much to be said for and
against, which can best be put in the way of
special pleading — at least that's the way it's
wanted ; so I, having gone over the whole ground
and cherishing no petty prejudices, argue for
protection in the *Forum*, and for free trade in the
Battle-Axe. I'm not riding a personal hobby, you
see ; I'm enlightening the community. Read
both papers, and you'd get about the entire truth
of the matter — so far as truth on this or any
subject is attainable by human faculties, with such

lights as have been afforded up to date. If people will be partisan, and hear only one side, that's not my fault. You might blame me if I had given only one, being able to see both. This was an act of exceptional conscientiousness, such as few could appreciate: in fact, when the *Forum* people found that I was answering myself in the *Battle-Axe*, they were absurdly angry, and dispensed with my further services."

We all sat silent for a minute or so, and I at least was pretty well convinced; but Dick said, "Let me ask one question, Mr. Prance, and forgive me if it sounds impertinent : you know it's not meant to be so. Would you have done that merely for your own pleasure — as an intellectual exercise, say — if there had been no question of pay ?"

"I might : I really don't know. You draw too heavily on my imagination, Grafton. Perhaps you can remember when you wrote for the fun of it, and what your manners and motives were then ; but I'm hanged if I can, it's so long ago. I've been writing for beef and potatoes and pudding these twenty years now; since before you were born, missie" — he put his arm around his daughter's chair — "and before this curious young man was interested in such recondite enquiries. The trade has its own laws, which are not imposed on amateurs. Humiliating, isn't it ?" He turned on me almost fiercely, as if I were an enemy come there to spy out the nakedness of the land.

I made haste to mollify his wrath. "Well," I said, "it's considered a mighty good thing for a fellow to be thrown on his own resources. My poor father used to say I needed just that discipline to make a man of me. He threatened more than once to cut me off with a shilling: you must remember, Dick, how scared I was that time at college, after I nearly flunked out. Once he even talked of failing — a real failure, you know, honest Injun — so as to bring me to hard pan and put me on my mettle. I half believed he would have done it but for Harry and Jane and my mother ; but he couldn't thrash them for my sins, because that wasn't biblical. With Grafton, somehow, the prescription didn't seem to work — not till you took him in hand ; as I said, you've licked him into tolerably decent shape."

It was my cue to be a listener when at Mr. Prance's, and not talk much ; but I said all this to show that there was no purse-pride about me, that I respected intellect and Roman virtue though in rags, and in their presence was properly meek and humbleminded. My remarks, however, had not a very good effect : Miss Louise looked at me indignantly, and her parent somewhat contemptuously, I thought. "You must have been a fine boy," he observed. "Grafton is getting along, as you say ; within a year or two he'll probably

learn to come indoors when it rains. Before he's
my age you may see him not only upholding and
denouncing revenue reform, but supporting all
the various presidential candidates — they'll have
at least six then — and earning big wages. That
sort of talent is coming more and more into demand."

Louise looked pained. "O no, papa. What
you did was all right, of course — right for you,
I mean, since you thought so. You're a — what
was it Mr. Leaf called you? O yes, a casuist.
But Mr. Grafton might not be able to take that
view ; he's young yet, you see, and not — not so —"

" Not so depraved? My dear, you have no idea
of the depth of his depravity. He does things
every day that you wouldn't suspect ; much worse
than I did at his time of life. Grafton, have you
forgotten what a horrible hole you got into when
you undertook to review Weesbax' book with a
view to the whole truth and nothing but the
truth? You put the notice in without consulting
me, but Perkins chanced to look at it, and came
to me — luckily you were out at lunch — as black
as thunder. 'Leave it to me,' I said, 'and this
will not occur again.' I had to tell him you were
sensitive, and take the whole responsibility myself,
and keep you away from the office all that afternoon. And then at night I talked to you like a
father, and laid bare the enormity of your offence."

" Well," said Dick, rather sheepishly, " I was
very sorry to give you so much trouble, of course ;
but you know what the book was, and that it
deserved all I said."

"As a private individual, certainly I do ; but,
shade of Giordano Bruno ! the naked truth mustn't
be always on exhibition. Have you no sense of
decency ? Have you forgotten the illustrious Pom-
ponatius ? I made you see, officially, that the firm
brings out none but good and admirable works,
and that we are on hand to testify accordingly.
Daughter, he heeded the words of wisdom, and
ever since he practises his Socratic principle
only on books that come in from outside. Of
our own publications he displays merely the
shining merits : when he has anything bad to say
of them he disguises it in French or Sanskrit, or
in that fine vein of irony of his which nobody can
detect. That's the way he salves his conscience
with a double meaning and a hidden esoteric sense,
this dissembling Gnostic whom you think so
guileless."

"Well, Mr. Prance," said Dick, resignedly, " I'm
a tree of your grafting ; and according to you, my
backsliding is growth in grace."

"Now, papa," the maiden cried, reproachfully,
"you're joking again. I don't mind it " (though
she looked much hurt), "and Mr. Grafton is
getting used to it, but strangers might not understand."

"You needn't mind Bob," my friend soothingly remarked; "he's said worse things to me than your father does — often and often."

"Then I don't see what people want to say such hateful things for," she almost snapped. The gentle creature's motherly instincts seemed to be aroused, as if she were charged with the defence of helpless innocence. Her father and his *protégé* were the only persons in her little world just then: they were right in all things, were to be defended even against their oldest friends: whoever opposed them was a heathen man and publican, whoever criticised them a heretic and blasphemer.

CHAPTER XXXVIII.

COSMIC PHILOSOPHY.

"Miss Prance," said I, rising to relight my pipe. "Are you quite sure you don't mind smoke?" Of course I had said this before, when we began.

"No," she answered, shortly, "but I can go into the next room if you want to talk secrets. Only it's so lonesome, and my father and Mr. Grafton never mind my being here." Her tone added, plainly enough, "And I don't see what right *you* have to send me out."

"O, not at all," I had to say. The truth was, I felt the time had come for asserting my claim to a place in this symposium, and making a contribution of some value to the fund of ideas; and I was not quite sure whether she ought to hear it. "Far from it, on the contrary. But we're getting rather blue in here — I refer to the physical atmosphere; and some of the thoughts expressed, Grafton's more especially, are rather free. I only feared you might find it tiresome, not to say oppressive — "

"She's used to it," said her father, with his hand on hers : "she has to take us as we are, for want of better. The air here is nightly polluted with vile fumes and conversation unfit for unaccustomed ears — when Grafton is present, as you remark. So out with your oracle."

Thus urged, though with some reluctance, I eased my bosom of its perilous stuff. A man of tact adapts his conversation to the company, and I had worked this selection up at leisure, with reference to Mr. Prance, whose measure I had taken previously.

"I speak under correction," I began, "and you will know how much importance to attach to the observation ; but it seems to me difficult to reconcile some of those old texts with modern facts. 'Cast your bread on the waters.' Now that's not a safe operation ; the chances are you'd never see it again. 'Consider the lilies.' If you do, how are you going to get in your crops ? 'I have not seen the righteous forsaken, nor his seed begging bread.' Why, you may see it on any street corner, if you look up their genealogy."

I paused, for a smile not wholly pensive was spreading over Grafton's countenance, while that of Mr. Prance was disfigured by a positive grin. The former inquired, "What does your wife say to this, Bob?" and the latter, composing his facial muscles to that air of gravity which best becomes gray hairs, replied in an unnecessarily oratorical tone.

"You put it bluntly, and I fear they would scarcely let you take a class in Sunday School. But you need not look so shocked, Louise. Our friend is a strict constructionist, but I think I can in part explain his difficulty. He quotes from a book at once oriental, therefore highly figurative, and ancient, therefore not immediately aimed at our present manners. In fact, geographically, politically, and generally, the distance between former times and our own is vast; witness their sad lack of newspapers, and of great publishing houses. Of old, wars, pestilences, and tyranny kept down the surplus population: civilization has stopped most of these amenities, and substituted an improved and decorous form of the Struggle for Existence, developed to proportions the old world never imagined. In those warm climates necessary expenses were light and wants easily supplied, for people lived out of doors and required hardly any clothing and but little food. Only epicures and men in politics needed much money; common folks, so long as they could keep their heads on their shoulders, had no appearances to preserve and small fear for their suppers. Their drawbacks were wholly different from ours, for they had no personal rights, no security against raids, and but the roughest and vaguest conception of liberty.

They were far more picturesque than we, and far less practical. Their notion of life was war; ours is peace. They cared for glory; we care for cash, and comforts to be procured therewith. They crawled at the heels of a patron; we stand on our own pins — or profess to — and push each his own fortunes. The wonder is that they have anything to say to us, except through the imagination. Homer is but a more venerable and less edifying Hans Andersen, and Thucydides the recorder of conditions that seem to us ludicrously impossible. Why should the gods intervene to punish Ajax and protect Ulysses, or lengthen the day to enable one barbarous tribe to complete the scalping of another? Such favoritism, such glorification of mere force, seems to us neither just nor wise. The personal element, with all its faults, is apotheosized, alike in heaven and among a few aristocrats on earth; the mass is but a herd to be driven, slaves to obey the law or feel the lash. Of course their legislation, civil and religious, proceeds on a basis of ideas widely variant from ours. And yet, that wonderful, deathless, unaccountable Syrian stock, that has given us poets greater than Shakspeare, and ethical principles far beyond Plato — we must make a reservation in their favor. This at least they have done: they have dreamed for all time, and it may be for eternity. Be it but a dream, it is so large, so beautiful — the most beautiful thing in life." The old man's tone was solemn; he seemed to have forgotten our presence, to be talking to himself.

"Father," said Louise very earnestly, "you believe more than that; I know you do."

He shook off his abstraction. "My dear, hadn't we better save up our beliefs for Sunday? Few people have enough to go round the week."

"For all that," said Dick, "I should like to have lived in the Bible lands and times — the further back the better, before the crowd came."

"That's merely because you're of a patriarchal turn," said I; "and I doubt if it was any better than the Eastern Shore. You must remember that 'they didn't know everything down in Judee.'"

"He is right," said Mr. Prance; "they knew little of the laws of competition, and the stringency of the literary market, and the rules of Lybert & Co. You see one can't have everything. So inquisitive a mind as yours, Grafton, could hardly have been satisfied with the company of Samson and Elijah, or even of Ezra and Joel. Their horizon was very narrow, and narrower the further back you go."

"One could dispense with some kinds of knowledge," Dick replied, "to be allowed to walk on one straight simple line, with no doubtings or windings; to deal with a few great primary truths, and stand erect in their light."

"Why, so you do," cried our female chorus.

"Father says you wouldn't do a dishonest thing to save your life; that's why he liked you so much from the start. I know you wouldn't tell a fib, not to him or me at least — no, not for a thousand dollars. And I don't believe you would to anybody, if you could help it."

"Not unless in the way of business, I hope," he answered. "That's the attraction of those old days to me; they hadn't any business to speak of."

"And they won't have any in heaven," said she, consolingly. "Poor papa, you wont have to be away from me all day, and to write so hard at night. Maybe they have books there, but not any newspapers, I'm sure."

"Just so, my dear. We'll have nothing to do but twang on gold harps, and listen to the sweet little cherubim singing, and put on clean collars every morning and fine white clothes, and sit by a beautiful purling stream."

"But that wont suit Dick," I remarked. "He'll want to go fishing in it, and to hunt up Socrates and Epictetus, and bore them to death till he hears all the nonsense they can think of."

"Mr. Prance," said Dick, "I didn't bring up these abstruse and elevated topics; but since we're on them, if you don't mind, I'd like to hear your scheme of being. It might do Bob here a great deal of good, and he needs it." He meant nothing by this hit at me; it was merely one of his efforts to be facetious, and he never had any talent as a humorist.

"His what?" Louise enquired. "What on earth do you mean?"

"His scheme, his theory. Of course he's got one — men of marked ability always have. His way of solving the infinite, and making darkness light and crookedness straight, and justifying the ways of Providence, Miss Louise; or, if you prefer, his plan for the conduct of life."

"Why, that's perfectly plain," the girl cried with full assurance, "and I don't see how you could ask such a question. His plan of life is simply to discharge all his duties faultlessly, and do a great many kind and generous things besides, and set a noble example to you and all other young men."

"That's right, Louie," the parent commented; "mix in all the colors of the rainbow. But I fear your Portrait of a Gentleman as drawn by his Daughter will not be recognized outside the family. Nor do I propose to unwind the labyrinth of fate for you, Grafton, as you modestly request; you'd better go to a fortune-teller. You're not as lucid as usual either. What he wants, little girl, is that I should try to reconcile the dual elements of Character, or what some now call the two lobes of the brain, and explain how honest men can descend to the tricks we perform every day."

"There are no tricks, papa, as you're perfectly well aware ; that is only your funny way of talking. I know all about lobes, and I've heard of duality ; if Mr. Grafton meant them, why couldn't he say so? But you'll have to explain now, or some of us wont understand."

She glanced at me, so I said, "That's true, Mr. Prance. I should like it of all things." If none of them cared to hear what more I had to say, that was their loss, not mine. Thus adjured by all present, he yielded.

"My scheme of life, as Grafton calls it, is as simple as the complexity of things will allow. We can't be just our own men, and go our own way. I doubt if anybody can ; certainly not those who are situated as we are. Necessity is laid on one man to preach the gospel, and on another to hunt for the North Pole, and on us to get our living between Lore Street and the *Battle-Axe* office. Yet we don't wish to become wholly the slaves of circumstance, nor to starve the soul any more than the body. The only way out of this dilemma is to compromise, to keep two sets of accounts, one with God and the other with Mrs. Grundy. One life we live invisibly because we ought ; the visible one because we must, and that brings its duties too. If they clash, we can't help that ; our business is to keep each account balanced by itself, and in as little conflict with the other as may be. Not only every politician

and retail tradesman, but every man who has any
work to do in the world, I suppose, has to connive
at humbugs, and crook the supple hinges of the
knee more or less, and do and bear things that
run counter to his ideal, if he has one ; it's either
that, or step down and out. Where the venial
ends and the inadmissible begins, each must judge
for himself. The extremes are plain enough: fail
on one side, and you're a cad, a worldling, a tool
and prey of the adversary ; fail on the other,
you're an imbecile. Even Scripture says he that
doesn't provide for his own house is worse than
an infidel. Curious, by the way, the number of
scoundrels who have all the domestic virtues :
they think kindness to wives and children gives
them license to be foxes and wolves outside, and
I presume they're not wholly wrong — better that
way than the other. It's not an angelic situation,
and I would no more have chosen it than you
would, Grafton. You can't do as you would, and
you're forced to do as you wouldn't if you were a
free agent, or to go further and fare worse. We're
let in to it, as the boys say ; by whom, or why, or
how, is useless to inquire. Most men either accept it without question and go on like machines,
or else try to persuade themselves that what they
do is sufficiently fine to justify the lapses they
commit in doing it, and to bring out their account
on the credit side ; but that's a delusive consola-
tion mostly. Why should we pretend that our

work is especially congenial, or inspiring, or grand
in its results ?   Making books and magazines and
newspapers ranks a little higher than raising cab-
bages, and much lower than speculating in real
estate or watering stocks.   We haven't the ability
for these more useful avocations, you see, and we
must expect to be looked down upon accordingly.
It's a grind, and humble at that ; but it keeps our
heads above water, and allows us to feel that we're
not absolutely cumberers of the ground.   Ask any
salaried man what is the most satisfactory element
of his position, and if he's honest he'll say the
monthly checks.   Not that the noble mind can
respect base lucre ; but so quaintly obnoxious are
the arrangements of this planet, the noble mind
can't continue to occupy its present tenement
without the assistance of cash."

"That's what I've been telling Grafton these
ten years," said I, seeing that our entertainer
paused ; "but he wouldn't believe it."

"And that's why I prefer the Old Testament
times," he asserted; "the earlier ones, I mean,
before mints were invented."

"Grafton's doing fairly now," said Mr. Prance,
"though with one or two wrong turnings he might
easily have joined the ignoble army of martyrs
who are never canonized, because they suffer in
nobody's cause.   As it is, I suppose he and I
ought to be thankful that we are privileged to
show some small fruits of our education, and in a

not flagrantly dishonest way to earn our mutton and occasional beer. Yes, Louie " — the girl had left the room, and now returned with several pint bottles, flanked by crackers and cheese — "it was time for that. And when we think that there are fellows just as good as we who can't afford these unassuming delicacies, who go to bed hungry and get up tired with seeking places they can't find — "

The old man came to a stop in the middle of his sentence, and Dick exclaimed, " You can't get a devotional exercise out of that, can you? It doesn't make me feel any better to think that others are worse off than I."

Louise answered him reproachfully. " Don't you see that he's worrying because he can't invite them all to supper, and find good places for them to-morrow? He would if he could. You ought to have known that."

" So I ought," said Dick, penitently. " Thank you, Miss Louise."

" I don't keep an intelligence office," her father retorted. " You thought I was hard on the would-be authors, Grafton; but my hands were full just then with your case, which seemed to be the duty that lay nearest; and I've cudgelled my brains over them longer than you have. I don't like the system; it's not merely that of our shop, but of the universe. But what the devil can I do? — There's a nickel to put in the

church plate, Louie. It's my fine for using cuss-
words," he explained to us.

"But you owe me another, papa," the girl
urged; "you're very bad to-night."

"So I do; it's the demoralizing atmosphere
of these young men. Here's a dime then; take
it and be quiet. Grafton, you may possibly have
heard, or suspected from your own observation,
that the world as a corporation is soulless. It
has a hardening influence on us who live in it,
and bears heavily on those who don't get on in
it — the lower stratum, a few feet beneath us.
Ah, bah, we say; he's out, let him stay out:
he has nothing, therefore he deserves nothing,
can do nothing, and is good for nothing. That
is liable to be like most snap-judgments. He
may be a good workman but a poor salesman;
he may have skill to raise fine pigs, but none
to get them to market. People are starving or
cutting their throats every other week who can
converse in six languages, calculate an eclipse,
and explain exhaustively the true inwardness of
the Thusandso. They go out of life because
they can't find any room in it; they take their
learning along because it seems to be of no use
here, and possibly it may be in some other planet.
Once they had a place, very likely, which gave
them bread and cheese, and perhaps a little *vin
ordinaire* and the plaudits of a limited community;
but they slipped out of it, and never slipped into

anything else. They had plenty of knowledge, but they couldn't apply it so as to turn it into power; they couldn't bring themselves to bear, because that branch was not attended to when they were laying in supplies. What should be done with these folks? Obviously one of two things : either get up wars and plagues as of old, and decently kill off enough to make room for them and thus avoid scandal, or set up bureaus for the Training and Utilizing of Intelligence, and so put them at their proper work. You might write a prize essay on that topic some time, Grafton. When philanthropy grows tired of its murderers and burglars, perhaps it will think of these people."

"But," said I, "don't you believe most of 'em are no account ?"

"Just so," Dick added ; "naturally, being ' the world's poor routed leavings.' "

"Not necessarily," Mr. Prance replied ; "not all. Some of them could pick oakum neatly after a little practice ; others would make very fair bartenders or district school teachers ; and some, no doubt, could govern an empire almost as well as the Czar or Queen Victoria. But they have no luck, that is, they don't understand the arts of trade and advertising ; they never attended Shyster and Grab's Commercial Academy — that is their difficulty. It was awfully stupid of them, or of their parents, who should have known that pipelaying, and wirepulling, and trumpetblowing, and making yourself solid in several quarters, and commanding various channels of usefulness, are the most important accomplishments man can possess, more so even than the rule of three and signing your name. O, confound it all!—Louie, you'll break me at this rate : you ought to go to bed."

"I'll let you off this time, papa dear," said the girl, who was listening with shining eyes. "You've told us all about the account with Mrs. Grundy, and it's very interesting. Now tell us about the other, please: or was this last part of it? Didn't you get them mixed a little?"

"Perhaps I did, my child, though it's against my own rule and all rules ; to do so is highly improper. Of the other account the less said the better; talking about it doesn't help to keep it straight, nor pottering much over it either. I've known men to have a good balance there without suspecting it ; and I've known lots to overdraw and go smash when they thought they'd been laying up wealth — though failures of this kind mostly make no noise. With these it was talk ; their banking was in word and name, not in deed and in truth. Judging by to-night, my place is among the goats, for 'gabble's the short road to ruin.'"

When we were in the street, Dick asked, "What do you think of him?" I said he ought to have been a preacher. "He is, but his best preaching is done at home. Down town they choose his texts, and limit him as to time; up here it's spontaneous."

"He's all right," I said, "and I'm content to leave you in his hands; but another question is, what do you think of his daughter?"

Dick flushed in his idiotic fashion, and replied, "We are quite brother and sister. As you can see for yourself, she is a child, inexperienced, ingenuous, loyal, and devoted to her father."

"And disposed to be devoted to you too, eh?" I rashly added. "If you don't look out, old man, you'll —"

I stopped, for he turned on me savagely. "Condemnation," he said (or something worse), and his violence shocked me. "I don't want to be rough on you, Bob, but you surely have sense enough to know that you ought not to say such things. The privileges of friendship have their limits, and I want you to understand that these people are my friends too. How would you like it if I were to speak in that way of your sister?"

It did not strike me that I should mind it much, for in those days Jane and I were not on the closest terms; besides, the cases were not parallel. When a young fellow talks about a strange girl as his sister, that means something else; but Grafton always was a cross between an early Christian and a government mule, and I could not manage him at all. Still, I wished he would go less to Prance's and much oftener to De Grout's, where he was just as welcome; but, as you have already seen, that affair came to nothing, through his pigheaded pride.

CHAPTER XXXIX.

MISFORTUNES COME DOUBLE.

ABOUT a year after this, and during Dick's second winter in the metropolis, he saw his senior's desk vacant one day, and toward noon was called into the inner office by Mr. Perkins. "Mr. Grafton, I am pained to say that Mr. Prance has had a slight paralytic stroke. There is no immediate danger, as I gather from the message, but he cannot be here for a week or two at least. You will have to take his work, as far as possible. You know him well, I think? Then see him to-day, and get his instructions."

He found the veteran tranquil and entirely himself. The daughter, as women will, had risen to meet sudden calamity : she hovered about the bed, jealous even of this intruder, and had to be ordered away. "Go and take a rest, my dear," the patient said. "No, it wont hurt me to talk ; the doctor said so. — Well, Dick, pride must have a fall ; I've not been on my back in the daytime for ten years or more, and now I'm paying up for

long exemption.   It's a bore, but we can't help it.
You're to take my work at the shop?   So I hinted
to Perkins: you may as well have my place if I
don't get back.   What, the *Battle-Axe* too?   Do
you think you can do both?   I fear it'll be too
much for you."

"My dear sir, at twenty-eight I ought to be able
to carry what you do at twice that.   Of course I
haven't your skill, but you've been training me,
and if they will let me try —"

"It's merely the facility of long practice, my
boy; your brains are full as good as mine.   But I
don't want you to overtax nature, and break down
before your time.   Well, try if you must."

He did try, and succeeded; though he omitted
to state that his temoprary arrangements with
the *Battle-Axe* had been made before seeing Mr.
Prance.   By stinting sleep, by eating his breakfast
on the cars and carrying lunch in his pocket, by
staying down town till eight or nine P.M., he was
able to give daily reports and care to his friend,
whose habits made sleep before midnight impossible.

This went on for a week; the invalid did not
mend, and the doctor spoke dubiously.   "Dick,"
said the veteran one evening, "I shall not get out
of this: it's borne in upon me somehow.   Another stroke is coming, and that will end it; at
least I hope so, for I can't afford to be an uncon-
scionable time dying, like Charles Second.   Of

course some cases hang fire for a year or two, but
that would swallow up all my savings, and be an
indecent extravagance. I'm not used to idleness,
and I've no desire to become a burden and 'a
driveller and a show.' If I have anything to say
about it, I'll go as soon as it's clear — to others, I
mean — that I can't get well. There's nothing to
regret in going, except Louise. Poor child, it will
be a blow to her ; she doesn't understand yet."

Whether Dick was prepared for this or not, he
spoke up on the instant. "I will take care of
her, if she will let me. O yes," — for he noticed
a curious look on the sick man's face, — "I've
intended for some time to speak to you about this
— later, after I got a little further on. As things
are, it's best to say so now."

"Have you spoken to her about it?" the parent
inquired.

Dick had some very oldfashioned ideas. "Of
course not. I couldn't, you know, till I had told
you. But she's pretty well used to me, and shows
no strong dislike for me personally, and so —"

"And so you feel bound to step into my place
here, as well as at the shop and the office?" He
spoke irritably, a thing unusual. "That's quite
another matter. I wouldn't mind letting you do
my work for a week or two, and reaping the benefit, if I were going to get up and take it again ;
but I don't propose to tie a millstone round your
neck for life. A girl and a boy can be on friendly

terms without his being under obligation to marry
her.   Louie's a good child, and all that, but I
don't see what the deuce the fact is to you ; you're
not in a position to go into sentiment.   If you
have no understanding with her, you're in no way
bound to sacrifice yourself, and I don't propose to
have it."

"Mr. Prance," said Dick coolly, "certainly I
haven't much to offer, but if I keep on with your
work I'll make what you've been earning, or near
it.   Have you any objection to my family, or
habits, or character?"

"That's not the point.   Not to your family anyway, as it's comprised in yourself.   There are no
relatives to object to the proposed alliance, and
that's about the only thing to be said in its favor.
Keep still now ; can't you see I'm talking in your
interest ?   You've taken up this quixotic notion of
immolating yourself for your friends, that I may
say, ' Bless you, my children,' and go off the stage
with an easy mind.   It's not necessary, Dick, and
I can't take advantage of your unprotected youth.
The Prances were somebody once as well as the
Graftons, and they still cling to the rags of self-
respect.   My girl is not an object of charity yet ;
she'll have a thousand or two — provided I retire
without any foolish delays — and six thousand of
life insurance ; and she can have a home at the
farm in New Hampshire.   They are good people
and fond of her, and she likes it well enough
there."

"Still, if she prefers to stay here with me, you ought to let her. She's nearly of age now, and I mean to give her the choice."

"It's a poor idea, Grafton; it will be a bad thing for both of you. If you could live in the country I might not object so much, but you know you can't, any more than I could, with this night work. It's an incessant, everlasting grind; a demnition grind, as the prophet Mantalini expressed it — or if it wasn't he I don't know who it was : my memory is going, I believe. It's folly, at your age and in your situation, to think of marrying. Your wife will be no better off than you, remember ; and when children come, it will be worse for both of you. You read Malthus before you move in this. Haven't I been through it all ? It has broken me down at fifty-six, and you'll repeat the tale, and not last so long. Being what you are, you'll have bound yourself to do what you can't ; every day you will feel that those nearest you have rights which you can't supply. You'll be down with them in a bearpit, with just a glimpse of sun and sky, climbing your pole for no more return than daily food. You know only what this treadmill is for one : what right have you to condemn another to it ? Tell me that."

"I simply keep her where I found her, Mr. Prance. I wish I had five thousand a year and the old place to give her ; as I haven't, would I stand in the way if better things were in her reach? I come between her and desolation: if she has other resources, if she thinks differently, well and good. As you say, it's not for me to put this thing on grounds of sentiment — not just here and now ; nor is it for you and me to settle the matter. We'll leave that to her."

" You'll have your way of course, and I suppose I know how it will end, for she likes you, and she's seen nobody else. If I saw any way out of this infernal round for you, it would be right enough. I only hope you'll not have to curse the fate you entail on others, as I've done — not out loud, to be sure. You're a fine lad, Dick, and I hate to think that I and mine are taking a mean advantage of you. Poor girl, she's as innocent as a babe about these things, and as for me, my help-lessness and not my will consents. If I were on my feet and doing my stint, you'd put this off awhile at least. I can't wish you luck, my boy, for I see no luck in it: you and I are not the lucky kind."

Grafton cared little for opposition, once the way was clear to his unworldly mind; like Jim Bludso, when he saw his duty, a dead-sure thing, he went for it there and then. He had less difficulty with the daughter; her only idea of finance was to make the few dollars that came into her hands go as far as might be, and the thought of being a burden to any one never entered her head. She had been indispensable to her father, or so she imagined, and Dick was the next man in the world to her father — in fact, there were no others deserving mention. If she had been offered a queen's position and income to leave these two, she would have rejected it with disdain; but no such temptation had come her way, or was likely to. Her mind was simple and direct, and she had been very imperfectly taught, having no mother to tell her how things are done in society. She had read that young men were in the habit of marrying young women, and saw no impropriety in Grafton's entertaining views of this nature concerning herself; but before she could understand the need for speedy action in the premises, her father's condition had to be explained to her. Then she gave way for a moment, but presently remembered that filial love must find its expression now in fortitude. For the rest, it is the nature of the vine to cling, and when the parent oak is shattered by the tempest, it is well if there be a vigorous young tree at hand to take its place. Not that she thought of this — questions of self-interest were not in her way; but Dick knew it, and assumed his new part with courage.

He had the manliness to come to me, few as were his hours of leisure then, and tell me what had occurred. "I don't expect your approval, Bob," he said, frankly, "but it's only fair that you should know what I mean to do."

I knew that he could not be shaken, but the

bride-elect was not fond of me, and self-respect required that I should put myself on record; politely of course, and with due consideration for his feelings, but still unmistakably. "Well, Grafton," I said, "I've got nothing to say against the girl, but —"

"No," he interrupted; "not at this time of day, I should judge." There was a warning gleam in his eye which was wholly uncalled for.

"Still, I had other views for you, and I quite agree with Mr. Prance." I had made him tell me the whole story, and he had not the skill or prudence to conceal that wise man's objections. "You are going into this thing simply from a quixotic sense of honor and generosity, and, so far as I see, the sacrifice on your part is entirely unnecessary. It's not your funeral —"

He again broke in upon my discourse, and in an unpleasantly sarcastic tone. "It will soon be the funeral of my best friend: would you advise me to drop the acquaintance of the family just at this time?"

"Not that," I replied with dignity, "but there are intermediate stages between dropping and marrying them. The latter, I repeat, is a needless sacrifice."

"Sacrifice!" he cried. "Why will you make me out a martyr? I told you long ago that I was as selfish as other men. To say the truth, Bob, it's a damnably lonesome and aimless life;

and I don't believe a man is good for much so
long as he has only himself to care for. Friends
are all very well in their way, but it's not good
for man to be alone, as you used to remind me.
I'm not as callous and independent as I once was;
time seems to take the stiffening out of a man,
and give him a sneaking desire for sympathy and
ties of his own. You can't blame me, for you set
the example." He was plainly conscious of the
gross imprudence of his course.

"O, if you put it on that ground : though you
talked differently not many months ago." I alluded to a conversation which you will find recorded in Chapter X X I X. But I spared him
any further reference to that episode, and went
on with well-deserved irony. "Of course there
were no other women in New York, at least
within your reach ; and as it was impossible for
you to form a union which would promote your
prospects in life — " I paused there : such a
pause is sometimes more impressive than the
completion of your sentence.

He disregarded the innuendo, and said quietly,
"I understand your point of view : we've discussed these topics before in a general way, and
must agree to differ. Well, old man, you can cut
me if you like : it will come to much the same
thing, as I shall be more closely occupied than
ever, and have no time to leave my work." He
looked me in the eye, and we both felt that more

was meant than the words expressed. "I don't blame you : we'll part friends at any rate."

He held out his hand : I took it, and in that moment our hearts went out to each other, and knew that I could forgive him even this. "Let me know when it's to be, and I'll come if you want me," I said in low and agitated tones. A man of my temperament can be almost unpardonably foolish where the comrades of his youth are concerned, and I never professed — except now and then for some particular purpose — to be a sage.

CHAPTER XL.

DEATH AND MATRIMONY.

GRAFTON's courtship, I imagine, was a prosaic and melancholy one; the circumstances afforded little room or reason for any other. The wedding was quiet, not to say sombre; the unhappy pair took no trip, and the groom left his duties for but an hour or two that day, for he knew a longer absence would be required soon. Mr. Prance was failing: Dick told me of one deliverance of his as the end approached.

"No, I can get through this without a minister," the sick man said: "you'll have to call one in shortly, and it's not fair to ask too much of him, for I'm not a valuable parishioner. You'll do for a confessor, if any last words are required. I'm quite content to leave this vale of tears, dear boy: as your friend Marcus says, why should one desire a longer stay, things being as they are? Yes, the accommodations and arrangements are far from perfect; if asked, I really could not recommend the Globe Hotel. Do you know, I

have an idea they do things better at the opposition house. It's erratic, I admit; if it's imbecile,
kindly credit the weakness to my failing powers ;
but I believe there's something beyond — I do,
indeed. If there isn't, this business of existence
is a put-up job, a most disreputable swindle ;
and that, you see, is what some call unthinkable
— at least one would rather not think it. No,
I fancy the Demiurge's reign is limited to this
mundane sphere. Excellent people, those Gnos-
tics, though ahead of their time ; they devised
the only plausible explanation of this planet. Put
your head nearer, Dick, and let me ‘ whisper :
don't tell anybody, but I believe the Man of
Nazareth was not altogether mistaken. Curious
instinct, isn't it, to print all His titles in capitals ?
Curious, but sound. So far as we know, He
never did any editing, or even writing, except
with His finger in the dust, so that it couldn't
be preserved — fine, strong idea that : but I believe He would understand. You think I'm
wandering ? Well, maybe I am. A little further,
and I'll wander over the edge and take the plunge,
and then perhaps I'll be in the way to know more
about it."

　　At the funeral I chanced to be put in a carriage
with Mr. Leaf. " I am not what is called a
religious man," said he, " nor was our friend ; but
to me he represented the Power that made him.
John is my favorite author, not James ; but James

has a noble word about those being happy who
endure. Yes, we are following to the grave an
athlete, crowned at last and victorious. When
stripped bare and smitten to earth, he never
whined, but rose and girded himself, and went
soberly about his humble duties. He disdained
the success that comes by puffery and lying : it
strengthens my soul to think how that man ab-
horred a lie. How brave he was, and how gentle !
His fine spirit revolted against its bonds, and
he loved to deride himself and his work ; but
many have been the better for him and none
the worse. If his light was not set on a hill,
nor in any lofty candlestick, the blame was not
his. When the city turned its back on him, he
drew apart into himself, and there lived, a modern
hermit, in patience and purity. Had he been a
Voltairean, he had reason and excuse ; but amid
all the doubts that life forced upon him he retained faith enough to stand erect and be a man.
His keen analysis went to the root of things, and
severed the perishable from the permanent ; so
much, the husk, the routine, for bread and a roof,
in necessary deference to the powers that rule
here and now ; but the inner part, the self, was
not for sale, but kept unmarred for better use
in the hereafter. Under that accursed system
he was held down, hidden, chained as a galley-
slave to his oar : now he is freed, enlarged. Few
knew him here ; but the Master Artist arranges

His figures and spreads His colors on a plan of His own, and those of whom the world was not worthy shall shine as the brightness of the firmament. For such as he are the palm branches, the reward and the repose." The old painter turned his head aside and drew out his handkerchief: he was not thinking whether I listened and understood or not.

I was careful not to ask the De Grouts what they thought of Dick's marriage; but as soon as it was decent to do so, Edith induced her mother to countenance her in a call on the mourning bride. They wore their plainest clothes and left their carriage around the corner; but even so, their presence must have caused some astonishment, and the meeting could hardly be enjoyable on either side. No doubt they were gracious, and Mrs. Grafton, if otherwise placed, would have borne sufficient signs of birth and breeding; but she shared her husband's views as to keeping in their own sphere. Her bereavement afforded a sufficient excuse for not returning the visit till it and her existence might be supposed to be alike forgotten.

We all thought better of the poor young couple for taking this stand; it avoided trouble. What is the use of mincing matters, or pretending that things are otherwise than as they are? As Mr. Prance used to say, the solid concrete, and not the airy abstract, makes the best pavement to walk on. A man can go anywhere, after dark at least, but ladies of established position have no business in that part of East Sixteenth Street — it is too incongruous. I am not responsible for these social arrangements, and they may be open to criticism in some of their details or applications, but any one can see that in the main they are reasonable and inevitable. No one cares where a bachelor sleeps; so long as he dresses properly and behaves himself, there is nothing in our usages to prevent his being welcome anywhere; but in marrying a poor girl he simply ties a millstone round his neck, as Grafton's father-in-law had fairly warned him. His respectable friends cannot recognize her without grave risk of embarrassing complications; if they push philanthropy so far as to call, they are out of place, and if she attempts to respond, she feels much more so. She has no fit rooms to receive company; she probably has no cards, they are not needed in her way of life; and — really it is needless to pursue such an unpleasant subject. As I have said, the Graftons quite understood all this; but Dick's absurd mistake was in supposing that he was under the ban before marriage, and obliged to perpetuate his impoverished condition instead of escaping from it. I had endeavored fifty times to expose this fallacy, but it was useless.

I never entirely abandoned him, I am proud to say, but no great encouragement was offered on his side to continued intimacy. When he had been married about fifteen months, a new incumbrance arrived; they always do with such people, I believe. Not long after this I met him on the street; he was looking worn and jaded.

"Old man," I said, "we never see you now."

"Too much to do," he answered, "business is brisk, and I work like a drayhorse."

"Well," said I, "you'll come along now and have some lunch;" and I took him into Zweikopf's.

"This hock is good," he admitted; "I haven't tasted any in ages."

"Dick, you're running it too hard. You should take a vacation."

"How can I, when it would increase the outlay and stop the supplies? Two thousand is less for me here than six hundred was in Tackville and Miletus. You used to want me to be up and doing, and I'm at it now; I can't stop for a week, or even a day off."

"But can't you branch out? With your brains, which ought to be growing all the time; you might do something original, and get higher pay."

"There's no time to think of anything original. The regular routine sucks your brains dry, and takes all ambition out of you. I suppose that's what Mr. Prance meant by his early warnings."

After a pause he went on. " Bob, do you remember Tennyson's prince who had 'weird seizures'
now and then, and 'seemed to move among a
world of ghosts, and feel himself the shadow of a
dream'? That has been my normal state since I
can remember, though not always equally. You,
and this table, and these oysters, and my desk in
Lore Street, and what I write, and all the rest of
it, pass before me like a poor play badly acted. I
am a part of it all, but I'm hardly real to myself;
when anything happens, good or bad, the first
thought that rises is, It doesn't matter; this is but
a form to be gone through with, a series of images
passing before the eye, a waking vision, a third-
class puppet-show. The solidest part of it is
home and the ties there; that's something to work
for, something to fall back on. I used to feel as
if I could drop out of life from sheer lack of any
interest in it; I had no hold, no purchase; but
wife and child give one a sort of anchorage, as I
once fancied the old place might have done. I
believe Mrs. Prance, dead twenty years, was nearer
and more authentic to her husband than the things
around him."

Some, hearing Grafton talk thus, would have
questioned his sanity; but I knew it was merely
his old disease of impracticable idealism. He always
preferred trains of thought that led nowhere, or
straight away from utility and common sense.
After this, I had small hopes of him.

CHAPTER XLI.

GREAT NEWS.

It is time this tiresome tale was ended. A flat, lustreless, dismal chronicle it is, and my spirits sink as I try to make the best of it; for I give you my word that I have selected the least undramatic episodes of Grafton's life, and such of the conversational encounters he engaged in as would best bear repeating. When a man has no money and no faculty of making any, there cannot be much that is cheerful to say about him; but his unwise architecture may serve as a useful lesson to more fortunate builders, and the principal end of literature, I take it, is the moral instruction of youth. The ending of the narrative will surprise you, as it did me: it is not at all in keeping with what goes before — there is no sort of fitness, or coherence, or even poetical justice; but I cannot help that.

It was a blustrous morning in March, and the subject of this history had been grappling with domestic cares for full two years. I sat in my place on Water street, looking over market reports, when Clinton De Grout rushed in. He was growing portly now, and free in his language: he had recently set up an establishment of his own, having loved both wisely and well. "Zeuxis and Apelles," he cried; at least I substitute these harmless names for the ones which he mentioned. He sank into an arm-chair, and I would not be willing to show myself in such a blown and breathless state. "Have you heard this about Grafton?"

"No; what?" I asked, starting anxiously to my feet: "is his wife dead?"

"Get out," he replied with too little urbanity. "What the demon would she want to die for? Has she done anything to you? She's all right. But I only just heard —" And he told me what it was.

"Great Cæsar," I said, for I wished to show the loose youth that a gentleman can be emphatic without profanity; "is this a sure thing?"

"I don't know; I hope so. Let's go round and see."

We went, and found our friend in his quiet corner at Lybert's, seemingly employed as usual. "Old horse," Clinton began, "we've come to congratulate you."

"Yes," I added, "provided the story's true. We want the particulars first."

"What story?" he asked. "Let us have no misunderstanding now: I don't wish to obtain congratulations on false pretences. We'd better get at the alleged facts in order. You claim —"

"That's what we're after," I said. "Somebody told Clint that you had come into a big fortune."

"O no," Dick corrected; "merely a decent competence."

"Thunder," Clinton observed. "Why, they said it was a solid million."

"It's more, as I understand; but you don't call that a big fortune, do you?"

We both stared at him. "You're a pretty blanked cool hand, you are," said my companion.

"There's nothing to be hot about," Grafton replied, "but there will be presently, if you shout so. This isn't a football ground. We don't allow dime novels in this establishment, nor noise, nor bad language; if you try to demoralize our young clerks, Lybert & Co. will be about your ears. Wait two minutes, will you?" He gave some directions to a subordinate, who listened with marked deference. "Now let's go out to lunch; it's early, but you can get up an appetite in honor of this reunion. Bob, you choose the place, and Clint, you can select the dishes — you're what Mrs. Gauche calls an ipecac; but it's my spread. First time I've had the honor, but I trust not the last."

"I must say, Dick," I remarked as soon as I could get in a word edgeways, "your ideas have

gone up several pegs. To talk so irreverently of
a million —"

"My ideas are just where they always were,"
he answered, "though my tax-rate will go up, I
suppose."

"Don't you see," Clinton put in, "he's posing
for the ancient sage, no more elated by prosperity
than cast down by t'other thing? You couldn't
expect any less of him. Well, bully boy, you've
kept a stiff upper lip in the shade, and now you
can enjoy the shine — but don't be too dashed
philosophic about it."

We found an upstairs room in a high-class hash-
ery, and secured the sole tenancy of it for an hour.
"Now, Dick," I said, "tell us the whole story. Is
it true that old uncle of yours has turned up at
last?"

"He's turned up defunct, and it would not be
the correct thing for me to say that no action of
his life became him like the leaving it; but between us, I suspect he was a hard case. He left
home, you know, when I was a baby, and we
thought his career was soon ended; but it seems
he drifted to the Pacific slope, went through various queer adventures, and under a false name
amassed all this money. He never was much of a
Grafton, in that or anything else; but being un-
married, and sick for some months, he disclosed
himself to a lawyer out there, set on foot inquiries
about the family, and made his will in my favor.

I was his only relative and natural heir, and I might feel more obliged to him if he had taken these steps some years ago."

"Then," said I, "you can buy back the old place, after all?"

"I should do so in any case, but he has expressed a desire to that effect, which carries the force of a command. Natural feeling, or I might say conscience, awoke in him toward the end and better late than never."

A shadow came over his face as he thought of the years of needless narrowness and gloom. I hastened to cheer him up. "But I say, old man, with your high and mighty notions you couldn't have taken help from him while he was alive, you know."

"You forget my patriarchal views, and our Maryland prejudice in behalf of family ties, Bob. As my father's brother and head of the house, he had a right to restore its fortunes and to direct my life, if he had chosen to take the trouble." I could see that he felt more aggrieved by that silence of near thirty years than gratified by his sudden inheritance.

Young De Grout, who was looking rather sour and pugnacious, now asked, "When did you get all this fine news, Monte Christo? It sounds as as if you'd been in correspondence with your lawyer since New Year's."

"O no; he wrote at length, and I got it only

yesterday, with authority to draw on him to any extent through a bank here; he'd satisfied himself about me some time ago, it appears. I would have sent you word, or looked you up, presently — both of you. Did you suppose I wanted to keep it to myself? I've had no time to turn round yet, till I made this sacrifice to friendship.

" And now you'll cut Lybert & Co., of course?"

"As soon as I can get things straight — in a month or so. They've done the fair thing by me, and I can't leave them in the lurch. I've got a young man in training for my place, and another at the *Battle-Axe.* There's no such violent hurry."

" And then, what are your plans?"

"We'll go to California and look after the property; curious, my having property to look after, isn't it? Beyond that, we'll see. *Sat die bonum suum.*"

"You'll want to stop at Tackville on the way," I suggested. "But how about securing the Manor?"

" I wrote last night: I may have to go there soon. And I might stop to shake hands with Mrs. Claybank and Major Way and Rustler, but that it would look like flaunting; the natives would think I thought myself a better man than I was in the old days, and had come to show off. I judge my wife will be content to take Tackville and Miletus at second hand."

Here a sudden thought struck me; connubial relations must be duly respected. "Dick, can I go up and call on Mrs. Grafton?"

"Why not? She'll be glad to see you, of course. It's no longer necessary to keep our friends at arm's length, thank Heaven."

"It never was necessary," Clinton exclaimed in his uproarious way; "that was your dashed pharisaism, thinking that folks who chanced to have a little more cash than you couldn't be fit to associate with. By Jove, Grafton, if you're going to acknowledge me as a friend simply because you've come into this bonanza, you may spare yourself the trouble. I can speak for sis and the old people, too; we're no more your friends now than we've been all this time, only you wouldn't let us show it."

"My dear boy," said Dick with a very sweet smile, "I'm quite aware of it. Having made allowances for my confounded position and pardoned my enforced rudeness through these four years, you needn't quarrel with me now. I was tied hand and foot, with results that no one can appreciate who hasn't been disgustingly and ludicrously poor. I'm free now, and one of the chief pleasures of emancipation is that it will enable me to show my respect and regard for your family." He made his grandest bow, and held up a bumper of Pommery. "Permit me to drink their health, and yours." We responded in silence, and the past was as if it had not been.

"Well, Dick," I presently remarked, "this new deal suits me first rate, though it puts you well above me in the social scale, so that I'll not be justified in giving you any more advice. But, if I may criticise, I should have expected something more original from you. California uncles are commonplace."

He hardly listened to this observation, the playful character of which was intended to rouse him to a frame of mind befitting the festive occasion. "Had it been left to me, I should have arranged it differently, as I've hinted. For myself it doesn't matter, but my wife has never been able to get about as I should like, or to indulge her taste in bonnets. She's young yet, however, and this comes in time for the children."

"The children?" Clinton exclaimed, with the thoughtless roughness of a man whose domestic experience is but just begun. "What the — O yes, I see; I beg pardon. Of course," and he laughed awkwardly.

"It doesn't matter, Dick," I said soothingly; "you can afford such things now."

A virginal blush mounted to his brow. "Well, you see it's best to have more than one, in case of accidents — when there is anything to inherit."

I understood his feelings perfectly: he could not at once break from the old sense of being

bound to apologize for any imprudence to friends
who might possibly (though not by his volition)
in one way or another have to pay the bill; and he
had got a little mixed, as the brightest intellects
will at times, for the excuse he offered applied
only to his newly arrived condition, which removed the necessity of any.

We parted from De Grout, and walked back
toward Lore Street. "I didn't care to say it before
Clinton," Dick went on, "but this takes a dreadful load from my mind. Now I can get out of the
treadmill, and do as I please. If only Mr. Prance
had lived to see this! You've always taken vaca-
tions when you liked, Bob, and been free to go
and come, so you can't understand what it is to
be my own man." He raised himself to his full
height, and shook off as it were a stoop which his
shoulders had contracted of late.

"Yes," I said, "now you can work in your own
way, and think about making a position and a
name." This I said, thinking to chime in with his
views in the way of literary ambition; but it did
not seem to please him.

"The Grafton name is good enough for me, now
that it no longer covers a beggar. I don't care
for your positions, old man, and the work may go
hang. I want to get away from it all, and look at
life dispassionately from outside, as I've not been
able to do since I was a boy. And I want to see
something of my wife, and give her open air and

sunshine: she's been shut up in a vault so far, poor child. Then my boy — or my boys, perhaps — must grow up in a very different atmosphere from what their parents have been breathing. The thing for us is to wander about, and have the Manor to fall back on when we're tired of travelling — for one must have the home feeling, you know — and come to a hotel here in the fall. Yes, I think a week or two in the year will be enough for New York."

"That's a pretty good program, Dick, except that we shall see too little of you. But I should think you'd want to write some books and things — by and by, after you've rested a bit. You'll have a vantage-ground now, and I presume Lybert would be glad to publish 'em."

"Not now, thank you, and probably never. What have I to say to the world? Simply that I am bored and that it is a humbug. Let me get off to the woods and waters and rehabilitate. I'm sick of ink and paper : I can buy all the literature I'll want for months to come of the trainboys and at the news-stands."

I was received with unprecedented cordiality in East Sixteenth Street, and spent a most agreeable hour. "Do you know," Mrs. Grafton said — she had caught certain tricks of speech from her father and her husband — "that I've had a weight on my conscience all this time? When I married, I was

so young, and so ignorant of practical things, it
never occurred to me that I was coming between
Dick and his friends, and might be spoiling his
life. I suppose you thought me dreadfully selfish
and unprincipled and designing, now didn't you?
— though, goodness knows, he was no great catch
then, and I never dreamed of such luck as this.
I've thought a great deal since, and it seems
incredible I should have been so stupid; but it
seemed perfectly natural and right then, and he's
so firm and positive that if I had resisted it would
have been of no use, probably. But when I realized that I had cut him off from his friends, I
knew that wasn't right, and it troubled me. They
couldn't come here — O, I know you tried, but
you didn't feel comfortable, and what was the
use? It was my fault, and I felt very badly about
it; but he wouldn't go anywhere without me, and
— he's so patient, you know. It doesn't matter
about me, but O, I'm so glad for his sake that
he's come to his own! I speak to you as his
oldest friend, and I want you to know that he
was never ungrateful or disloyal — it isn't in him
to be that. And I want his friends to share in
our joy over his good fortune. You understand,
don't you?"

"That's all right," I hastened to assure her, and
explained that De Grout and myself had been
with Dick but two hours before. In my secret
heart I was much indebted to her for thus tak-

ing the whole responsibility for any coolness or estrangement that might have appeared to exist. These terms are too strong, for I had carefully avoided any breach between us; but when a stock goes up suddenly and violently like this, you feel remorseful for not having invested in it more heavily while it was down. "You don't mean to stay here, of course," I asked somewhat anxiously.

"No," she replied. "Dick wants to stay till we leave the city, and it's the only home I can remember, but I will not keep him any longer from his true position. Of course we will keep the books and pictures and furniture — all that was my father's; they can be stored till we are ready to send them to the Manor." The pride with which she said 'the Manor,' as if she had also been born and bred there, was touching; I remembered that the Prances too had been Somebody once, and now their solitary remnant was coming to her own as well as the last Grafton. "I want to go there, if it is possible, before we start for California. We will make our home there, you know; that is the place for his boy to grow up in. But meanwhile we shall go to a hotel just as soon as I can persuade Dick to it. O yes, you can trust me for that," she added confidently, "and he will let you know as soon as we move."

I renewed my congratulations on the windfall. "Dick says he cares for it chiefly on your account.

He wants you to see people, and things, and places."

"Yes, that is his view," she said very brightly; "he so is unselfish. It will be a great change, of course, and no doubt I shall enjoy it; but I don't care very much about meeting people. I have always been contented, and a wife lives for her husband. I am glad because he will be free now, and not have to work so hard all day and most of the evening, but be able to follow his own tastes. You know," she said with brave simplicity, "he is a very able man. My father often said he had too fine an intellect to be chained to mere drudgery at the desk. I didn't understand it then, a girl takes things so for granted; but I've often thought since, that poor father never escaped that drudgery himself, and feared Dick never would. And now I thank God that he has escaped it before his mind was stunted, and his spirits broken, and his youth and health entirely gone. Didn't you know I would feel that way about it?" she cried, for I was looking at her in some surprise at this vehemence. "Did you suppose I would think of myself in comparison with him? Why, he is the best man in the world. *Of course* he comes first: who else should I think of?"

"Well," I said suggestively, "there's the boy."

She laughed. "O, that's entirely different. I don't suppose you could understand, being a man: one loves a child ever so much, and does every-

thing for him, but others might take an equa'
place in your heart — without your caring any less
for him, I mean." She blushed a little. "Some
mothers, you know, have several. But one's husband is separate, and nobody could ever be like
him — not possibly. O, I can't explain it; perhaps your wife can. O yes, certainly, I'm glad
that Archie will have an easier time than his
father has had ; but I mean to bring him up to be
exactly like his father."

"There's another thing," I said, "that maybe
you can effect, and nobody else can. Dick has
very fine brains, as you say, but he lacks ambition.
I want him to write a book or two, or do something to distinguish himself, and show what's in
him. We've often talked it over ; and now he has
a fine chance, but he wont hear of it — says he's
sick of ink and paper."

"Naturally," she answered ; "but he'll get over
that feeling, I think, and use his pen in a higher
way. He's so tired now, poor boy ; but I have
some ambition for him, if he hasn't. I knew you
appreciated him. Of course his mind can't be
idle, and the world ought to know him. I think I
can manage that in time."

CHAPTER XLII.

A LAME CONCLUSION.

I WENT home with my mental equilibrium somewhat disturbed (for I had always thought of Dick's wife in the light of a mistake and an incumbrance), and sought to regain a proper tone in the bosom of my family, by a relation of the day's events, omitting De Grout's improper language. The ladies of my household had seen very much less of Dick than I had, but I thought any news would gratify them.

"Well," said Clarice, when my judicious abridgment was finished, "Mr. Grafton has fallen in *my* opinion. From all you have told us about him, I should have expected him to do something striking, and this is so vulgarly flat and feeble. Rich uncles are continually dying in the West; it happens to every other carpenter and laundress."

"It never happened to us yet, dear," my wife urged. "Still, as you say, it was an ordinary thing to do; but I suppose they don't mind that, as they couldn't afford to be particular."

"Would you have had the poor man die of brain fever, and leave his widow and orphan to charity?" asked my sister Jane. "That was not unlikely to occur, I understand, if this good fortune had not come to them."

"It would be more picturesque," said Clarice, "more harmonious. I have never met him, but Robert said he was a cultivated person, and far from commonplace ; and this was such a stale and greasy thing to do. Probably the money was made in groceries."

"Let us trust not," I said. "I don't believe a Grafton would stoop to that, and Dick shares your effete antipathy to trade. More likely by gambling and murdering about the mines ; that would more nearly meet your views, Clarice. The old man was a tough customer, it is said. I urged your objection to his accepting the legacy ; but it really isn't Dick's fault that he had an uncle in California. He said he would have fixed it differently if it had been left to him ; give him credit for that."

"I presume," Clarice languidly went on, "you think the uncle ought to have died four years ago and let your friend marry Edith De Grout."

"That's just the way Robert would feel about it, of course," Jane chimed in. "Did you advise him to stop at Chicago on his way out and get a divorce, brother?"

"No," I replied calmly, for I was used to these

carpings. " His present wife is good enough for
him. In fact, my opinion of her has altered ; she's
improved wonderfully."

"In looks, do you mean ? " they all asked.

" Yes ; in looks, and manners, and intelligence,
and character. She received me most courteously,
and talked with charming frankness. There was a
delicate flush on her cheek, and a fine soft light in
her eye. Her hair was always good, for a blonde,
and she has a nice neck and shoulders, and small
hands. She wouldn't compare with any of you, of
course, but she's entirely a lady, and some might
call her almost beautiful."

" Then that accounts for it," Jane cried. " She
never was polite to Robert before, fearing, no doubt,
that he would lead her husband astray. Now they
are going off, she wants to part on friendly terms,
which is to her credit, I'm sure ; and any tolerable-
looking woman who is decently civil to him he
thinks an angel."

" Jane," I said mildly, " Mahomet must have
been acquainted with you in some pre-existent
state." My wife asked why, and I explained that
that fact would account for his excluding ladies
from the heaven of his persuasion. " If he had
met only women like you, and Clarice when she
behaves herself, and Mrs. Grafton, he would have
known better. But," I went on, " you ought to
call on her now."

" Why," said Mabel, " Jane and I were going
there long ago, and you wouldn't let us."

" She didn't want visitors in those small rooms, and you wouldn't either if you had to live in such a place, which God forbid. But now they are going to a hotel, and she'll be ready to receive. You see, the situation is totally changed. They both came of very good stock, and now they'll be where they would have been all along, if their parents had had more sense."

" So they were a prince and princess in disguise, were they ? " Clarice inquired.

" Just so ; so disguised that you never would have known them — through no particular fault of their own. But now they've come out in their proper character, and are to be respected accordingly. I want you all to remember that."

Dick and his wife had to attend sundry domestic dinings, at which she acquitted herself as creditably as if she had been brought up in society ; a certain unconventional freshness about her called forth only admiration from the men, and sympathetic no less than hostile comments from her own sex. It was interesting to see how many people now recalled Grafton's existence ; Van Snoozer and a hundred others, some of whom neither he nor I could remember. But he was cool to all except the De Grouts and my family.

" I've known you through fair weather and foul," he said, " principally the latter, and we're not going to part now. But I don't care for new acquaintances, and as for those who value a man

by his bank account, let them go to the bank and
nose it over; they and I haven't two ideas in
common." But I made him see that such rational-
ism was vulgar and levelling, and that he now had
a stake in the community, involving certain duties.

"Remember, you've got the Grafton name to
keep up," I said: "that implies an exchange of
courtesies with your peers. The money is merely
the outward and visible sign of gentility : without
the sign, you couldn't expect to be recognized;
with it, you take and keep your proper place."
He growled and grumbled, and I think hastened
his departure ; but that touch-me-not air, which
Mrs. Claybank had noticed at Tackville and Jandyke at Miletus, sat well upon him now, and a
certain hauteur, which he put on to guard against
intruders, added to his importance.

His wife came to be great friends with Edith
and her mother, and was made much of in his antique manner by the senior De Grout. "Madam,"
said he, "I knew your father well, long before
you were born ; his reverses and determined
withdrawal from society were a source of grief to
myself and others, who sought in vain to lure him
from his retirement. He was the soul of honor,
but a prouder man never lived. Your husband
is not unlike him. My dear — if you will let
me call you so — teach your children, in happy
days to come, that pride has its limits ; it is a
good armor of defence, but not a weapon to be

turned against one's friends. Your mother was one of the loveliest women of her day ; you have her eyes, her forehead. Her grandfather married a distant cousin of my own, so that I may claim you as a relative. I trust that you will not yield to the charm of California ; it is a fine country, but too new. Grafton Manor is not so far away. and next summer we rely on your spending some weeks at Oaklands."

Clinton and I, being satiated with these correct festivities, determined on a little stag party at Delmonico's on the eve of Dick's going. Mr. Lybert heard of the plan, and, somewhat to our disgust, begged to be admitted on the ground floor, a favor which we saw no way to refuse. The worthy publisher, unaccustomed to these re-laxations, became effusive, and made a tearful speech over his late employé. "A brilliant young man," he said ; "a most excellent man, an inval-uable man, whose loss to the city will be deeply and widely felt. His departure leaves an aching void in all our breasts, and most of all in mine. Gentlemen, his was the master mind to superin-tend all our periodicals. I offered him a partner-ship, sirs, which he refused, as Cæsar did the kingly crown."

"Dick," Clinton remarked as we turned home-ward, "it would appear that you're considerable pumpkins of a huckleberry, after all. Did the boss really want you in the firm ? "

"O," Dick returned lightly, "he's enlarging his business, and it would meet his views to have my uncle's cash added to the capital; but it didn't meet mine to go in. Speaking poetically, I'm not on that lay."

"I guess not," said young De Grout. "When you want to go into business, there's ours. If you'd had any leaning that way, we'd have taken you in long ago, and made a partner of you before now, and be dashed to your million. Do you know that, man of sin?"

"I don't doubt it, dear boy," said Dick.

I do not believe Grafton will ever amount to anything. He is a very good fellow, and greatly respected now, of course, and enjoying life rather more than he did of old; but he has no earnestness, no faith, no real respect for the established Order of Things. His boys will probably come to something, because they have their mother's blood in them, and are getting her training; but if Dick ever wakes from his dream, and comes into sympathy with the Cosmos, and asserts himself by taking some voluntary part in it, it will be his wife's doing.

THE END.

CUPPLES & HURD, THE ALGONQUIN PRESS, BOSTON.

Y^e Bookworme

Y^e Olde Colonial Time

Extracts from

Cupples & Hurd's List,

✳ 𝕿𝖍𝖊 𝕬𝖑𝖌𝖔𝖓𝖖𝖚𝖎𝖓 𝕻𝖗𝖊𝖘𝖘 ✳

Boston.

The Algonquin Press Library.

Pictures of American Life and Character, Past and Present.

Each complete in one volume, cr. 8vo, cloth, elegant.

I.

THE AUTOBIOGRAPHY OF A NEW ENGLAND FARM HOUSE. By N. H. Chamberlain. Illustrated. Third edition. $1.50.

A book that will take its place, on the shelves of the library, by the side of "The Vicar of Wakefield." Born and bred on Cape Cod, the author, at the winter firesides of country people very conservative of old English customs now gone, heard curious talk of kings, Puritan ministers, the war and precedent struggle of our Revolution, and touched a race of men and women now passed away. He also heard, chiefly from ancient women, the traditions of ghosts, witches, and Indians, as they are preserved, and to a degree believed, by honest Christian folk, in the very teeth of modern progress. These things are embodied in this book.

II.

THE SPHINX IN AUBREY PARISH. By N. H. Chamberlain. Illustrated. $1.50.

The instantaneous popularity of "A New England Farm House," the author's first venture in the field of fiction (which has been read and re-read by all classes, with an eagerness little short of that which hailed the appearance of "Scarlet Letter" a generation ago), has led the publishers to induce Mr. Chamberlain to consent to a companion volume. Wholly distinct from that first book in its plot, scenery, and location, it will be found as interesting, and equally as strong in its animation and sustained energy of action.

III.

OLD NEW ENGLAND DAYS: A Story of True Life. By Sophie M. Damon. Illustrated. Fourth edition. $1.25.

IV.

AUNT PEN'S AMERICAN NIECES AT BLEDISLOE. By Ada M. Trotter. Illustrated. Second Edition. $1.50.

V.

AROUND THE GOLDEN DEEP. A Romance of the Sierras. By A. P. Reeder. $1.50.

VI.

CLEOPATRA'S DAUGHTER. A Romance of a branch of Roses. *[In press.*

VII.

AN ALIEN FROM THE COMMONWEALTH. The Romance of an odd young man. *[In press.*

VIII.

A WINTER EVENING'S TALE. A Californian Romance. *[In press.*

THOMAS CARLYLE'S COUNSELS TO A LITERARY ASPI-
RANT (a Hitherto Unpublished Letter of 1842), and What Came of Them. With a brief estimate of the man. By JAMES HUTCHINSON STIR-LING, LL. D. 12mo, boards, 50 cents.

Gives a side of the rugged old Scotchman which will be new to most readers. It shows that he was not always gruff and bearish, and that he could at times think of somebody besides himself. *The letter is one which every young man who has a leaning towards literary work will read and ponder over.*

SOCIAL LIFE AND LITERATURE FIFTY YEARS AGO.
16mo, cloth, white paper labels, gilt top. $1.00.

By a well-known *litterateur.* It will take a high place among the literature treating of the period. A quaint and delightful book, exquisitely printed in the Pickering style.

CIVILIZATION IN THE UNITED STATES. By MATTHEW
ARNOLD. And Other Essays concerning America. 16mo, unique paper boards. 75 cents. Cloth, uncut, $1.25. *The cloth binding matches the uniform edition of his collected works.*

Comprises the critical essays, which created so much discussion, namely, "General Grant, an Estimate." "A Word about America," "A Word more about America," and "Civilization in the United States."

. This collection gathers in the great critic's *last* contributions to literature.

LEGENDS OF THE RHINE. From the German of PF. A. BERNARD.
Translated by FR. ARNOLD. Finely Illustrated. Small 4to. Cloth.

An admirable collection of the popular historical traditions of the Rhine, told with taste and picturesque simplicity. [*In press.*

A SELECTION FROM THE POEMS OF PUSHKIN.
Translated, with Critical Notes and a Bibliography. By IVAN PANIN. author of "Thoughts." Foolscap 8vo. Unique binding. $2.00.

The first published translation by the brilliant young Russian, Ivan Panin, whose lectures in Boston on the literature of Russia, during the autumn of last ear, attracted crowded houses.

WIT, WISDOM, AND PATHOS, from the prose of HEINRICH HEINE,
with a few pieces from the "Book of Songs" Selected and translated by J. SNODGRASS. *Second edition, thoroughly revised.* Cr. 8vo, 338 pp. Cloth, $2.00

"A treasure of almost priceless thought and criticism."—*Contemporary Review.*

Cupples and Hurd,   *Publishers,*   BOSTON.
                                 Booksellers
                                 Library Agents,

TRAVESTIES, PARODIES, AND JEUX D'ESPRIT.

THE IMAGINARY CONVERSATIONS OF HIS EXCELLENCY AND DAN. By C. W. TAYLOR. With 40 full-page silhouette illustrations by F. H. BLAIR. 90 pp. 16mo Paper. 25 cents.

"It is fun for the masses, wholly irrespective of political parties,— such good-natured fun that even those that it satirizes might well laugh. . . Probably the most humorous skit ever produced"

THE LITTLE TIN-GODS-ON-WHEELS; OR, SOCIETY IN OUR MODERN ATHENS. A Trilogy, after the manner of the Greek. By ROBERT GRANT. Illustrated by F. G ATTWOOD. *Tenth edition.* Pamphlet. Small 4to. 50 cents.

Divided into Three Parts: The Wall Flowers; the Little Tin-Gods-on-Wheels; The Chaperons. A broad burlesque of Boston society scenes.

ROLLO'S JOURNEY TO CAMBRIDGE. A Tale of the Adventures of the Historic Holiday Family at Harvard under the New Regime. With twenty-six illustrations, full-page frontispiece, and an illuminated cover of striking gorgeousness. By FRANCIS G. ATTWOOD. 1 vol. imperial 8vo Limp. London toy-book style. Third and enlarged edition. 75 cents.

"All will certainly relish the delicious satire in both text and illustrations."— *Boston Traveller.*
"A brilliant and witty piece of fun." — *Chicago Tribune.*

EVERY MAN HIS OWN POET; OR, THE INSPIRED SINGER'S RECIPE BOOK. By W. H. MALLOCK, author of "New Republic," etc. *Eleventh Edition.* 16mo. 25 cents.

A most enjoyable piece of satire, witty, clever, and refined. In society and literary circles its success, both here and abroad, has been immense.

TWO COMEDIES: AN ILL WIND; AN ABJECT APOLOGY. By F. DONALDSON, JR. Fcap. 8vo. Paper, elegant. 50 cents.

These comedies belong to the same class of literature as do the lightest of Austin Dobson's lyrics and Andrew Lang's least serious essays, and their form is admirably suited to the depicting of the foibles and rather weak passions of that indefinite caste, American society. They are evidently modelled on the French vaudeville, and their characters are clever people, who say bright things. Why should we not choose the people we describe from the clever minority, instead of making them, as is sometimes done, unnecessarily dull, although perhaps more true to nature at large? Mr. Donaldson has done so, and much of the dialogue in these comedies is clever as well as amusing.

Cupples and Hurd, *Publishers, Booksellers, Library Agents,* **BOSTON.**

Important New Books.

HOW TO WRITE THE HISTORY OF A FAMILY. By W. P.

W. PHILLIMORE, M. A., B. C. L. 1 vol. Cr. 8vo. *Tastefully printed in antique style, handsomely bound.* $2.00.

Unassuming, practical, essentially useful, Mr. Phillimore's book should be in the hands of every one who aspires to search for his ancestors and to learn his family history. — *Athenæum.*

This is the best compendious genealogist's guide that has yet been published, and Mr. Phillimore deserves the thanks and appreciation of all lovers of family history. — *Reliquary.*

Notice. — Large Paper Edition. A few copies, on hand-made paper, wide margins, bound in half morocco, may be obtained, price $6.50 *net.*

THE KINSHIP OF MEN : An Argument from Pedigrees ; or, Genealogy

Viewed as a Science. By HENRY KENDALL. Cr. 8vo. Cloth, $2.00.

The old pedigree-hunting was a sign of pride and pretension ; the modern is simply dictated by the desire to know whatever can be known. The one advanced itself by the methods of immoral advocacy ; the other proceeds by those of scientific research. — *Spectator* (London).

RECORDS AND RECORD SEARCHING. A Guide to the Genealo-

gist and Topographer. By WALTER RYE. 8vo, cloth. Price $2.50.

This book places in the hands of the Antiquary and Genealogist, and others interested in kindred studies, a comprehensive guide to the enormous mass of material which is available in his researches, showing what it consists of, and where it can be found.

ANCESTRAL TABLETS. A Collections of Diagrams for Pedigrees, so

arranged that Eight Generations of the Ancestors of any Person may be recorded in a connected and simple form. By WILLIAM II. WHITMORE, A. M. SEVENTH EDITION. *On heavy parchment paper, large 4to, tastefully and strongly bound, Roxburgh style.* Price $2.00.

" No one with the least bent for genealogical research ever examined this ingeniously compact substitute for the 'family tree' without longing to own it. It provides for the recording of eight lineal generations, and is a perpetual incentive to the pursuit of one's ancestry." — *Nation.*

THE ELEMENTS OF HERALDRY. A practical manual, showing

what heraldry is, where it comes from, and to what extent it is applicable to American usage ; to which is added a Glossary in English, French and Latin of the forms employed. Profusely Illustrated. By W. H. WHITMORE, author of " Ancestral Tablets," etc. [*In press.*

Cupples and Hurd,   *Publishers,*   *Booksellers,*   *Library Agents,*   BOSTON.

JOHN BROWN. By Hermann Von Holst, author of "Constitutional History of the United States," &c., together with an introduction and appendix by Frank P. Stearns, a poem by Mr. Wason, and a letter describing John Brown's grave. Illustrated. 16mo, gilt top. $1.50.

This book, the author of which is so well known by his "Constitutional History," and by his biography of John C. Calhoun, cannot fail to be of interest to all students of American history, who appreciate a calm, impartial criticism of a man and an episode which have been universally and powerfully discussed.

MARGARET; and THE SINGER'S STORY. By Effie Douglass Putnam. Daintily bound in white, stamped in gold and color, gilt edges. 16mo. $1.25.

A collection of charming poems, many of which are familiar through the medium of the magazines and newspaper press, with some more ambitious flights, amply fulfilling the promise of the shorter efforts. Tender and pastoral, breathing the simple atmosphere of the fields and woods.

AROUND THE GOLDEN DEEP. A Romance of the Sierras. By A. P. Reeder. 500 pages. 12mo. Cloth. $1.50.

A novel of incident and adventure, depicting with a strong hand the virile life of the mine that gives its name to the story, and contrasting it with the more refined touches of society in the larger cities; well written and interesting.

SIGNOR I. By Salvatore Farina. Translated by the Baroness Langenau. 12mo. Cloth. $1.25.

A dainty story by an Italian author, recalling in the unique handling of its incidents, and in the development of its plot, the delicate charm of "Marjorie Daw."

MIDNIGHT SUNBEAMS, OR BITS OF TRAVEL THROUGH THE LAND OF THE NORSEMAN. By Edwin Coolidge Kimball. On fine paper, foolscap 8vo, tastefully and strongly bound, with vignette. Cloth. $1.25.

Pronounced by Scandinavians to be accurate in its facts and descriptions, and of great interest to all who intend to travel in or have come from Norway or Sweden.

WOODNOTES IN THE GLOAMING. Poems and Translations by Mary Morgan. Square 16mo. Cloth, full gilt. $1.25.

A collection of poems and sonnets showing great talent, and valuable translations from Gautier, Heine, Uhland, Sully-Prudhomme, Gottschalk, Michael Angelo, and others. Also prose translations from the German, edited and prefaced by Max Müller.

Cupples and Hurd,   *Publishers,* *Booksellers,* *Library Agents,*   BOSTON.

Important New Books.

SCOTTISH HUMOR.

DAVID KENNEDY, THE SCOTTISH SINGER: Reminiscences
of his Life and Work by MARJORY KENNEDY. With portrait and illustrations. 8vo. Cloth. 479 pp. $2.00.

A highly interesting narrative of this humorous and pathetic singer, who will be remembered the world over, not only by Scotchmen, but by all those who, at any time, have formed a part of his delighted audiences, and who recall the inimitable manner in which he rendered all that is best in Scottish poetry and song. Genuine fun and drollery, keen observation of men and manners, notes of travel in many cities, the vicissitudes of an artistic career, are all depicted here with force and style.

NEW AND CHARMING WORK ON JAPAN.

NINE YEARS IN NIPON: SKETCHES OF JAPANESE LIFE AND MANNERS. By HENRY FAULDS, L. F. P. S., *Surgeon of* TSUKIJI *Hospital, Tokio ; Member of the Royal Asiatic Society.* With lithographed frontispiece, and initial letters and illustrations on wood by Japanese artists. 1 vol. 304 pp. 8vo. Cloth. With appropriate and original cover designs. $2.00.

The best inexpensive book on Japan that has yet appeared ; valuable as the record of the observations and experiences of one who, by virtue of his profession and his long residence, was admitted into the inner life of that conservative people, the Japanese. Teeming with accurate information and eloquent description, especially of the social life of the people, of which the ordinary traveller sees practically nothing, it is a valuable addition to the literature of geographical, ethnological, and social science.

THE TERRACE OF MON DÉSIR. A Novel of Russian Life. By SOPHIE RADFORD DE MEISSNER. 12mo. Cloth limp, elegant. $1.25. 3rd edition.

This novel is written by the American wife of a Russian diplomat, who, by virtue of her position, is well qualified to describe the scenes and characters which she has chosen to present; she writes with the clear, unbiassed view of her native country, and shows, perhaps for the first time, an unprejudiced picture of Russian society.

Her literary style has been pronounced easy and flowing, with a certain opulence in its swift panorama of bright scenes and high personages, and readers who recall the charming story of Switzerland which appeared in a late number of "Scribner" will need no further recommendation to the perusal of this work.

In these days when so much interest and sympathy is evoked by the narration of the miseries of the *moujik* this novel comes very à *propos*, as it presents a picture of the social and domestic life of that other branch of the Russians, the aristocratic, governing class; who, notwithstanding their adherence to French models, still have that indefinite touch of their Oriental ancestry which gives them their romance and passion, and renders them as emphatically Russian as the most humble peasant.

Cupples and Hurd, Publishers, Booksellers, Library Agents, *BOSTON.*

Important New Books.

Standard Books by the Author of "Madge" and "Sherbrooke."

A distinguished critic says: "There is nothing sensational or dramatic about the writings of Mrs. H. B. Goodwin. Her books are natural, heartfelt, and a true mirror of this not altogether unromantic life of ours."

DR. HOWELL'S FAMILY. 1 vol. 16mo. Cloth elegant. $1.00. New and popular edition.

"Of the merits of this work it is difficult to speak too highly. It is written in a style as near perfection as it is possible to conceive. Better books a parent cannot put into the hands of a son or daughter."—*Watchman.*

CHRISTINE'S FORTUNE. 1 vol. 16mo. Cloth elegant. $1.00. New and popular edition.

Like a pearl on the sands of the seashore is the story of Christine among the average novels of the day. The interest is sustained, and no one who begins the book will lay it down until he has finished reading it, and will rise from it with the feeling that he has been in excellent company. The style, the sentiments, and the teachings are faultless and ennobling.

ONE AMONG MANY. 1 vol. 16mo. Cloth elegant. $1.00.

The author has not drawn imaginary and impossible characters, but has selected a few from the vast theatre of life to portray the loveliness of that wisdom "which is first pure, then peaceable, gentle, and easy to be entreated, full of mercy and good fruits."

OUR PARTY OF FOUR. A story of Travel. 1 vol. 16mo. Cloth elegant. $1.00.

Readers will find great pleasure in following the fortunes of the kind-hearted narrator and her three friends in their Europe an tour, and in the glimpses of their subsequent careers at home. A rare combination of travel, intellectual discussion, exciting adventure, and the portrayal of earnest feeling and refined sentiment.

THE ANGEL OF THE VILLAGE. By L. M. Ohorn. Translated by Mrs. Mathews. 16mo. Cloth. $1.25.

"A work possessing unusually high merit. It is such fiction as elevates and makes beneficent influences keenly manifest; . . abounding in deepest interest, and written in the most fascinating style."—*Journal,* Philipsburg, Pa.
"Purely and pleasantly written."—*Christian Register.*
"Honest and pure in tone, with a distinctly religious inspiration."—*American,* Philadelphia.
"Elevated in tone, and healthy in its suggestions and influence."—*Universalist Quarterly.*

Cupples and Hurd, *Publishers, Booksellers, Library Agents,* **BOSTON.**

Important New Books.

Important New Books.

BOOKS ABOUT RALPH WALDO EMERSON.

RALPH WALDO EMERSON : PHILOSOPHER AND SEER. By
BRONSON A. ALCOTT. *Second edition.* Portraits, etc. Cr. 8vo. Cloth. $1.00.

A book about Emerson, written by the one man who stood nearest to him of all men. It is an original and vital contribution to *Emersoniana* ; like a portrait of one of the old masters painted by his own brush.

"A beautiful little book." — *Boston Transcript.*

"This book, more than any other which Alcott published, shows his highest quality as a writer." — *Boston Unitarian.*

RALPH WALDO EMERSON : HIS MATERNAL ANCESTORS, WITH SOME REMINISCENCES OF HIM. By his cousin, D. G.
HASKINS, D.D. With illustrations reproduced from portraits and silhouettes never before made public. 12mo. Large paper, $5.00; cloth, $1.50.

Printed in the antique style, and a very choice book. The illustrations are exceedingly interesting, while the work itself throws unique and valuable sidelights on the life and character of its subject.

THE OPTIMISM OF RALPH WALDO EMERSON. By WILLIAM F.
DANA. 16mo. Cloth. 75 cents.

An essay of reach, insight, and ripeness of judgment, showing the teaching of Emerson's philosophy in terse, well-chosen language. One of the best of many critical expositions.

THE INFLUENCE OF RALPH WALDO EMERSON. By W. R.
THAYER. 8vo. Paper. $0.50.

An eulogy of his work by one qualified to speak with authority by reason of his studies of philosophic systems, who compares Emerson's solution of the problems of the Infinite with those propounded by other great minds.

LONGFELLOW AND EMERSON. The Massachusetts Historical
Society's Memorial Volume, with portraits. Quarto boards, $2.00; cloth, $2.50.

Containing the addresses and eulogies by Dr. Oliver Wendell Holmes, Charles E. Norton, Dr. G. E. Ellis, and others, together with Mr. Emerson's tribute to Thomas Carlyle, and his earlier and much-sought-for addresses on Sir Walter Scott and Robert Burns. Illustrated with two full-page portraits in albertype after Mr. Notman's photograph of Mr. Longfellow, and Mr. Hawes's celebrated photograph of Mr. Emerson, taken in 1855, so highly prized by collectors.

Cupples and Hurd, *Publishers,* *Booksellers,* *Library Agents,* **BOSTON.**

Important New Books.

www.ingramcontent.com/pod-product-compliance
Lightning Source LLC
Chambersburg PA
CBHW030904270326
41929CB00008B/572